S. B. Corwin
Book

Very sincerely & truly
Yours
S. Nelson

PIONEER HISTORY;

OR,

CORTLAND COUNTY

AND THE

BORDER WARS OF NEW YORK.

From the Earliest Period to the Present Time.

BY H. C. GOODWIN,

AUTHOR OF THE LIFE OF "JOHN JACOB ASTOR," "LEGENDS OF POLAND," "THE ROSE OF PROVINCE," ITHACA AS IT WAS, AND ITHACA AS IT IS," "EDGAR WENTWORTH; A PRIZE STORY OF THE SECOND AMERICAN REVOLUTION," "CORRESPONDING MEM. OF THE ROYAL HISTORICAL SOCIETY OF HAVANA, DE LA CUBA," "HON. MEM. OF MASSACHUSETTS HISTORICAL SOCIETY," "CORRESPONDING MEM. STATE HISTORICAL SOCIETY OF WISCONSIN."

NEW YORK:
A. B. BURDICK, PUBLISHER,
No. 8 SPRUCE STREET.
1859.

EDWARD O. JENKINS,
Printer & Stereotyper,
No. 26 FRANKFORT STREET.

DEDICATION.

TO THE

SURVIVING PIONEERS

AND THE

DESCENDANTS OF PIONEERS OF CORTLAND COUNTY;

AND ESPECIALLY TO THE

VENERABLE DR. JOHN MILLER,

AND

MAJOR-GEN'L SAMUEL G. HATHEWAY,

This Volume is Respectfully Dedicated.

That their future days may be happy and pleasurable as those of the past have been arduous, honorable, and useful; and that the evening of their lives may draw on, gently as fades the light of day, is the sincere and devoted wish of their friend,

THE AUTHOR.

CORRESPONDENCE.

THE following letter, addressed by Hon. Joseph Reynolds, Prof. Hyde and others to the author of this volume, precludes the necessity of any additional prefatory remarks :

CORTLAND, May 22d, 1858.

H. C. GOODWIN, ESQ.—Dear Sir,—The undersigned are informed that you are now engaged in writing the history of "Central New York," a work which will, doubtless, be highly valued, and read with pleasure by those familiar with the efforts you put forth to obtain facts relative to the early history of localities, and the graphic manner in which you record important events.

A notice of the fact that you are still employed in writing upon subjects which interest the public generally, induces us to hope that you will revise and publish in book form the history of "*Cortland County and the Border Wars of New York*," in order that our citizens may be able to preserve the matter which you presented to them in one of our county papers two years since, and which proved to be highly interesting and instructive.

We are of opinion that the work would meet with a ready sale, and that you could not fail to secure a worthy compensation for your labor. It is with the hope that you may be induced to publish the history in a more desirable form that we address you, believing that by so doing you will perform a service ever to be remembered by the citizens of our county.

We are, sir, yours respectfully,

JOSEPH REYNOLDS,
HORATIO BALLARD,
FREDERICK HYDE,
HIRAM CRANDALL,
EDWIN F. GOULD.

CONTENTS.

CHAPTER I.

ABORIGINAL, FRENCH, AND ENGLISH HISTORY.

"First in the race, that won their country's fame."

THE historian is sometimes obliged to record events, over which, if truth could be as well accommodated, he would gladly cast the veil of forgetfulness, nor torture public sympathy with the narration of scenes that pain even while they instruct. We pity even the banditti of Judea whom Herod's soldiers subdued; for lawless as they were, their women, children, and all their hopes sank into the same ruin. But the aboriginals of America come up in the annals of the past, demanding our strongest sympathy, because their crime was simply the accident of birth; they were the possessors of this continent; its untold treasure of wealth invited the cupidity of strangers from the eastern climes, and in their presence the proud sons of the forest of America have withered away. When we contemplate our country as it is, filled with wealth and the most wonderful improvements; when we consider the almost exhaustless resources, agricultural and mineral, of our land; and when we look upon our educated, active, and indomitable people, with the Bible for their code, ready to use every available and righteous means to strengthen and perpetuate the Republic, and increase its moral, social, intellectual, and political light and liberty, we feel that in the inscrutable providence of God, the red man's period in time has about elapsed, and soon all that will remain to tell that he ever existed will be the imperfect record left by us, his exterminators.

To us, who, from this time, look back upon the events of the past, it does not look strange that the natives should have retired before the more powerful whites, and that they should have made some attempts to expel their invaders. Nor does it appear strange, that, after having seen the graves of their dead desecrated, their homes made desolate, and their ancient forests laid waste— after the apprehension had at last reached their darkened minds that they were to be eventually exterminated, they should have turned on their persecutors, nerved with destruction, and armed with the desire for "liberty or death." Sympathy for our countrymen who suffered from the chafed, desperate people whose homes we have wrested from them, and whose country we have appropriated to our use, should never mislead us into the supposition that the Indian of America possesses a more vindictive nature than ourselves. Could a people as much more highly cultivated than ourselves, as the early settlers were better informed than Indians, approach our shores, and by friendship at first, and then by fraud, theft, the deceitful use of powerful exhilerating drinks, and finally by force of arms, get possession of all our eastern cities and seaboard, would we quietly relinquish *all* of our homes, and tamely bend our necks to the conqueror's yoke? If not, then learn to appreciate the parallel case of the Indians.

In attempting to narrate any event of Indian warfare, we find the most insurmountable difficulties arising, unless we bring in the combined events that prompted the outrage or action. The truth is, the aborigines have no historians to record and publish to the world the virtues, the sufferings, or the heroism of their race, and from this fact has arisen the difficulty of presenting the red man as he really is. As the night retires leaving no trace behind, so the Indian has retired from his country. As the day drives the night away, and then paints a variegated dress for the landscape, so the white man has driven away his feebler neighbor, and left his own history.

The early settlers along the Atlantic coast had many things to retard their progress. The woodland abounded with game, and the rivers and creeks with fish, but the strong desire of most of the early emigrants to become *speedily rich*, prompted them to search for gold and silver ; and when they failed in this, they commenced a course of fraud,—capturing a native, in some instances, and then demanding a ransom of corn, land, and skins.

As might have been expected, the settlements following such a course were very soon reduced to abject want. The disaffection thus generated among the Indians at one settlement, soon spread through nearly the whole, and at a very early date after the settlement of our country commenced by the whites, the Indians became their deadly foes. After many lives, together with much time and money, had been needlessly expended, the New World assumed an aspect wholly changed ; people of industry, enterprise, and morality flocked to our shores, anxious to obtain the necessaries of life by hardy toil. The woodman's axe was heard, and soon the busy hum of mills and machinery mingled with the clatter of wagons, the ploughman's song, and the lowing of herds.

The English claimed the earliest possession of this territory, but the French, no less willing to extend their possessions and increase their power, began a settlement in the north. This led to much unpleasant feeling, and at length to open collision between the settlements and nations. These difficulties were all apparently settled by the treaty of Utrecht, in April, 1713. The apparent peace would have continued a permanent adjustment undoubtedly, but for the ever restless Jesuits. These zealots imagined that the Indians would gladly embrace their religious dogmas, and that the introduction of missionaries among them would eventuate in fixing Jesuitism on a firmer and more honorable basis. Prompted by such motives, this privileged sect of the Roman See commenced their missionary efforts among the Indians with a zeal peculiar to propagandists. The French, and especially the French colonists, lent aid to these missionaries and their abettors, who, in turn, explored the wilds, and greatly promoted the interests of the French in America, and by their glowing descriptions stimulated the desire of the French colonists to become masters of the trade, and if possible of the continent itself.

The fur trade presented inducements to both parties ; and to reap a rich return from it, it became necessary to win and retain the friendship of the Indians. The French, prompted by their subtlety, won many Indians in the west to their cause, and then commenced a series of encroachments upon Nova Scotia in the east; Crown Point in the north and west; attempted to establish a line of fortifications, extending from the head of the St. Lawrence to the Mississippi, and were encroaching far upon Virginia, while the English colonists had the unpleasant prospect before them of being surrounded by a belt of hostile French and Indians, closing rapidly upon them. With this prospect clearly in view, they commenced the most active measures to counteract the ruin that seemed about to hurry them swiftly along the way of the banished aborigines. Indian agents were appointed, whose duty it was to treat with them; to make them valuable presents; to redress their grievances, and to act at all times as the friend of the red man. These efforts of the English to establish amicable relations with the Indians, were crowned with happy results; many individual Indians became firm friends of the English, and eventually a majority of the tribes were found warmly attached to the ever-conquering English side.

Among the Indian agents, Sir William Johnson's name stands first among those with whom we need trace any definite connection with the incidental Indian history of which we shall treat in future chapters. This gentleman was for many years the Superintendent-General of the Indians, and by his friendship and wisdom attached the Five Nations so closely to him, that he exercised an almost unlimited control over them. After the death of his amiable wife, he received to his home "Mary Brant," sister of "Joseph Brant,*" the

* Thayendanegea.

celebrated captain and governor of the Six Nations, and lived with her in the full enjoyment of that affection and fidelity consequent upon a union of minds congenial, and love devoutly pure. This union, so far from being an insult to the Indians, was doubtless looked upon as a mark of real esteem. When an Indian becomes a warm friend of a white man, it is no uncommon thing for him to bring his wife, as a present, thinking, unquestionably, that as she is most valuable to him, so she will be most acceptable to his friend. Whether this relationship had any tendency to tighten the cords of confidence between him and the red men or not, we leave the reader to judge, barely remarking, that the influence he exerted over them was so powerful, that it gave the controlling motion to all the subsequent events of Indian history in this region of country.

Sir William Johnson was born in Ireland, in the year 1714. In 1734 he came to this country to superintend the estate of his uncle, Sir Peter Warren. His residence was located on the banks of the Mohawk river. He soon ingratiated himself into the esteem and confidence of the Six Nations. He studied the Indian character, became master of their language, and at particular seasons assumed their dress, invited them to his house, and labored on all suitable occasions to extend to them that attention and courtesy so well calculated to impress them with peculiar reverence. He was stern and unyielding in his disposition, yet possessed the superior faculty of controlling his passions, and when occasion required was conciliatory and courteous to the unlettered aborigines of the forest.

During the French war, which broke out in 1754, he

rendered very great assistance to the provincial army. At Lake George, where he held the post of Commander-in-Chief, he gained a most brilliant victory over the French and Indian forces of Baron Dieskau. In honor of this achievement, the House of Commons voted him a bequest of £5,000 sterling. The king most graciously favored him with the title of "Baronet, and Superintendent of Indian Affairs." Brigadier Gen. Prideaux fell at the siege of Fort Niagara, when Sir William assumed the office of Commander-in-Chief of the combined English forces. He conducted the siege with gallantry, compelled the Fort to surrender, and took the garrison prisoners. Under his command were 1000 Iroquois. With these well-trained warriors, he united with the forces of Gen. Amherst, at Oswego, in 1760, preparatory to his expedition into Canada, closing his distinguished military career at Montreal.

In his retirement from the bloody field of "glorious war," he lived like an eastern lord, supporting much of the dignity of a nobleman.

He died in the sixtieth year of his age, and was interred under the "old stone church" at Johnstown. In 1806, his remains were "taken up and re-deposited." He had been rather seriously wounded at Lake George, and the ball, not having been extracted, was found in the mingled dust of the brave old man.

We have deemed it necessary to take this brief review of the early history of our country, that we might be enabled to understand why the Indians of the confederacy, and many other tribes, adopted the cause of the mother country during the Revolutionary struggle, and that we may be better prepared to present a general sketch of the border wars of New York, waged for the supremacy of soil, for power and plunder.

The most prominent language spoken by the aborigines was the Algonquin.

They believed in one Supreme God—the Great and Good Spirit—the Maker of Heaven and Earth—the Father and Master of life—the Creator of every animate being. They adored him, worshiped him, and regarded him as the author of all good. Different tribes knew him by different names, such as *Kiethan*, *Woonand*, *Cautanwoit* and *Mingo Ishto.* He lived far away to the warm south-west, amid perennial flowers, golden fruit, and sweet-scented zephyrs. They saw him in the glassy water, foaming surge, sparkling fire, in the dazzling sun, silvery moon, and radiant stars.

Among them were many gifted and eloquent orators. Tall and majestic in appearance, with graceful attitude and noble bearing, they united in extreme harmony and degree both action and sentiment. Full of electrifying emotion, thrilling ideas, and pulsating, leaping words, every sentence was instinct with exuberant, all-motioned, panting life. They would fill the ear with music, the mind with fire. Their speeches were like streams of swift-running intellect, charmed and poetized by the sweetest flowers and fairest thoughts.

At a very remote period in the annals of the past, the aborigines had penetrated into different parts of the territory, now embraced within the State ; and as early as 1535 had erected the seat of their empire at *Ganentuha,* or Onondaga.

In 1600, the Five Confederative Nations,—the Mohawks, Oneidas, Onondagas, Cayugas, and Senecas,—

had become very numerous and warlike. They had gradually spread over the territory extending from the borders of Vermont and central western New York, from the great northern chain of lakes to the head waters of the Ohio, the Susquehanna, and the Delaware. The French called them the Iroquois, and the English the Five Nations. Their war-paths extended beyond the Connecticut, the Mississippi, and the Gulf of Mexico.

The French made their first permanent settlement in Canada during the year 1608. Governor Champlain was the guiding spirit, and under his direction and efficient action, Quebec was founded.

From 1609 to 1759, central and western New York formed a portion of French Canada, or New France. The St. Lawrence river and its shores had been explored by Cartier and portions of his crew, as early as August, 1535 ; but no permanent settlement was made previous to 1608.

The French looked upon the aborigines as a kind of groveling beings, having few wants, desires, or thoughts above the instinct of the brute creation, and labored to locate them in villages, the first of which was founded near the settlements of Montreal and Quebec. But the general habits, customs and sentiments of the whites were so dissimilar to those of the Indians, that the attempt proved a failure. The presence of the "pale face" tended rather to corrupt than improve the natives. The plan was therefore abandoned, and another mode adopted to induce them to favor the French, while they should exhibit their hostility to the English.

In 1608, the Iroquois, or Five Nations, were engaged in a bloody and exterminating war with the Adirondacks, a confederacy of the Algonquins. They had been driven from their possessions and hunting grounds around Montreal, and compelled to fly for safety to the southern coast of Lake Ontario, but in turn they fell upon their invaders with the ferocity of tigers, and forced them to abandon their lands, situated above the Three Rivers, and seek a rampart behind the straits of Quebec.

Governor Champlain, unhappily for the colonists, and unwisely for himself, entered into an alliance with the Adirondacks, furnishing them with men and munitions of war, which tended strongly to turn the current of success. Their pomp, parade, and haughty movements, their glittering armor and polished steel, waving plumes and richly decorated banners, the blaze of musketry and the roar of the deep-mouthed bellowing cannon that flashed lightning and spouted thunder, bewildered their untutored minds, and sent horror and consternation among the combined forces of the Iroquois, and they were as a consequence defeated in several battles, and finally driven from Canada. Undismayed, however, by their reverses, they turned their arms against the Satanaus or Shawnees, defeated them, and set about a renewal of the contest with their rival foes.

A Dutch ship had entered the Hudson river, having on board the colonists who made a location where we now see the city of Albany. It was an easy task to obtain of them weapons similar to those which had been so successfully used in their defeat and dishonor. Being now fully prepared for a more severe contest for power, they resumed the fight with their old enemies. Their efforts were attended with the fullest success, and the Adirondacks were completely annihilated. Gov. Champlain, too late to retrieve his mistake, learned that he and his friends had united their fortunes with the conquered instead of the conquerors. This action on the part of the French originated that bitter enmity and undying hatred which for a long period existed between them and the Five Confederated Nations.

From this time the confederacy rapidly rose to the first power east of the Mississippi. Their war parties ranged from Hudson's Bay on the north to the mountains of Tennessee on the south, from the Connecticut on the east to the Mississippi on the west; and every nation within these vast boundaries trembled at the name of the Akonoshioni, or united people.

During the reign of the Dutch governor, Peter Stuyvesant, the province of New York, in 1644, was surrendered to the English, who exerted themselves to preserve the friendly feelings which were created between the Five Nations and the Dutch, through the agency of the latter, who were so opportune in lending that species of arms which enabled the former to conquer the Adirondacks, and regain their former honor, their homes and hunting grounds. This timely aid on the part of the Dutch, enabled the hardy German to penetrate with safety into the Indian settlements, and traffic with the natives. The English were successful. They called conventions at Albany, were liberal, and even extravagant in distributing among the Indians munitions of war, merchandize, and various gaudy tinselled trappings of fancy. The French, unwilling to see the English reap all the fame and glory derived from Indian friendship, redoubled their exertions to win their favor and weaken their alliance with the English. If the confederacy could be dismembered, they presumed it an easy matter to conquer the English.

In 1665, Courcelles, Governor of Canada, dispatched a party of the French to attack the Five Nations ; but being unaccustomed to long and secret expeditions, they lost their way amid the wastes of snow which retarded their progress, benumbed their faculties, and reduced them to a state bordering on starvation, and finally, without knowing where they were, made a stand at Schenectady, then but recently founded. Reduced by cold, starvation, and the consequent results of a rapid march, they resembled an army of beggars over which the buzzard and vulture had hovered, and were ready to descend and devour. The appetite of a hyena would hardly have been satisfied with a meal from their wasted forms. Many Indians were then in the village, and could have easily destroyed them, and perhaps would, had not the friendly aid of a Dutchman interfered, by way of advice and artifice, to spare them, that they might be the more fully prepared to meet and contend with a stronger foe, which he contrived to make them believe was advancing.

The French were not so anxious to instill morality and the more noble lessons of virtue into the minds of the savages, as they were to make allies for France. That they partially succeeded is evident from the fact that they induced the Caughnawagas, in 1671, to leave the banks of the Mohawk and locate in Canada. French vanity, and their advantages of polite bearing, were better calculated to influence the native, than the stiff, overbearing pride and self-conceit of the English ; and although they could not for any great length of time retain the good graces of the Indians, yet it is recorded that one of the French Jesuits so far won their favor as to be adopted into one of the tribes, and was afterwards chosen a sachem.

The Dinodadies, a tribe who were in alliance with France, were at war with the Five Nations in 1688, and by treachery and falsehood contrived to intercept their ambassadors while on their way to hold a conference in Canada, and with a cowardly meanness and savage barbarity peculiar to themselves, killed several of them, pretending to be influenced by the French Governor, thus violating their faith and making their enmity still stronger, and the breach wider. Resolved upon having vengeance, they soon landed 1,200 Iroquois warriors at Montreal, slew 1,000 French, "and carried away twenty-six prisoners." These, after being subjected to their scoffs and jeers, were burned alive. The French, no less willing to submit, made stealthy incursions into their country, and during the dark hours of night applied the incendiary torch to the Indians' home, thus reducing several of their villages to ashes.

In 1690 Schenectady was secretly attacked by a band of French and Caughnawaga Indians. The hour chosen was the dead of night. The village was completely surrounded, and before the inhabitants were aware of it the torch had been applied, and every dwelling was being devoured by the devastating element. Then commenced the sacrifice,—cruel, unrelenting. Murder and rapine went hand in hand. Infants had their brains dashed out, or with fathers, mothers, brothers and sisters, were cast into the burning dwellings, while the red-hot flames, like ten thousand fiery serpents, wreathed their consuming folds around them. Sixty persons thus perished to appease their unhallowed wrath, while thirty were taken captive. The few that escaped the awful massacre fled naked through the drifting snow in the direction of Albany. Many perished on the way, and twenty-five of the unhappy fugitives lost their limbs.

To avenge the wrong, a party of young Albanians united with a tribe of the Five Nations, and pursued the invaders, overtook them, and killed and captured about thirty.

Previous to this inhuman massacre, the colony of New York had not been regarded as being in any immediate danger of an attack from the French. The colonists felt more especially secure, from the fact that the negociations which were then pending in Europe were likely to bring about an amicable adjustment of the difficulties originating from the conflicting claims of the two rival powers in the New World.

The red leaguers still remained firm to the English cause, and exhibited considerable tact and ingenuity in harrassing their enemies.

In 1701 a general peace was concluded between the French and the Five Nations.

In the year 1712 the Corees and Monecons, or Tuscaroras, were waging a cruel and bloody war against the Carolinas. They were defeated with great loss, and driven from their country. Thus vanquished in their endeavors to subjugate the inhabitants of those colonies, the Tuscaroras left the seat of their ancient renown and journeyed northward, and finally united their destinies with the confederacy of the Five Nations, receiving a tract of land to dwell on; after which the allied powers were known by the name of the Six Nations.

From the commencement of the eighteenth century down to 1750, the Jesuit missionaries were very successful in influencing the Six Nations to favor their cause. They dazzled their uncultivated minds with the tinselled glare of Romish ceremonies, accommodated themselves to the tastes of savages, and held out to view the rich resources, the magnificent splendor of their king's golden throne, and thus ingratiated themselves so far into their good graces as to succeed in obtaining permission to build forts in their territory : and when the last French war broke out in 1754, four of the tribes were found raising the tomahawk against their former friends, the British colonists; and yet, singular as it may appear, before the last decisive blow was struck which defeated the French and gave power and dominion to the English, the red men had abandoned the French and the "magnificence of *le grand monarque*," and were once more allied with the English.

CHAPTER II.

LINDESAY'S PATENT.—CHERRY VALLEY.—BRITISH OPPRESSION.

"There was heard the sound of a coming foe,
There was sent through Tryon a bended bow,
And a voice was heard on the free winds far,
As the strong rose up at the sign of war."

GILLIES, the celebrated historian, presumes that men "in the infancy of society" were "occupied with the business of the present hour, forgetful of the past, and regardless of the future." There may have been instances where the truth of this declaration has appeared evident. We however doubt its general application. Not so with our *Pilgrim Fathers*, who two hundred years ago braved the dangers of the stormy ocean, when the May Flower came to this western continent laden with the destinies of this great nation. They left the land of persecution, where religious fanaticism and political tyranny were at their work of oppression, that they and their children might enjoy the rights and privileges of freemen in the new world of promise. Not so with our patriot fathers, who, rather than endure the injustice of British tyranny, or British insolence, made bare their bosoms to the shafts of battle, and shrunk not from the bloody horrors of a seven years' war. Not so with the dauntless champions, who, from the day of peril when they wrestled with the savage for his birthright, to the day of glory when they proclaimed a new charter to man, were giving a new nation to the world. Not so with the annointed few who came to sow the good seed, to grapple with infidelity as they rallied around the banner of the cross and descried on the far-off shore of the *heavenly Canaan* that celestial diadem that was bought with the hues of *Calvary*. Not so with the early pioneers of our country, who abandoned the soft endearments of home, social ties, and struggled to form new settlements in the wilderness, where before the hand of civilization had not contributed its strength to rear the domestic domicil. They toiled, not alone for themselves, but for their children—for posterity. We glory in the achievements of such men. We take pride in witnessing their success. They are the great benefactors of mankind—nature's true noblemen. And it will be our humble effort "to rescue from oblivion the names" of those who first warred with the mountain oak, or enriched our valleys by hardy toil; and it will be, too, our province and pleasure to record the deeds of those stern actors, over whose labors the rust of time has gathered, and over whose hallowed dust the green turf has grown, and wild flowers have sprung up in beautiful luxuriance. Nor shall we pass unmindful by those whose whitened locks and trembling limbs point like sentinels to the tomb. We should cherish their worth, emulate their virtues,—for they toiled that we might enjoy the rich fruits of their labor.

Albany county, in 1771, embraced all the northern and western part of the province of New York, extending from the Hudson river to the Niagara. Tryon county was organized in 1772. It was named in honor of Sir William Tryon, the provincial governor. It embraced in its boundaries a very large territory of country, containing all that part of the State lying west of a north and south line running nearly through the centre of the present county of Schoharie. The county seat was at Johnstown, the residence of Sir Wm. Johnson.

By examining our State map, it will be seen that Tryon was made up in part of Franklin, Hamilton, Fulton, Montgomery, Delaware, Ulster, Sullivan, and Orange, and the whole of St. Lawrence, Lewis, Herkimer, Otsego, Broome, Chenango, Madison, Cortland, Onondaga, Oneida, Oswego, Cayuga, Wayne, Seneca, Tompkins, Schuyler, Chemung, Tioga, Steuben, Yates, Ontario, Monroe, Livingston, Alleghany, Cattaraugus, Genesee, Orleans, Niagara, Erie, and Chautauque counties. It was changed to Montgomery in 1784.

The boundary between the British and Indian territory, as agreed upon in the treaty of 1768, run from Fort Stanwix, near Oneida creek, southward to the Susquehanna and Delaware.

Various portions of country embraced within the boundary lines of Tryon county have been hallowed and consecrated by the toils, the sacrifices and blood of those who fought and fell in freedom's holy cause. The blood chills as we look back to those days of rapine and carnage, and the pulse throbs with wild emotion as we recur to the stealthy march and midnight massacre—scenes which have made our country classic to those who delight in the recital of tales which send the blood curdling to the heart.

We see the long defile of painted savages as they wind along the Indian trail,—now issuing from the dark forest upon some defenceless settlement; now robbing some happy home of its brightest jewels, or applying the midnight torch to the pioneer's domicil, while savage yells rend the heavens and mingle in horrid discord with the groans of the dying who have fallen by the intruder's hand.

The Revolutionary struggle has lent an additional charm to those battle fields where freedom and tyranny met and struggled for the mastery ; fields hallowed by time, and made consecrate by the uncoffined bones of many a brave warrior. No country presents such scenes of grandeur and glory. In no country has passion stamped its vitality, energy, and sublimity more indelibly in popular traditions and in historic reminiscences.

In the early part of the 18th century, about 3000 German Palitinates, under the protection of Queen Anne, emigrated to this country. A large number of them made locations in Pennsylvania, while a few passed from Albany, by way of the Helderberg, in 1713, to the rich flats which border Scoharie creek. Here, wearied and wayworn, they paused for rest. Explorations were made, and finally a settlement agreed upon. In 1722, the country bordering the Mohawk had become dotted with small settlements, and the footprints of civilization had reached the German Flats.

In 1738 a patent was granted by the Lieutenant Governor of the province of New York to John Lindesay, Joseph Roseboom, Lendert Gansevoort, and Sabrant Van Schaick. This patent contained 8,000 acres of land, situated in the northern part of the [now] county of Otsego, and embraced a part of the town and village of Cherry Valley.

In 1739 Cherry Valley was founded by John Lindesay, a Scotch emigrant. In a few years improvements were so far made as to render the little band of pioneers comparatively comfortable, though they had endured the horrors of an almost living, lingering death by starvation.

In 1740 the snow fell, during the middle winter month, to the depth of several feet, precluding all intercourse or communication between the settlers of Cherry Valley and those bordering the Mohawk. Mr. Lindesay and family were placed in a most critical and truly alarming condition. Unprepared for the close quarters to which the severity of the weather had reduced them,—without food, with scanty raiment, and none of the conveniences which were calculated to encourage or improve their unhappy condition,—they looked on all around as one wide waste of dreary, blank desolation. He looked upon his wife, the partner of his early love, and as he saw the pearly tear start from her once sparkling eye, and steal its way down her pallid cheek, where he was wont to see the blush of vestal modesty start, he inwardly prayed that a good Providence might protect, and that the angel of mercy might rend aside the curtain that hid the present from the unknown future. And his children—who will protect and answer to their appeals for food? The cold, bleak blast, as it comes on its storm-beaten pinions, sweeping over the great lakes and wide-spread prairies, moans and howls among the tops of the forest trees, and sends a colder chill to the sinking heart of the stricken parent.

'Tis night! The sky is filled with snow, the wind sings its sad requiem. Without, all is cold and cheerless. Within the frugal home of our ill-protected pioneer sits an aged Indian of the Iroquois tribe. He is listening to the sad tale of the starving family. Touched with pity, the tear of sympathy steals down his furrowed cheek. His majestic form rises from the oaken chair. He is resolved to alleviate their sufferings. He pauses but a moment to light his pipe, or calumet of peace, as an indication of friendship with the pale face, then stroking the flaxen hair of the little infant that sat upon its mother's knee, and waving a good-bye with his brawny hand, he left the confines of the pioneer's little empire with slow and measured pace. His course is in the direction of the magnificent Mohawk.

And now, amid the darkness and solitude of a bleak winter's night, the native red man, dressed in the simple Indian garb, wearing heavy snow-shoes, is wending his lonely way to his rustic home, embosomed amid an amphitheatre of hills just back of that majestic river. Could we have fathomed the thoughts of that "aged hemlock," we should have learned that his mind was deeply impressed with the forlorn situation of his white friends, whose relief was the immediate object of his night march through the drifting snow. His sentiments and grateful emotions were akin to those which actuated the simple aboriginals long before their minds were polluted with the inhumanity of the transatlantic lords, whose object was the subjugation and annihilation of the red men of the wilderness. In due time the old scarred warrior returned laden with provisions, which he freely presented to Mr. Lindesay and family. With what grateful emotions they were received can be better imagined than told.

Mr. Lindesay was deserving of the Indian's friendship, for it had been his endeavor to cultivate the good will of his tawny brethren.

The old Indian made him frequent visits during that long and unpropitious winter, and continued to relieve the wants of himself and family — an act worthy of being written in letters of living light on the tablets of immortality.

The enterprising and spirit-stirring Harpers settled at Harpersfield in 1768. They had received a patent for twenty-two thousand acres of land, located in the present county of Delaware.

At about the same time settlements were made near Unadilla, and scattered families were found locating in various parts of the "plains,"—at Springfield, Middlefield,* Laurens, and Otego.† The population of Cherry Valley fell a little short of 300, and the whole of Tryon county did not exceed 10,000 when the British lion began to thunder defiance on the continent of America.

As yet the citizens of Tryon county had made no open resistance to the measures of the crown of Great Britain, political or ecclesiastical. They did, however, believe in the true and real freedom of all mankind—the right of speech, and the freedom of the press—those inherent rights which are God-given and inalien-

* Early called Freetown Martin. † Old England District.

able. They justly complained of the course which had been taken by the British authorities to incite, with foreign gold and foreign rum, the ruthless savage against the infant, and defenceless matron. They had time and again heard the Indian war-whoop, and had vainly sought the protection of the dear ones at home, for in that horrid yell they heard the doom of their wives and children.

Enjoying the name of freemen, they felt that they were becoming mere vassals to an arbitrary power. They knew that the hand that should aid and assist them was wielding an influence to crush and destroy them. They were sensible that the parent government had stretched a rod over them, and had threatened them with a despot's revenge; and long before the Revolutionary curtain rose on the memorable plains of Lexington, the Tryon county freemen were found engaged in holding meetings, and denouncing the arbitrary measures of the king and his governors, and freely took part with their brethren in other colonies in uttering their opposition to the Stamp act, and various other anti-republican measures which had emanated from the British Parliament. And they resolved to give their adhesion to those measures which finally resulted in the calling of a Congress, which convened in the city of New York in 1665.

After the death of Sir William Johnson, which occurred in the midst of an Indian council, held at Johnstown, July 11th, 1774, the difficulties increased, and rapine and massacre were of more frequent occurrence. He had possessed a powerful and commanding influence over the Indians, and displayed an administrative genius superior to any who had before been at the service of the British government in America.

Convened at this war council were a large number of the most active and rebellious spirits of the Six Nations, besides numerous high civil dignitaries of the provinces of New York and New Jersey.

Sir William had held the office of Superintendent of Indian affairs for the northern provinces for upwards of twenty years; and, at the time of his decease, his department included 130,000 Indians, more than one fifth of whom were "fighting men." The Six Nations numbered about 10,000, and could bring into action over 2,000 bold and skillful warriors.

Col. Guy Johnson, son-in-law of Sir William, was his successor in office. But he was a man of an entirely different temperament, possessing but a small share of his talent and judgment, was illiberal, crafty, full of vain-glory, and delighted in playing the tyrant.

The political elements which, for a long time, had been gathering in the eastern provinces, broke forth in a spirit of angry defiance, which was hailed by the Tryon county friends of freedom with a spirit bordering on enthusiasm. They exhibited a devoted love of country worthy of freemen. To animate their New England friends, and cheer them on in the good work of reform, they forthwith met and organized an association, the avowed object of which was to diffuse a spirit of opposition to the kingly sway and menacing power of British tyranny in the provinces of the New World. They were resolved to enjoy the freedom of their own views, and assist in propagating the principles of equal and exact justice to all men. And yet they knew not but that they would be hunted down with savage vengeance, and that infamy would cling unrelentingly to their names. But what had this to do with freemen? They were opposed to taxation without their consent, and were resolved to cherish the sentiment while a single " arm could beat the larum to rebellion."

Guy Johnson became the leader of the loyalists. Discussions sharp and spirited took place between them, until finally the Colonel discovered the determined will of the revolutionists, and becoming satisfied of his waning influence, abandoned his royal palace at Guy Park, and with a formidable band of tory and Indian adherents, such as Col. Claus, Brant, and the Butlers, made his head-quarters at Fort Stanwix, subsequently at Oswego, and finally at Montreal. Here Sir John Johnson followed with a body of three hundred loyalists, chiefly Scotch.

England, excited to madness by the daring effort, covered our country not only with her own legions, but the insurrectionary negro, the Hessian, the savage, and the dastardly parricidal American tory, all animated by a reckless spirit of revenge, blighting our fair fields and waging a cruel war against the helpless woman and innocent child. But our immense forests, interminable plains, extensive rivers, with the exalted spirit which prompted to emigration, had imparted to the naturalized American a principle of noble independence, invincible firmness, and a daring intrepidity, which exhibited to astonished Europe a picture of the moral sublime.

The provincial supporters of the royal throne united with the home government in the determination, black-hearted and infamous, cruel and cowardly as it was, of setting ten thousand reckless, pampered, paid savages upon the scattered frontier settlements of the United Colonies, to glut their unhallowed desire for blood, to rob, plunder, and massacre the defenceless citizen, to strike terror into the peaceful and unguarded community of republican pioneers, to destroy their property, fire their dwellings, tomahawk and scalp the weak, the innocent and decrepit, to torture their prisoners in the most barbarous and unrelenting manner, to dig out their eyes, cut off their tongues, or roast them alive in the devouring element that was consuming their otherwise peaceful homes ; and as the red-hot flames lit up the heavens with a lurid glare, to yell and shout like incarnate devils over their work of devastation and death.

The Johnsons were in possession of great wealth, and had long lived in princely grandeur. Allied by marriage to families of foreign birth and royal blood, and holding important posts by British appointment, shrewd, sagacious and artful, they were found, when united with the Butlers, fit dispensers of massacre to the northern frontiers.

Little thought the British king as he sat upon his throne of regal grandeur, fattening on the blood and bones of murdered and oppressed humanity, that in prosecuting and urging forward the bloody frontier wars of New York and Pennsylvania he was digging his grave of moral infamy, or that the haughty foe, after waging for years a cruel and unrelenting warfare, was to be driven from our shore in sullen gloom and disappointment, having lost the brightest jewels that glittered in his crown of royalty. He did not for a moment presume that the heroic actors against whom he warred were destined to gain an immortality of fame and glory, in consequence of the noble and exalted stand they had taken in defense of home, kindred, and country—that their names were to be honored through successive generations,—the penman's theme and the poet's inspiration,—or that when the historian should write his country's annals, he would erect to them a monument, at whose base the falsehoods and prejudices of their enemies should wither, and around whose summit the lightnings of immortality would play.

CHAPTER III.

BORDER WARS—BRITISH INFLUENCE—BATTLE OF ORISKANY—SIEGE OF FORT SCHUYLER.

"Heard ye not the battle horn?
Reaper, leave thy golden corn,
Leave it for the birds of heaven,
Swords must flash, and shields be riven!
Leave it for the winds to shed—
Arm! ere Tryon's turf grows red!

"Mother! stay thou not thy boy!
He must learn the battle's joy.
Sister! bring the sword and spear,
Give thy brother word of cheer!
Maiden! bid thy lover part,
Tryon calls the strong in heart."

Border warfare, in all ages and in all countries, has presented an unrestrained exhibition of human passion; and the frontier wars of New York exhibit to the moralist one of the darkest pages that has yet seen the light, embodying a mass of depravity and misery, which the mind of man contemplates with mingled emotions of amazement, horror and disgust; and presenting a picture of weakness and wickedness, of turpitude and guilt, which has few parallels in any work of fiction. Humanity mourned over these devastations upon the beauty and brightness of her primeval empire, and lifted aloud her voice for their abatement.

The British possessed a very decided advantage over the colonists. They had agents who were appointed and paid by the king, to traffic and coöperate with the Indians in every possible way. The Indians were taught to believe that the king was their natural ruler and protector ; that it was the object and intention of the colonists to defeat, if possible, the English, and then wage an exterminating war against the red men; that, unless they united with the king's people, and assisted in conquering the revolutionists, their hunting grounds would be taken from them, their villages burnt, their homes pillaged, and themselves tortured, massacred, or made menial slaves to wear the white man's chains and the tyrant's fetters. Presents in great profusion were frequently made in the name of their royal father, to these unlettered aborigines ; and we are not surprised that a favorable impression should have been made, or that the savages were preëngaged in favor of English tyranny, nor do we regard them as having been alone to blame. Far from it. The cupidity and base mendacity of the royal leaders were continually urging forward marauding parties, and instigating them to massacre and blood ! And bitter were the fruits of these unhallowed attempts in Tryon county.

Though the stealthy incursions of the Indians had been severely felt by the inhabitants, previous to the campaign of 1777, they were afterwards attended with a more deadly vengeance.

In July of that year, General Herkimer marched to Unadilla at the head of 380 men of the Tryon county militia, and was there met by Brant, having with him 130 men. A conference was had between Gen. Herkimer and Capt. Brant, which finally terminated without tending to the furtherance of the American or Republican cause, leaving no doubt, in the minds of those present, of the determination of Brant and his followers to unite their destinies with the tories.

On the 17th of July, Gen. Herkimer issued his celebrated proclamation. It breathed the true spirit of the patriot, and was worthy of having emanated from the head and heart of the gallant hero who penned it; and it was very generally well received, notwithstanding the tory spirit which had been infused into the minds of a number of influential citizens, through the agency of the Johnsons, Col. Claus, and Walter Butler, son of Col. John Butler, of Wyoming notoriety.

When Burgoyne, with his well-disciplined army of over 7,500 regulars, besides Canadian and Indian auxiliaries, was rapidly advancing upon Crown Point, he detached Col. St. Leger with a body of light troops, Canadians, Indians, and tories, in all amounting to about 2,000, by the way of Oswego and the Mohawk river, with orders to take Fort Schuyler, and join him as he advanced to the Hudson, on his way to New York.

Eearly in August, Gen. St. Leger and his forces approached Fort Schuyler in all the "pomp and parade" of victorious troops fresh from the tented field of blood. The fortification was a rude structure formed of logs, and located on a well-selected elevation near the source of the Mohawk river. It was garrisoned by about six hundred continentals under the order and control of Col. Gansevoort. It undoubtedly appeared to St. Leger as an undertaking of no very great effort to reduce the fort and hang the rebels. The garlands of immortal fame were to cluster around his brow, and his name to be recorded upon the fairest page of English history! Nodding plumes were to droop and wither at his approach, and the revolutionists to seek mercy at the feet of the king's appointed dignitary! But how sadly was he disappointed. On the 3d he invested the place with about two-thirds of his army, and demanded a surrender of the fort. The reply of Gen. Gansevoort was, that he would defend it to the last extremity.

Gen. Herkimer, with 800 troops, had marched to reïnforce the garrison. During the forenoon of the sixth day he sent forward a messenger, who informed the defenders of the fort that he was within eight miles of them, and expected to be able during the day to force a passage and enter the garrison.

Of this fact Gen. St. Leger had been by some means apprised, and forthwith detached a strong body of regulars and Indians, under the command of Brant and Butler, with orders to ambuscade, and if possible, intercept and cut off the forces of Gen. Herkimer. The plan was adopted, and told with awful and heart-rending effect upon the approaching army. The spot was admirably chosen, being along a ravine which swept through a deep-cut gorge thickly studded with the "dark forest trees" of Oriskany.

There is a sublime and imposing appearance in a well-equipped and well-drilled army. You see generals and their aids clad in rich and tasteful uniform, with glittering shields and nodding plumes, mounted on richly caparisoned steeds, giving their hurried orders as the battalions wheel into columns and prepare for the deadly conflict. To see the two opposing forces rapidly closing in upon each other, and suddenly swayed back like the surging waves of the ocean, as their ranks are opened by shot or chain belched from the mouths of brazen cannons, is indeed an awful scene. The earth trembles as if convulsed by some mighty volcanic eruption, and the red-hot balls and bursting shells resemble so many fiery orbs gemming the earth. Not so, however, in the battle scene we are about to record.

The tory and savage forces were crouched, tiger-like, along the banks of the ravine, entirely secluded from the sight of General Herkimer and his little gallant army of well-tried soldiers, yet ready to pounce upon them with the ferocity of hungry hyenas. The heroic forces of Herkimer, unapprised of danger, were moving along the winding gorge, but were suddenly startled by a heavy discharge of musketry, followed by the war-whoop of the painted savages and royal allies, who came rushing down the banks, screeching and yelling like ten thousand demons fresh from the portals of the infernal pit. This precipitate movement on the part of the enemy, so unexpected, so sudden, and so furious, threw the army of Herkimer into considerable disorder. Indeed, the greatest consternation spread throughout the ranks. The rear division of the column broke and fell back on the first attack, and fled. The forward division had no alternative left but to fight, and gallantly they defended themselves in the unequal contest. The royal troops and the militia became so closely pressed together as to be unable to use their fire-arms, and one of the most deadly hand to hand conflicts ensued that is recorded in either ancient or modern history. Confusion and carnage reigned supreme, and hundreds fell, pierced to the heart with the deadly steel. The earth was red with the blood of the dead and dying, and the purple current was seen mingling with the crystal element as it swept along in its hurrying course. Those who fled at the first onset, sought for safety behind trees, from which they poured the most raking and disastrous shots into the enemy's ranks. But the wily savages, not willing to be outmanaged, especially in their own mode of fighting, watched for the smoke of each discharged gun, then suddenly sallied forth, tomahawked and scalped the unerring marksman before he had time to reload. This way of taking scalps was, however, soon checked. Two men were directed to take a position behind the forest rampart, and while the one should bring down his foe, the other to reserve his charge for the seeker of scalps. In this way sad havoc was made with the savage foe.

In this severe struggle, General Herkimer's loss was computed to amount to four hundred men ; the gallant leader himself was found among the slain. Many of the most active political characters of that unfortunate portion of country were either made prisoners, wounded, or fell—gloriously fell—in the defense of that principle which has established republics, demolished thrones, wrecked kingdoms, and divided empires. Nor was the loss less severely felt by the allied party. The dusky chieftain mourned the fate of his brave warriors, who lay thick as autumn leaves around him. His grief was almost bordering on despair. He wept as the red man was unused to weep, for he plainly saw the wide-spread desolation that was at almost every point staring him in the face. And while the few remaining sons of the forest bewailed the loss of their friends, and exhibited the deepest sorrow and distress of mind, as they saw the result of their inhumanity in the mangled forms, in the blasted hopes, in the unutterable agony of the fallen braves, and, while their doleful yells rent the air, the old scarred chieftain stood still and motionless as the sleeping marble. His countenance, however, soon changed to that of a demon, for the spirit of vengeance was at work in his breast, and his dark eye flashed a falcon glance at the heroic warriors who passed hurriedly by with their dead and dying, who, but a little while before, were flushed with manly pride and noble bearing. That glance was indicative of his deep and undying hatred towards the Americans, and was ominous of future devastation, of massacre, and blood.

During this severe contest Col. Willett made a successful sally, killed a number of the enemy, destroyed their provisions, carried off their spoils and plunder, and returned to the fort without losing a man.

In the meantime Arnold had been dispatched with a respectable force of Continentals for the purpose of preventing a junction of St. Leger with General Burgoyne. St. Leger had become aware of the expected arrival of Arnold, and after again demanding, in the most haughty manner, the surrender of the fort, and meeting with the same patriotic and prompt refusal, began to make arrangements for its destruction. But just at this important crisis of affairs, Arnold apprehended an American of wealth and influence, whom he strongly suspected of being a traitor. He agreed, however, to spare his life and fortune, on the condition that he would go forthwith to the British camp before Fort Schuyler, and circulate a report to the effect that an overwhelming force was rapidly approaching. The prisoner consented ; and, true to his word, entered the camp, and very greatly magnified the force that was marching against it. As was anticipated, this report spread consternation and alarm throughout the forces of St. Leger. The Indians had no notion of remaining there to be overpowered by Arnold. They had rather take scalps than to be marks for the keen-eyed revolutionists. St. Leger was fully satisfied as regarded his strength and ability to defend the position he had taken, as also, of the weakness of the fort, and reluctantly listened to his Indian allies, who were open in avowing their disappointment. They had presumed it an easy matter to triumph over the Americans, and were to share equally with the British in the division of the spoils of conquest. Thus defeated and deceived, they resolved to fly for safety, and seek trophies in another quarter. And all the art and genius of Leger failed to detain them. Many left, and the remainder declared they would if the siege was persevered in. Thus he was compelled to abandon the siege, and, on the 22d of August, retired in great confusion ; the tents were left standing, the artillery abandoned, and the greater part of the baggage, ammunition, and provisions fell into the hands of the garrison, a detachment from which pursued the retreating enemy as he bent his course in the direction of Montreal.

CHAPTER IV.

FLIGHT OF ST. LEGER.—BRANT GATHERING HIS FORCES.
—THE MASSACRE.

> "Hark! hark! methinks I hear some melancholy moan,
> Stealing upon my listening ear,
> As tho' some departing spirit was about
> To soar, amid the horrors of a massacre!
> Yes! the savage fiend, with glittering knife,
> And tomahawk, reeking with infant blood,
> Stands in awful prospect before my vision."

THE circumstances under which St. Leger made his hurried flight from Fort Schuyler, were by no means flattering to his vain-glorious disposition. He had the command of an army which boasted of being in the enjoyment of the full powers of health, discipline and valor, and into whose minds he had labored to infuse a spirit of opposition to republican liberty, as well as to prejudice them in favor of the crown of Great Britain. He had endeavored to prove that the government of the mother country, with all her fading splendors of anarchy, was in every respect superior to the one designed to be established in the colonies. He was peculiarly lavish with his promises to all who would assist in redeeming the cause of the king from the usurpers, and continue submissive to his arrogant behests, and tyrannic acts of his minion serfs in Parliament. The children of the colonists were to receive their full measure of vengeance and wrath from the ministers of justice, who were to visit with devastation, famine, and the long train of unmitigated horrors of a scourging war, all who refused to acknowledge the "Divine Right of Kings." Yet after having exhausted his powers in rhetorical flourishes, begging, promising and threatening those under his command, he suddenly abandons the siege, and retires from the "field" in the utmost confusion.

The Indians continued their depredations, for massacre and murder had become the cherished objects of their lives.

In the summer of 1778 Brant made his head quarters at Oquago,* and Unadilla, and gathered around him several hundred Indians and tories, ready for any emergency,—to pillage and devastate the country.

A fort was erected at Cherry Valley by order of General Lafayette, and became a retreat when the incursions of the Indians gave alarm to the surrounding inhabitants. Brant resolved upon its destruction, was prepared for an attack, and was only prevented by being frightened by a band of boys who, in honor of their patriotic fathers, were marching out in the direction of Brant's hiding place, where they were to engage in a sham battle. Brant, presuming it to be an approaching army, discharged a few scattering shots, killing Lieut. Wormwood, and Capt. Peter Sitz, and decamped, leaving the boys

> "To beat the sheepskin, blow the fife,
> And march in trainin' order."

In July, Wyoming, a new and flourishing settlement on

* Now Windsor.

the eastern branch of the Susquehanna, was devastated and laid waste, many of the inhabitants were ruthlessly murdered, others burned at the stake, or tortured in the most barbarous and unrelenting manner.

In the following November, Brant, at the head of 700 warriors, 500 of whom were his own men, accompanied by Capt. Walter Butler, son of Col. John Butler, the devastator of Wyoming, who had obtained 200 Butler Rangers of his father, marched upon Cherry Valley, where was perpetrated one of the most inhuman massacres recorded in history, and which proves to an absolute certainty the tory commander to be a most implacable enemy to freemen, a reckless tyrant, a barbarian well suited to the capacity of his calling, a midnight marauder, and wanton ravager of the innocent.

Col. Ichabod Alden was in command of the fort, and through his inexcusable neglect the surrounding inhabitants did not take shelter in the fort, as he had promised to keep scouts out, who, in case of danger, would sound the alarm. His scouts built a large fire, around which they were enjoying a comfortable nap. Brant and his allies fell upon them just before daylight had dawned on the ill-fated settlement, capturing them, and making the surprise most complete. Back settlers were surprised in their dwellings, and murdered with every circumstance of fiendish barbarity. The village was invested in all parts at the same moment, and then ensued a scene at which humanity would shudder and angels might weep. Fathers, mothers, brothers, sisters and friends, were inhumanly tomahawked and scalped, to appease the Indian and tory spirit of revenge. Even lisping infancy was made to share the like fate, cruel and barbarous as it was.

The commander of the rude fortification, refusing to yield to the usurper's call to surrender, fell by the tomahawk. Brant and his Mohawks nerved themselves for the scene of blood and woe that was to follow, but were less furious, less depraved, and still less cruel, torturing and fiendlike, than were the Senecas; for they, as if inspired by the *arch demon of Hades*, sprung upon the innocent, the helpless and unoffending, and murdered them without exhibiting one touch of remorse, or emotion of sympathy. So, too, with the tory, or renegade *allies*,—they were ripe for massa cre and blood.

The troops in the fort made a gallant and noble defence; but they were not sufficiently strong to make a successful sally from their entrenchments.

When darkness had again curtained the earth, the invaders, with about forty prisoners, were hurrying from the scenes of devastation and death.

The next day a detachment of militia arrived from the Mohawk, just in time to see the last of the prowling foe disappear from the settlement. To them the cruelties and disastrous effects were exhibited in all their hateful and sickening deformities. The inhabitants who escaped the tomahawk and scalping knife, fled from their homes, seeking the protection of others whose hearts and desires were with the advocates and supporters of republican freedom and entire independence.

A volume might be filled with incidents, cold-blooded and heart-chilling, detailing the horrid massacres where whole families were indiscriminately murdered.

Robert Wells, his mother, wife, four children, his brother and sister, with three domestics,—twelve in all,—were cruelly slaughtered by the Indians, leaving only one of this large and interesting family to tell the fate of the others. The blood runs cold as we contemplate the inhumanity exhibited towards Miss Jane Wells, the sister, an amiable and worthy young lady, who, on seeing her brother cut down while bowed in prayer, fled from the house and secreted herself behind some wood. Pale and trembling with fear, she was discovered by a Seneca Indian, who, as he approached her, very coolly wiped the blood from the glittering steel on his leggins, and sheathed it by his side; then seized her by the arm and dragged her from her covert. Looking up imploringly in his face, and in Indian accents, she begged him to spare her life. Vain supplication! Raising his tomahawk, yet red with the blood of her kindred, he buried it in her brains.

The wife of the Rev. Samuel Dunlap was cloven down before his eyes, and he barely escaped, through the interposition of a young chief of the Oquago branch of the Mohawks.

In the absence of William Mitchell, his wife and four children were ruthlessly murdered by the cowardly assassins; the house plundered and set on fire. The husband and father returned just in time to put out the fire, and discover the faint glimmerings of life remaining in one of his children. He had conveyed it to the door, and was in the act of stopping the flowing blood, when he saw to his horror another band approaching; he hastily secluded himself from sight, and there beheld a blood-thirsty tory extinguish with a blow of his hatchet the last spark of life that remained in the breast of his child. What a scene to meet a parent's eye!

The day following was one of sorrow and sadness to him. Without the assistance of a single friendly arm, he conveyed the remains of his dear ones to the Fort, where they were entombed in the "cold earth." Who can refrain from weeping at his loss! What eye can remain dry, or what heart untouched!

A Mrs. Campbell and her four children were taken prisoners and carried away into captivity. Long, long years of suffering, worse than death, passed away, before the husband and father learned the fate of his wretched family.

Many escaped to the mountains, and looking down into the valley saw their houses wrapped in flames, and heard the yells of the savages as they triumphed in their work of death.

Girls in their teens, mothers with infants at the breast, fled to the woods without clothing, and for twelve or fifteen hours endured the most excruciating agony. A cold November wind whistled through the tree-tops, and moaned over the mountain gorges. The earth was covered with snow, and a drizzling rain added to the sufferings of the fugitives.

Retributive justice will, however, sooner or later, overtake the vile oppressor. Capt. Walter Butler, the acknowledged instigator of all this havoc, was captured at Johnstown in 1781. He had been defeated, and fled. Swimming his horse across the river, the moment he gained the shore he turned and defied those in pursuit; a ball from one of the Yankee rifles brought him to the ground. An Indian of the Oneida tribe, who favored the American cause, sprang into the stream and swam across, when Butler immediately cried for quarter. But the old chieftain shouted in his ear, "Sherry Valley! Remember Sherry Valley!" and instantly clove his skull with a tomahawk. Hastily pulling off his scalp, he held it up to the gaze of his followers while his yet bleeding victim was gasping out his death groans.

CHAPTER V.

SULLIVAN'S CAMPAIGN—INTERESTING INCIDENTS.

> "Go, seek the covert of the savage foe,
> Disperse them at thy weal or woe."

During the year 1779, General Sullivan made a successful expedition into the Indian territory, destroyed forty of their towns, and put the enemy to flight.

Influenced by the numerous presents and promises made by the British agents and tory adherents, and with the desire to plunder, five of the confederated Indian tribes invaded the north-western frontiers, spreading devastation and death wherever they went.* Their object was to ravage, burn, and kill. To check the career of these lawless intruders, and to mete out to them a due amount of retributive justice, Congress placed three thousand continental troops under the command of General Sullivan.

When the savage allies received the first news relative to the projected expedition against them, they immediately began to fortify their strongholds and prepare themselves for a determined resistance. They well knew that the horrid murders and midnight massacres, in addition to the rapine and plunder which they had

* The Oneidas alone remained favorable to the American cause.

committed, were laid up against them, and that if unable to withstand the force which was marching through the wilderness, they would be indiscriminately cut down and despoiled of their country.

General Sullivan marched from Easton, Pennsylvania, and arrived with his army at Wyoming on the 24th day of June. The enemy having fled before him, and learning that they were committing outrages of the grossest character, he determined to pursue, and if possible drive them from the country.

On the 31st of July he left, with his forces, for the Indian settlements farther up the Susquehanna and its tributaries. His stores and artillery were conveyed up the river in one hundred and fifty boats, and presented a grand and imposing appearance. The lurking savages, who still hovered about the country for the sake of plunder, were not only surprised but greatly frightened, as they viewed them from the long range of mountains which bordered the majestic Susquehanna. The horses, as they moved along in single file, formed a continuous line of six miles in length. They numbered about two thousand.

The forces arrived at Tioga Point on the 11th of August, and were joined by Gen. Clinton on the 22d, he having marched from the Mohawk with a detachment of one thousand troops, thus swelling the command of General Sullivan to four thousand. The Indians had taken a position near Newtown, where they had strongly entrenched themselves, determined to resist the advance of Gen. Sullivan. Their combined forces numbered eight hundred Indians and two hundred tories, and were commanded by Brant and Butler. On the 29th the

Americans were drawn up before their breastworks, and commenced a most deadly attack. The Indians withstood the fierce shocks of a terrible cannonade for upwards of two hours, making the most determined efforts at resistance recorded in our country's history. They fought with desperation, while the shot and chain from the well-drilled forces of Sullivan were making terrible havoc in their ranks. But though they warred for country and home, and sought for victory as a last forlorn hope to their sinking cause, it was vain, for it was impossible to withstand the perfect shower of balls that were poured in among them, answered by the cries and groans of the wounded and dying. The tories faltered ; the Indians broke and made a precipitate retreat. The victory was achieved.

The contest was one which has but few parallels. The enemy yielded, inch by inch, and when finally forced at the point of the bayonet to leave their entrenchments and flee, terror-stricken, to the mountain gorges or almost impassable *lagoons*, the ground they had occupied was found literally drenched with the blood of the fallen victims. Eleven of the dead remained upon the field, and fourteen were found but partially covered with leaves. Two canoes were very much stained with blood, and their trail, even in the mind of Col. Stone, author of the life of Brant, exhibited "the most indubitable proof that a portion of their dead and wounded had been carried off." The Americans lost, according to the highest account which we have found on record, "only six men," and from forty to fifty were wounded. Among these were Major Titcomb, Captain Clayes, and Lieut. M'Colley.

The Indians who had escaped the terrible fire of Sullivan's artillery, saw with horror the destruction of their orchards, cornfields and cabins. It was to them a scene of utter desolation. They had, it is true, made some preparation to intercept and cut off the progress of Sullivan, but had no idea that such a formidable force could successfully penetrate through an almost unbroken forest, convey their heavy baggage, and drive them from their strongholds.

Like a tornado sweeping over the country, destroying everything in its onward march, passed the army of Generals Sullivan and Clinton, spreading the most utter desolation on every side.

At Knawaholee, twenty cabins with their contents were consumed. The corn, which looked very promising, was also destroyed.

At Catharine Town,—the home of Catharine Montour, the wife of the stern Canadesaga chief,—the wigwams, orchards and cornfields were entirely destroyed, the inhabitants having, previous to the approach of the army, deserted their homes.

Their cluster of houses on the east side of Seneca lake, and near the old Indian Peach Orchard, in the [now] town of Hector, shared a like fate.

The army, like so many vultures, hovered for an hour about Apple Tree Town, leaving nothing but desolation to mark the destroyer's course.

Arriving at Kandaia, an old town of twenty houses, which exhibited considerable taste, the warriors paused for a short time, making a few general flourishes in true knight-errant style. The houses, as represented by one who shared the honors and privations attending the campaign, were large and elegant, some beautifully painted ; their tombs likewise, especially of their chief warriors.

Still the army strode forward, hoping to come up with the retreating foe. But they were not to be so easily caught.

At the capital of the Senecas, Kanadesaga, at least something like a flourish at resistance was expected ; but when the emboldened army drew up before their entrenchments, eager, anxious, thirsting for the blood of the poor unlettered red men, lo ! they, too, had fled. But in their sudden flight they left behind them, asleep, a white boy of seven or eight years.

Kanadesaga was located about one and a half miles north of the present flourishing village of Geneva, and contained about sixty houses. It was the last stronghold of the Senecas, though destined to fall into the spoilers' hands. In after time, however, a few of the surviving remnants of that once powerful and far-famed tribe, returned, and once more reared their rude homes over the ashes of their former wigwams. When their lands were ceded to the State, it was explicitly agreed that this, the home of their ancient grandeur, should never be cultivated by the white man's hand. "Here," said the red man, "sleep our fathers, and they cannot rest well if they hear the plow of the white man above them." The rude traces of their olden fortress are still distinctly visible.

Near the shores of the Canandaigua lake, another flourishing settlement was approached and fired, with many of the products of Indian toil. There were twenty-three houses, many of them framed, and very elegantly painted.

From this place the army moved forward to Honeoye, a small town of about ten houses, situated near Conesus lake. The houses were fired and consumed. Here General Sullivan left a portion of the heavy stores and one field-piece, under the charge of a competent garrison. He had no doubt but that the Indians would show some resistance at the Genesee Castle, and he desired to be unencumbered with every unnecessary article. The next day he left for the capital. The enemy had held a council of war, and were almost unanimously in favor of making at least one more bold stand in the defence of their homes and their hunting-grounds. Their women and children were therefore directed to secrete themselves some miles ahead, in the direction of Fort Niagara. The preliminaries having been thus arranged, the warriors prepared for the contest. They took a favorable position between Honeoye creek and the head of Conesus lake, near what is now called Henderson's Flats. They had carefully ambushed, and awaited the arrival of the American forces. As soon as Sullivan's advance guard reached their position, the Indians appeared and commenced the attack. It was in the main a rather bloodless effort, and terminated in the enemy taking two Oneida Indians prisoners,—one a guide to Sullivan's army. He had on several occasions been of important service to the American force,—a fact fully apparent to his captors,—and hence he was a prisoner of consequence. He had a brother in Butler's corps, who in the early progress of the war had endeavored to persuade him to unite his destiny with his British brethren. But to no purpose. Soon after the prisoners were conducted into the enemy's camp, the brothers met—not, however, as friends who had been long separated. The eldest of the two, deeming it a proper time to vent upon his weaker brother the envenomed shafts of his deep and undying malice, approached, and thus addressed him: —

"Brother! You have merited death! The hatchet or the war-club shall finish your career! When I begged of you to follow me in the fortunes of war, you were deaf to my cries: you spurned my entreaties!

"Brother! You have merited death, and shall have your deserts! When the rebels raised their hatchets to fight their good master, you sharpened your knife, you brightened your rifle, and led on our foe to the fields of our fathers!

"Brother! You have merited death, and shall die by our hands! When those rebels had driven us from the fields of our fathers to seek out new homes, it was you who could dare to step forth as their pilot, and conduct them even to the doors of our wigwams, to butcher our children and put us to death! No crime can be greater! But though you have merited death, and shall die on this spot, my hands shall not be stained with the blood of a brother! Who will strike?"

There was a pause of one moment—a moment of awful suspense—and the next, the bright hatchet of Little Beard cleft his skull, and his spirit passed to the brighter land of promise.

While at Honeoye, General Sullivan detached Lieut. William Boyd, of the Rifle corps, with a select party of twenty-six men to reconnoitre Little Beard's Town, (now known as Leicester.) On arriving at the settlement, the party discovered that the Indians were absent, though certain indications led them to presume that in all probability they would soon return, and they therefore concluded to remain sleeping upon their arms.

Just after Aurora had begun to ascend the eastern sky, two Indians were discovered lurking about the place, and unfortunately for the party, were instantly shot and hastily scalped. Considering the unsafe position in which this act of indiscretion had placed them, they determined to hasten their return back to the main army. But when within one and a half miles of Gen. Sullivan's force, their progress was intercepted by the sudden appearance of five hundred Indians, and nearly an equal number of tory Rangers; the former under command of Capt. Brant, and the latter under Col. Butler, of infamous memory. We have been told by one who served in the campaign, that these border pirates had not for a single day lost sight of Sullivan's army after their defeat at Newtown. Boyd and his party made a number of attempts to cut their way through the strong lines of the enemy, but were unsuccessful. All fell save Boyd and an Oneida Indian, who served as pilot, and who had distinguished himself in the battle of Oriskany.* Boyd and Hanyerry surrendered and were made prisoners. Under the direction of Butler they were conducted to Little Beard's castle. Boyd had an interview with Brant, who promised that his life should be spared. But he was unexpectedly called away. In his absence, Butler delivered them over to the tender mercies of a chosen number of barbarians that would disgrace any army and blacken the character of any

* They were buried at what is now called Groveland.

commander. The Indian was literally hewn to pieces. But the fate of Lieut. Boyd,—the high-souled, gallant Boyd,—was of a more terrible and disgusting character. The heart sickens as we record the inhumanity of his captors. We read of no parallel in the records of ancient wars, when bigotry blotted its pathway with blood, or when tyrants, clad in iron mail, waged long and unrelenting wars, severed kingdoms and divided empires, in order that their names might be enrolled on the scroll of immortal fame.

He was disrobed of his clothing, his hands pinioned behind him, and his person tied with a hempen cord to a small tree. Then commenced the work of torture, Little Beard leading the way. He was one of those reckless wretches whose barbarity did much towards injuring the English cause, as well as in tarnishing the Indian character. Their tomahawks were whirled over his head with great fury, accompanied with horrid yells, until the tree was completely hewed and shivered to pieces. Then, like so many infuriated demons, they approached him, brandishing their scalping knives, frantic with rage, and thirsting for his blood. "His nails were pulled out, his nose cut off, one of his eyes plucked out, and his tongue cut off."* An incision was made in his side, from which protruded an intestine. This was immediately attached to the branch of a small tree ; the hempen cord loosened from his pinioned arms ; and now goaded and scourged by means the most heartless, he was compelled to march round and round until his intestines disappeared from his body,

* Stone's Life of Brant.

and he fell like a lump of clay to the earth. Then louder, louder were the yells of the demoniac devils—wilder, wilder were their frantic gesticulations, for on his brow they saw the large drops of sweat—his lips quivered, his eyes rolled in agony, and all was over,—for Heaven in mercy had thrown the sleep of death over the gallant Boyd, who was thus horribly scourged in his passage to the tomb.

Not yet satisfied, they added still another act of fiendish ferocity to the already unparalleled outrage. His head was severed from his body and attached to the end of a pole, with the expanded jaws of a dog just above it. And thus it was exhibited amidst the laughter and jeers of the more than half intoxicated tory and Indian faction.

When Gen. Sullivan learned the fate of Lieut. Boyd and Hanyerry, he made every possible effort to ferret out the dastard foe, hoping to avenge the barbarous act.

These unfortunate men, as reported by the journalist of Sullivan's campaign, were found in Little Beard's castle, bearing the marks of the most inhuman torture. Gen. Sullivan saw them respectably buried on the banks of Beard's Creek, in the midst of a number of Indian plum trees. In 1849 we visited the place, and looked upon the humble grave made consecrate by the remains of these brave and heroic men.

The Genesee castle as well as their town, which included one hundred and twenty-eight houses, fell into the conquerer's hands, but the artful foe had disappeared. Great efforts were made to ferret out their hiding-place, but in vain ; they were beyond the devastator's power.

Vast quantities of corn, beans and potatoes were collected and placed in the houses, to which fire was applied, and they were consumed. One of their numerous orchards contained fifteen hundred trees. But they, too, were devastated of their beauty.

The author of the Journal from which we have gathered our materials for this chapter, lived to tell us in his own glowing language how beautiful and Eden-like the Genesee valley, with its rich and waving products —the result of Indian toil—appeared previous to its being devastated by the victorious army.

The work of desolation was now complete. Forty of the Indian towns were laid in ruins. Not a house was left ; and the poor Indians felt that the ravagers' hands were upon them, for they had not left even food enough to sustain an infant's life for twenty-four hours.

When Gen. Sullivan arrived on his return march at the outlet of Seneca lake, he detached Col. Zebulon Butler, with the Rifle corps and five hundred men, to the east side of Cayuga lake, to lay waste the Indian settlements. The next day, and while encamped near Kandaia, Lieut. Col. Dearborn was detached with two hundred men for the purpose of destroying the settlement south of the lake, and but a little distant from the present prospective city of Ithaca.

Col. Butler pushed forward with his forces, and faithfully performed the task assigned him. At that time the natives had large fields of corn, which presented a most luxuriant growth, and of which the Cayugas were intending to garner up for their winter's use. Patches of beans and potatoes exhibited the like promising appearance. Nor was the fruit of their fine apple orchards less inviting to the soldier's eye, or gratifying to the Colonel's taste. Yet these trees of two hundred years' growth were felled to the ground. The products of the field—of hardy toil—were gathered into the Indian's rude dwellings and with them consumed by fire.

Three villages, to them of considerable importance, one of which was the capital of the Cayugas, were located near the shore of that magnificent sheet of water. Smaller settlements were scattered along the banks at various distances apart. But all, all were destroyed. Their cabins and castles were swept away, for the fatal element from the "white man's torch" was communicated to them, and soon all that remained to tell the wandering pioneer, as his eye caught sight of the flames as they gleamed heavenward, was a mass of smouldering ruins. Here the brave but unlettered red men had lived in unadorned peace ; and their council fire had burned for upwards of three centuries, serving as a beacon light to the returning warriors.

The mission of Col. Dearborn was alike successfully performed. Their wigwams were consumed, their maize burned up, and the home of their ancient grandeur made desolate. Truly they were a wandering and stricken people. If the Indians in their stealthy marches had been cruel, the white man had been equally so. The one had oppressed for the sake of gain, while the other sought revenge as a just retaliation for the conduct of his unmanly oppressor.

A little west of the residence of Dr. J. F. Burdick, and where he now has a flourishing peach orchard, were some eighteen or twenty cabins. Here lived a tall, swarthy Indian chief, generally known among the warriors of the Six Nations, as Long Jim, with whom he was a great favorite. He was of the Mohawk and Oneida extraction, and possessed many of the more prominent characteristics for which the two tribes have been so justly celebrated. He was usually kind, benevolent and just, but if insulted without proper cause, would assume the ferocity of a tiger, and act the part of a demoniac monster. He was an orator and a warrior, and possessed the art of swaying the multitude at his will. He believed in witches, hobgoblins and wizards, and often pretended to be influenced by a tutelary goddess, or guardian spirit. Shrewd and artful, dignified and generous, yet at times deceptive and malevolent, he studied to acquire influence and power, and in most of his marauding depredations, was successful in keeping the *arcana* of his heart as in a "sealed fountain." His unwritten history represents him as acting a conspicuous part in numerous tragical events which were perpetrated by detached parties from Burgoyne's army. A venerable chief, who resides on the New York Indian Reservation, informed us that, according to the tradition of his tribe, Long Jim was the main cause, instigator, and perpetrator of the bloody massacre which we are about to record.

A gentleman of character and fortune, and holding an honorable commission in the British army, had succeeded in winning the affections of Miss Jane M'Crea, a young, intelligent and lovely girl, over whose head had passed scarce seventeen summers. Her father resided near Fort Edward, and was a prominent actor in the royal cause. Circumstances having required the services and personal attention of Mr. Jones, the plighted lover of Miss M'Crea, he was stationed at some distance from the paternal roof of her father, and becoming exceedingly anxious for her safety, offered various rewards as inducements to the Indians who would convey her in safety to his camp. At length the bold and hazardous enterprise was undertaken. A band of Winnebagoes set out for the home of the expectant bride, bearing a letter from the intended husband, in which he had made a faithful record of his unabated love for the cherished object of his heart. On their approach the family were much alarmed, and were about flying in terror from the house, that safety, if possible, might be found, if not nearer, at least in the fort. But just at this moment, the young and gallant chief of the band bade his followers to retire a little; then beckoning to the frightened family, he held up the affectionate epistle, which unfortunately caught the attention of the mother, who readily conjectured the object of their mission. A token of friendship and welcome was returned, and the Indians, much pleased with the success of their chief, laughed heartily as they approached the worthy matron, each of whom she shook by the hand.

The seal of the little message was broken—the contents read and hastily considered—when Miss M'Crea prepared herself to accompany them to the British camp.

Thus far the expedition had been attended with the most perfect success, and they set out on their return with high hopes and lofty aspirations, for a keg of English rum was the price to be paid for her safe escort to the fortress of her lover!

But when about half way back, they were met by a

second party who had left for the achievement of the same purpose. Long Jim was the controlling spirit of his party, and was desirous of obtaining the prize. An altercation ensued, which finally rose to a warm dispute. Long Jim, unwilling to see the Winnebago chieftain proceed with the spotless object of the expedition, and presuming his party too weak to take her by force, suddenly seized her by the hair of the head, pulled her from the back of the noble steed, and with one demoniac stroke from the fatal tomahawk, cleft the scalp from the head of the fair young girl, and he bore it as a trophy to the astonished and heart-stricken lover.

This reckless and cold-blooded murder called forth a stern and feeling rebuke from Burgoyne ; and well it might, for it had a strong tendency to weaken the royal cause.

On the opposite side of the lake, where the Taughanic creek empties into the Tiohero, or Cayuga lake, the Indians had built a small town, and were growing corn, beans and potatoes on the rich flats. They had, also, apple trees of two and a half centuries' growth. This little town, called by the natives after the stream on which it was located, escaped the notice of Col. Butler, in consequence of his having passed up from East Cayuga, by way of Aurora and Lavana, to the head of the Cayuga settlements.

There was another settlement about six miles southwest of Taughanic, near the present village of Waterburg, which, from its back location, was not discovered by either of the detached forces which General Sullivan had sent out to make havoc with the Indians' property.

The traces of a remarkable trench enclosure were distinctly to be seen in 1840, when the author last visited the spot made consecrate by the uncoffined bones of a "once peculiar people." Near by was the burial place of their dead. At an earlier period many of the mounds were dug open, from which were collected numerous antiquated articles of Indian warfare, and which very closely resembled those used in a former age by Europeans. A few miles distant, William Carman found on his farm a number of human bones, while he was extracting some stumps of trees of over two hundred years' growth. These olden relics were presumed by many to be of a larger race of people than the Indians. The presumption is possible, as there is much evidence in support of that opinion. We have seen several ornaments, the texture and workmanship of which undoubtedly belong to a different race, and probably date back to a remote period of our country, on which neither tradition or history can throw any light.

But to return. General Sullivan, after having sent sufficient forces to cut off the Indians and lay waste their settlements bordering the Cayuga lake, marched to "Catharine Town," and thence up the Chemung valley. Wearied with over-exertion, he paused with his gallant troops for the night on the rich flats about six miles north of Newtown, (now Elmira,) and while here encamped, they concluded to abandon or dispose of about four hundred of their horses, in consequence of their worn-out and galled condition ; and to prevent their falling into the hands of the enemy, though not a Red Roman appeared in sight, they were led out in Indian file and shot down ; and hence originated the name of Horse Heads—a name familiar to the general reader of American history.

Arriving at Newtown, they received a heart-cheering salute of thirteen guns from the Fort which had been thrown up by Captain Reid and his force of two hundred men, who had been left in charge of some stores which were forwarded from Tioga Point for the support of Sullivan's army. While here, the news of Spain having declared war against Great Britain was received with unbounded joy. The event was celebrated in a manner which was well calculated to animate the drooping spirits of those who had periled health, happiness, and fortune in the support of American liberty. Five large oxen, one for each brigade, were killed and roasted, which, with the added trimmings and double rations, were dispatched in a way at once interesting and agreeable. During the festive proceedings, cannons were fired at intervals, which added much to the joy of the already excited heroes. Here Colonels Butler and Dearborn united with the main army.

Leaving Newtown, they returned by way of Tioga Point to Wyoming, where they arrived on the 7th of October, and in a few days after bent their course for Easton, and from thence to Morristown, New Jersey, where they took up their winter quarters.

There are very few expeditions on record, which proved so entirely successful in their general results, and which so fully met the hopes and expectations of the people and of Congress, as the one of which we have just given a hasty sketch.

The burning of Moscow was a terrible blow to Napoleon and his unrivaled army, and which forever clouded the hopes of the imperial hero. It involved the sumptuous palaces, monuments, and miracles of art, in one common flame. The devastation of the Indian country was as severe a chastisement inflicted upon the red men, and from the effects of which they never wholly recovered. Deprived of their homes and provisions, they were of necessity dependent upon the English for the necessaries of life. Provisions were extremely scarce and high. The winter was unusually severe, and hundreds "took the scurvy and died."

But though the Indians were greatly crippled, they were not subdued ; though defeated, they were not vanquished. They still made stealthy incursions into peaceable settlements, the history of whose attacks might be summed up in the fearful, sad, bloody, but brief record—surprise—massacre—conflagration—retreat.

As in the past so in the future, Brant was the ruling spirit. He could not brook the thought of being subdued. Disaster and defeat tended to make him the more daring and reckless. Yet Brant possessed many valuable traits of character—was often humane and benevolent. But we do not propose at this time to pen a sketch of his life—that is reserved for a future work, "The Indian Chiefs of America." As often as he was baffled in his endeavors to retrieve his loss upon the embattled field of glory, or failed in restoring to his nation the homes and hunting-grounds of their fathers, so often did the old chieftain gather his long-abused and often-betrayed followers around him, and with the envenomed rage of the famished tiger, when brought to bay by the hunters, make another and still another effort to regain the Indians' dominion—the Indians' ancient residence. If it was his custom to crouch and hide like the baited lion, it was but to leap with the greater vengeance—to dash with the greater force upon his antagonist—to make the victory more easy—the tragedy more terrible.

Soon after the close of Gen. Sullivan's campaign, a party consisting of between forty and fifty Indians and tories were found ranging about the wild mountain gorges of Wyoming, from whose dark retreats they stealthily made incursions, committing many and serious depredations. They were fit subjects for plunder, rapine, and murder. They were ripe for any outrage, however dark, bloody, and heart-rending it might be, and it is doubtful whether a more cruel and unrelenting band of heartless desperadoes cursed our land at any time during the long and painful period of our country's revolution. They delighted in having an opportunity to wreak vengeance upon an American. To torture by acts the most barbarous, seemed to be the highest object of their ambition.

Capt. Bedlock, who was taken prisoner at the fiendish massacre, afterwards fell into the hands of these heartless wretches. He was stripped of his clothing, had his body stuck full of pine splinters, his arms closely pinioned behind him, and his person attached by cords to a small tree. Around the wretched captive was then placed a mass of combustible matter, with a quantity of pine knots. Now commences the awful sacrifice. The fire is kindled around him, and when the terrific flames began to wreathe their death folds around his person, his two companions, Ransom and Durkee, were thrown into the middle of the crackling flames, where they all perished, martyrs to freedom's holy cause. An Indian, who figured conspicuously in the horrid scene, told us in 1849 that whenever any of the victims attempted to rise from the faggot and flame, they were instantly felled to the earth, and held down by means of poles and rails.

One of these tories, whose mother had married a second husband, butchered with his own hands both her, his father-in-law, his sister, and their infant children.

Another tory, of the same class, exterminated his whole family,—mother, brothers, and sisters,—and then mingled their blood in one common carnage with that of the aged father and husband.

It was, too, this same class of desperadoes who, not satisfied with effecting these heart-chilling scenes of massacre and blood, fired the houses, shot and destroyed their cattle, or cut out their tongues, leaving them still alive to roam the fields in agony.

To protect the settlement from the attacks of these piratical mountaineers, several companies were called out, with orders to hold themselves in readiness to avenge any wrong that might be inflicted upon the peaceable inhabitants of the valley. One of the companies had marched from Northampton county, and encamped on the banks of one of the tributary streams of the Nescopeck creek, and while partaking of their frugal repast, were surprised by these barbarians, who inhumanly slew eleven of the company and severely wounded two others. Recovering from the terrible shock, from the tempest of balls, bludgeons, and tomahawks, the Northampton boys returned them a complimentary salute from their Yankee rifles, causing an equal number to give death a *horrid grin.*

Wyoming will ever be memorable in history, for there occurred some of the most tragical scenes in our national annals. The green turf has been made classic and consecrate, and will ever be hallowed in the imagination of the heroic bard, for there are entombed the mouldering bones of many a brave warrior.

The ladies of Wilkesbarre, influenced by the true spirit of chivalry, have erected a monument over their sleeping dust. The pyramidal shaft of granite stands a memento of the white man's sufferings and a witness to the red man's cruelty.

CHAPTER VI.

PIONEER MOVEMENTS—INDIAN REFLECTIONS—REVENGE —DESTRUCTION OF THE MOHAWK VALLEY—INCIDENTS.

"But go, rouse your warriors."

The red men saw, as with prophetic eye, that their hunting-grounds were soon to pass into the control of the white invaders. They saw villages spring up, as if by magic, in various parts of their dominion, and traders were besieging them along every important trail, or offering rich inducements wherever the council fires blazed as beacon lights to returning warriors. Mill sites had been marked wherever the aristocratic adventurer had heard a cataract's roar, or seen a leaping cascade. The merchant and commissioner were seducing and bribing them of their most magnificent forests. And contrary to stipulation and expostulation, emigrants, like the frogs of Egypt, were coming in from every quarter, and laying the corner stones for royal palaces and cottage homes. British lords and French Sebastians saw thousands of castle builders ready for the work of progress, and imagined that to their dreaming vision appeared fields of rich fertility. Towns and counties were being carved out of their inheritance. The sharp crack of Yankee rifles was heard on the mountain tops, while New England axes were ringing in the valleys of Canisteo, Chemung, Susquehanna, Wyoming, Chenango, Otsego, Onondaga and Genesee. Ramparts were reared, behind which the invaders might gather and concoct plans for the annihilation of the natives. They had heard the roar of cannon and the rattle of grape shot under the bluffs of Ticonderoga. The music from Montcalm bugles, and Bradstreet drums, was still ringing in their ears. They saw provincial rangers, bloody Britons, and French chevaliers, and knew that fire and grape had done their work of carnage and desolation at Niagara, Oswego, and Frontenac. They had seen the army of General Sullivan sweeping over their country from the Delaware to the Great Council, or Big Tree in Genesee Valley, laying waste their cornfields, orchards and gardens. Forty of their towns were smouldering ruins. Or, if they turned their eyes to their rich locations bordering the Cayuga lake, nought but desolation greeted their vision, for Colonels Butler and Dearborn had despoiled them of their fondest hopes. Colonel Gansevoort had checked their ravages about Fort Schuyler, and Col. Van Schaick carried disaster among the Onondagas.

These expeditions, though attended with the fullest success, did not subdue the war spirit of the restless savages. They felt that they had been greatly wronged and abused by the "pale faces," who had thus unceremoniously deprived them of their birthright. They determined on revenge, for they were unwilling to brook the indignant insult. Their council fire had been put out, and their country laid waste. Desolation sat in gloomy silence, while the hooting owl flapped his wings over their deserted homes, marked only by the charred logs of their demolished cabins. All was dreary and desolate. But these wrongs were to be avenged. Hate, —bitter, unrelenting hate,—was most assiduously cultivated in the bosom of the native lords of the forest. Though defeated and driven from their castles and strongholds, they were not subdued The spirit, though "crushed, would rise again" with renewed vigor, and the haughty and stealthy foe was determined to crush and gloat over those who would thus wantonly deprive them of their rights—rights marked out and defined by the very finger of the Creator—guaranteed to them by patent or deed, by the Great Jehovah.

Nor did they long feel thus indignant, before an opportunity was offered to wreak vengeance on their white oppressors.

They made a stealthy march into the Mohawk valley, with a fixed purpose to ravage, burn and kill.

The inhabitants of that ill-fated region were regarded by the Indians and tories as enemies, and sad and heart-rending were the results of such a conclusion. Hordes of savages and loyalists incessantly emerged from the forests and mountain gorges, murdering and scalping all whom they met. Even innocent women and lisping infancy were cruelly butchered by the marauding assailants.

The whole valley was rendered most desolate. If a single dwelling remained to be seen, it was like a flowery oäsis looming up in the wide waste of ruin. What a sight to meet the eye of the hardy, industrious, yet gloomy and despondent pioneer! There were the smouldering ruins, the charred bones, the mangled bodies of domestic animals, and the blood-stained marks of ruthless violence.

There were many brave patriot pioneers who fell by the tomahawk or the Indian's arrow, and were left to moulder and wither in the desert air. But their names, their virtues and heroic acts, have been embalmed and consecrated in the hearts and affections of a grateful people. The orator has spoken their praise; the poet has strung anew his lyre, and breathed forth most feeling and tender sympathies.

"Ah! where are the soldiers that fought there of yore?
The sod is upon them, they'll struggle no more;
The hatchet is fallen, the red man is low:
But near him reposes the arm of his foe.

"The bugle is silent, the war-whoop is dead;
There's a murmur of waters and woods in their stead,
And the raven and owl chant a symphony drear,
From the dark waving pines o'er the combatants' bier.

"The light of the sun has just sunk in the wave,
And a long time ago set the sun of the brave.
The waters complain, as they roll o'er the stones,
And the rank grass encircles a few scattered bones.

"The names of the fallen the traveler leaves
Cut out with his knife in the bark of the trees;
But little avail his affectionate arts,
For the names of the fallen are graved in our hearts.

"The voice of the hunter is loud on the breeze;
There's a dashing of waters, a rustling of trees;
And the jangling of armor hath all passed away,—
No gushing of life-blood is seen there to-day.

"The eye that was sparkling, no longer is bright;
The arm of the mighty—death conquered its might;

The bosoms that once for their country beat high,
To those bosoms the sods of the valley are nigh.

"Sleep, soldiers of merit! sleep, gallants of yore!
The hatchet is fallen, the struggle is o'er.
While the fir-tree is green and the wind rolls a wave,
The tear-drop shall brighten the turf of the brave."

In many parts of the Mohawk valley, the inhabitants were reduced to a state of suffering which will hardly admit of comparison. Every thing in the line of property was destroyed. The tories, as in many other instances, were more cruel and barbarous than the savages. It was their object and desire to make the ravages most complete. They were not satisfied with burning, plundering, driving off and killing hundreds of cattle and horses, but were determined on drenching the green earth with the blood of the oppressed. Many were tortured in the most cruel and barbarous manner. Some were burned at the stake, while others were merely scalped and left to endure the pains and horrors of a living, lingering death.

Col. Fisher, who lived near Caughnawaga, when it was burned by the Indians, made a most noble effort at self-defence in his own house. His two brothers had fallen by his side, and himself being closely pressed to the wall by a band of savages and painted tories, whooping and yelling like incarnate demons,—nerved with desperation, he resolved to make one more bold stroke for liberty. At a single discharge of his rifle, two of the enemy fell locked in the embrace of death. Two more were felled to the floor by well-directed blows from the breech of his gun, while a fifth was made crazy in consequence of having come in contact with a bunch of bones which was attached to the extreme end of his arm. In this way he escaped from his castle, was pursued by the infuriated foe, captured, scalped, and left writhing in his terrible agonies. The day after, he was discovered by a friend who had fled to the mountains, and was conveyed to his house, where he received every attention which circumstances would permit ; and although the wound was of the most frightful and dangerous character, he survived its dreadful pains, recovered, and lived many years after peace had been restored to his country, an honorable member of society, as well as an ornament to the republic, the freedom of which he so dearly loved.

Lucretia Mott was one of the fifty prisoners taken after the burning of Schoharie. She fell into the hands of six tories, who were as heartless and inhuman, as reckless and perfidious, as the mind could well imagine. After being compelled to minister to their menial appetites, she had her right ear cropped, two of her fingers amputated, besides other barbarities of a similar character. She was then compelled to disrobe herself of her clothing, which was buried in her presence, after which she was left in the wilderness, many miles from any settlement, with no companion save the hooting owl, howling wolf and screeching panther, to protect her as she sought out, as best she could, her way to the desolate valley.

Mr. Sawyer was taken prisoner by a band of marauding Indians, who, after having proceeded with him several miles, stopped for the night in the gloomy recess of a mountain gorge. After being, as they presumed, securely bound, they directed him to lie down and sleep with them. As he had been a terror to the Indians, he expected little else than cruel, unrelenting torture at their hands. The night was one of intense darkness. The moon had descended beyond the western hills and "gone to rest." The stars put on their weeds of mourning, and refused to give their light, while thunders rolled and lightnings flashed athwart the darkened sky. The vivid flashes of lightning gave the prisoner an opportunity to view his situation. To his surprise he found means to loosen his hands. This was effected by carefully reaching his pinioned hands to the nearest Indian, and cautiously taking from his belt his scalping knife. His next object was to free his feet, which was soon done. He then with great care looked into the face of each of the seven savages by whom he was surrounded, and found them in a sound sleep. Just at this auspicious moment, the clouds dispersed, and the stars looked out from their hiding-places, which fully revealed the position of his oppressors. Carefully taking from the belt of the leader of the band, his tomahawk, he soon dispatched six of them, and mortally wounded the seventh. Thus having effected his release, he bent his course for a distant settlement, which he hoped the Indians had not visited, and which he reached during the afternoon of the next day.

The heart sickens as we contemplate some of the bloody tragedies and inhuman acts which were perpetrated by these marauding parties. We have read many a tale of horror, where revenge had instigated the fiend to seek out his victim during the dark hour of night, and when no eye could witness the awful deed, save the all-seeing eye of Omnipotence, plunge the dagger to the heart of her whose affections he was unworthy of possessing, and send her disembodied spirit uncalled for into the presence of the great Eternal. But we can recall no act so chilling to the heart, so dishonorable to humanity, as the one which we are about to sketch.

A family, consisting of father, mother and eight children, residing in one of the settlements adjoining Schoharie, and which had been laid in smoking ruins, was massacred with every attending circumstance of heartless cruelty. Near by where the mother lay weltering in her heart's blood, was a cradle containing a little babe. An old Sachem of the Iroquoy tribe, on discovering it, approached the cradle with his hatchet raised, with intent to dispatch it with a blow. A cherub smile played over its innocent face, which seemed to touch his heart, for his strong arm was at once nerveless, the hatchet fell from his hand, and he bent his weather-beaten, scarred frame, for the purpose of taking the little innocent in his arms, and pressing its tender form to his breast. But before he had time to effect his purpose, a painted tory, who had a far less feeling heart than his savage ally, plunged his bayonet in its bosom, and raising it up to the wall, cried out in tones which none but the *incarnate* could utter—"*This, too, is a rebel.*"

Maria Marshall was taken captive near Oswego, by a party of savages who were returning from one of their predatory incursions into the Mohawk Valley, where they massacred several families, and burned a number of houses.

Arriving within a few miles of Oswego, the party divided in hopes of securing more convenient quarters for the night with some of the scattered settlers who were occupying comfortable dwellings along the line of their ancient war-path.

Five of the party were kindly entertained at the house of Mr. Marshall. The family consisted of Mr. and Mrs. Marshall, and three children, the youngest of whom was but nineteen days old. After being freely treated with the best provisions of the house, they retired to rest. Mr. and Mrs. Marshall, presuming upon the good will of the Indians in return for their generosity, felt secure, and after retiring to bed, were soon wrapped in sound sleep. But they had mistaken the character of their visitors. They were less humane, less faithful than their charitable fidelity had supposed. The hellish plot of massacre had been conceived, the first intimation of which, that reached the ears of Mr. and Mrs. Marshall, was the crackling of the burning timbers. The faithless foe had secretly plundered and fired the house, and were now ready to take the lives of those whose bounty they had so liberally shared.

The cowardly assassins had taken positions on the outside of the house, where they stood with uplifted hatchets, ready to strike down whoever might attempt to escape from within. Suddenly their attention was arrested by Mr. Marshall, who was hurrying through the huge columns of smoke and flame, holding in his arms his two eldest children. Presently he sprang from the door, and was cloven down with the tomahawk, wielded by the strong arm of an athletic savage. In a moment the father and his precious burthens were weltering in their blood, and writhing in the agonies of death. Mrs. Marshall, with feeble step, and nearly suffocated with smoke, reached the door just as the roof fell in with a terrible crash. Closely folded to her bosom was her little babe. She was soon surrounded by her inhuman assailants who demanded of her the child, and on being refused, it was seized by one of the Indians, who immediately dashed out its brains on the door-step. This most detestable and horrible requital of evil for good was executed with a shameless barbarity alike frightful and revolting to the finest feelings of humanity.

Mrs. Marshall was made prisoner, and securely guarded by two of the Indians while the others secured the plunder.

Thus having completed the work of desolation, the marauders took up their march for Canada. When they reached Oswego, their number was increased to twenty-seven, two of whom were female captives. On the fifth day, one of them, the mother of the other, an infirm old lady, gave out; she could go no further. She begged for her life, but it was denied her, for at that moment a tomahawk went whirling through the air on its mission of death, and sunk deep into the brains and gore of the fallen captive.

The destination of the Indians was a settlement contiguous to the Three Rivers, near where the Adirondacks, early in the seventeenth century, were defeated in a bloody and exterminating war waged against them by the Five Confederative Nations.

Notwithstanding the poor health of Mrs. Marshall, occasioned by her recent confinement, she was forced to travel from ten to fifteen miles per day, which occasioned still greater debility of bodily powers, as well as tending to enervate the more noble powers of her exalted mind.

The day previous to the expected time of reaching the Three Rivers, the party divided, leaving Mrs. Marshall still in the hands of her original captors. Early in the evening they encamped for the night on an elevated spot of ground, kindled a fire, stacked their arms, partook of a scanty repast, and sought rest in the embrace of sleep. The savages had intimated to their captive the fact, that on their arrival at the end of their destination, she was to be delivered to one of the grand sachems, who would in turn give her in marriage to a young and distinguished brave of the Iroquoy nation. Shocked at the idea of becoming the wife of an Indian, she could hardly refrain from shedding tears, and otherwise bewailing her sad fate. Bereft of the protecting arm of a kind husband, mourning the loss of her dear children, all of whom had fallen by the hands of the inhuman monsters who were preparing to fetter her with the polluter's chain, far away from country and friends, and in the midst of a dense forest swarming with ravenous beasts and barbarous savages, and in the immediate power of five inhuman Indians who had wrecked her happiness and blighted her fairest hopes of life, she resolved upon death, or deliverance from a bondage more to be deprecated than the assassin's knife.

She cautiously rose from the cold, damp earth, on which she had vainly endeavored to repose her weary limbs, and noiselessly prepared for the work of massacre.

The moon was careering high in the vaulted dome.

The stars looked out in beauty from the radiant sky. The wind had died away. Not even a floating zephyr was heard among the tall trees. All was silent as the grave.

The weapons of the Indians were hastily removed out of their reach. She now examined the guns for the purpose of selecting two to assist her in carrying out the bold enterprise in which she had so determinedly engaged. They appeared in excellent order. There was one which particularly struck her fancy, as it had two barrels and was therefore better suited to her purpose than two of the ordinary kind. This, and a keen-edged hatchet, she deemed sufficient for her purpose. The gun was placed behind a tree near by the sleeping and unconscious foe. The hammers were drawn back, that each load might the more readily be discharged. The savages were arranged in a row—their usual habit of reposing. Nerved with desperation, she seized the tomahawk, and in less than a moment had buried it in the brains and gore of three of the depraved wretches. She then flew with great celerity to the tree, seized her gun and shot the fourth monster as he approached; he gave one terrific yell, and all with him was over. The fifth and last of her captors, unable to find the secreted weapons, now rushed upon her with his scalping knife; her gun having missed fire, was quickly reversed in her hands, and with a well-directed blow from the breech, she felled him to the earth, and with her hatchet gave him the finishing stroke, for he too was quivering in the last agonies of expiring nature.

Having thus exterminated her enemies, she lost no time in retreating from the scene of horror, with the hope of securing some friendly aid that might enable her once more to return to her friends if still alive, and to her home made desolate by savage violence and inhuman barbarity. For seven long days she wandered in the gloomy forest before meeting with any human being. As the sun was about retiring beyond the western horizon, faint from want of food, having subsisted on roots and plants, she was about to lay herself down for another night's rest, when she was suddenly started by the wild Indian whoop, and looking around, saw, to her consternation, a number of savages approaching the little mound upon which she reclined. They were of the Oneida tribe, and were on terms of friendship with the colonists. "Fear not, pale face," said a young brave, who saw the agitation and forlorn condition of Mrs. Marshall. He in a few words gave her to understand that his party was humane and benevolent, and would not in the least do her harm. She related to him how her husband and children had been sacrificed by a band of piratical invaders of the domestic hearth. He replied that he was going to pass within a few miles of her once peaceful abode, and that if she would place herself under his care, he would conduct her with safety to her home.

Thanking him for his generosity, she felt most happy in being thus protected. In a few days after she was in the midst of former friends. But how changed! Her home presented a mere mass of charred ruins. The hand of friendship had entombed the dear ones of her bosom, for whom she had mourned and wept while held in cruel and unrelenting captivity.

There are many recorded incidents establishing the

the patriotic character of the early pioneers, one of which relates particularly to Col. Harper, of Harpersfield. When McDonald, a tory who had acquired considerable celebrity for his daring deeds of cruelty, was ravaging the Dutch settlements of Schoharie, with his three hundred tories and Indian allies, Col. Harper, alarmed at the sacrifice of life and property, approached Col. Vrooman, who was in command of the Fort, and very feelingly said, "What shall be done?" To which the Dutch colonel replied, "O, nothing at all; we be so weak we cannot do anything." But Col. Harper was not the man to sit down in quietness, and calmly fold his arms while the country around him was being ravaged and made desolate. He called for his horse, and passed with an undaunted spirit and firm resolve through the scattered forces of the enemy, and bent his course for Albany, where he hoped to secure assistance to free his country of the rude despoilers. Reaching Fox's Creek, he stopped for the night at a tory tavern. After partaking of a hasty meal, he called for a room and retired to rest. Soon after, the Colonel was aroused by a loud rap at the door. "What is wanted?" said Harper, as he rose from his bed. "We wish to see Col. Harper," was the quick reply. The Colonel very coolly unlocked the door, and then seated himself on his bed, with pistols and sword by his side. Presently four men entered and closed the door. "Step one inch over that mark," said the Colonel, "and you are dead men." They stopped and showed evident signs of uneasiness. Not finding him, as they presumed, ready to bend the obsequious knee, and tremble like Belshazzar of old, they left his room. Again he closed and bolted the door, and seating himself on the bed, quietly awaited the approach of day.

Just as the sunbeams began to illuminate the orient sky, he ordered his horse, though the house was surrounded with savages, and was soon on his way for Albany. A swarthy old Indian pursued him to the very outskirts of the place. As often as the red skin pressed too closely upon Col. Harper, his speed was immediately checked by the appearance of an ill-looking pistol, which was aimed at his breast.

Arriving at Albany, he held a conference with Col. Gansevoort, which resulted in accordance with his wishes. A squadron of horse was placed under his direction. They immediately set out for Schoharie, reaching there quite early in the morning. The citizens were not aware of Col. Harper's movements, and were greatly surprised, on hearing the yells and shrieks of the enemy, to behold him with his troops making terrible havoc in their ranks. A very patriotic and successful sally was made from the fort, and the consequences were so alarmingly disastrous to the enemy, that they made a hasty retreat from the country.

CHAPTER VII.

THE REVOLUTION—ITS EFFECTS UPON EMIGRATION—SETTLEMENTS—INCIDENTS—THE THREE POINTS FROM WHICH EMIGRANTS PENETRATED CENTRAL NEW YORK.

"I'll note 'em in my book of memory."

THE Revolutionary curtain first rose upon the memorable soil of Lexington, and fell, in the closing scene of that eventful struggle for freedom in which the infant colonies were engaged, on the blood-drenched plains of Yorktown. Great Britain, in her endeavors to maintain and extend her supremacy over the primitive soil of the New World, was waging a war of oppression against the freemen of America, who were kindling fires that were to light them as they hewed their way through the embattled forces of his royal highness King George III. The Revolutionary war was emphatically a struggle between liberty and oppression. On the east side of the broad waters that separated the two continents, sat the crowned monarch, arrayed in royal splendor, devising plans for the subjugation or annihilation of the chivalrous spirits who were endeavoring to shake off the chains and manacles of the oppressor. The colonists warred for their liberties, their rights, and free institutions; and while the hostile banners of victorious generals were approaching the surf-beaten shore of "this land of the oppressed," and foreign armies were seen marching upon Columbia's soil, they were rallying to the field of slaughter with gleaming swords and glistening bayonets, ready to strike for liberty in freedom's holy cause. During this struggle, a period extending from 1775 to 1783, the spirit of emigration was greatly impeded. But after the stormy cloud of war had passed away, and the tempest of revolution had ceased to give alarm or threaten with danger, and when the contending elements were no longer agitated, and the incendiary's torch, which not unfrequently was applied by marauding parties to the cottagers' homes, had been extinguished, the sturdy and industrious pioneers again began to penetrate beyond the confines civilization.

John Doolittle, originally from Connecticut, was the first explorer of the Oquago valley, having made a permanent settlement near the present valley of Windsor, early in 1785. At this time the Indians were living near the spot where he erected his cabin.

During the same year James M'Master, made a location on the rich flats which border the classic Susquehanna, and the little hamlet which soon after sprung up as if by magic influence, has finally become the beautiful and enterprising village of Owego.

Capt. Joseph Leonard was the pioneer of Broome valley, having located in the vicinity of Binghamton in 1787.

In 1789, Peter Hinepaw, Jacob Yaple, and Isaac Dumond located on the Ithaca Flats. They were employed nineteen days in transporting their goods from Owego, a distance of twenty-nine miles.

Col. John Hendy was the pioneer at Elmira. He erected the first log cabin in 1788, having previously made a location at Tioga Point. His daughter, Rebecca, who subsequently became the wife of Mr. Culp, was the first white child that ever sat on the banks of the Chemung river. A few years since we shook the withered and fleshless hand of the old lady, then trembling on the verge of four score years. She was a woman of remarkable mind and memory. But she has passed the portals of death, and her sainted spirit is at rest. Col. Hendy was a veteran soldier of the Revolution, and became acquainted with the soil upon which he located while serving under Gen. Sullivan in his successful campaign against the Indians. He possessed great moral courage as well as physical strength. In his conflicts with the Indians, he proved a more than equal opponent, not only in originating schemes of artifice, but in carrying his plans into successful operation. And here permit us to relate a single incident.

An Indian who had offered an unpardonable insult to Mrs. Hendy, had been turned from the Colonel's house, with orders never to cross his path under the most severe penalties. A few weeks after, however, the old offender, thirsting for revenge upon his more worthy rival in all the general characteristics that constitute the man of moral and intellectual worth, had taken a secret position by the side of an Indian trail which ran nearly parallel with one of the little tributaries of the Chemung, and along which he expected Mr. Hendy would pass at a certain hour of the day. Reaching the secluded spot where his foe was crouched by the side of a huge old oak, he was suddenly surprised by the swarthy savage, who was making rapid strides towards him, brandishing his tomahawk and scalping knife, and uttering the most hideous yells. Col. Hendy was unarmed, having nothing with which to defend himself save a walking cane, which was immediately hurled with great force at the Indian, and which, quite unexpectedly to his copper-colored highness, made a most lasting impression on a very prominent organ of his face, from which the blood spirted as he measured his length upon the ground. In an instant Col. Hendy was by the side of his, for the moment, powerless assailant, and having seized his weapons, bade him in the most authoritative tone to lie still. But the savage determined on one more effort to disarm and subdue his rival conqueror. Quick as thought he sprang to his feet and grappled the Colonel, but was again brought in contact with the ground, and securely bound, certainly to his great displeasure. With his hands pinioned behind him, he was marched off to an Indian settlement and delivered to the Sachem of the tribe to which he belonged, and from which, after being appropriately dealt with, he was banished from the country. But to return.

Hon. Hugh White made the first location at Whitestown, within four miles of Utica, in 1784. Mr. White was one of the joint proprietors of the Sadquada Patent. The surrounding country was then a perfect wilderness, he having been the first pioneer who had ventured to trespass in that quarter beyond the footprints of civilization.

Ephraim Webster, a native of New Hampshire, was

the first white settler in Onondaga county. He located in 1786, and soon after was married to an Indian lady.

In 1793, Col. John L. Hardenburgh erected a log cabin on the present site of the city of Auburn, and up to 1800 the place was known by the name of Hardenburgh's Corners.

In 1789, a ferry across Cayuga lake was established by James Bennet and John Harris.

The Phelps and Gorham purchase of 2,600,000 acres of land for the sum of $100,000 was made in 1787. The next year, Mr. Phelps left his home in Massachusetts for the purpose of exploring this hitherto unexplored region.* On taking leave of his family and friends, they were found unable to suppress their sobs and tears, for they had but little expectation of meeting him again. The vast wilderness comprised in this Patent was infested with various Indian tribes, whose war triumphs had signalized them for deeds of cruelty and blood. At or near the present village of Canandaigua, he convened the Sachems of the Six Nations, and for a nominal sum extinguished their title to his land. The territory embraced in this purchase comprised the counties of Ontario, Yates, Steuben, Genesee, Alleghany, Niagara, Chatauque, Monroe, Livingston, Erie, the western half of Wayne, and a portion of Orleans.

In 1789 Canandaigua received its first white inhabitant, Mr. Phelps having erected a small log building, in which he opened a land office,—the first of the kind in America.

"Mr. Phelps may be considered the *Cecrops* of the

* General Sullivan and his army had passed through a portion of this tract in 1779, and gave glowing accounts of its fertility.

Genesee country. Its inhabitants owe a mausoleum to his memory, in gratitude for his having pioneered for them the wilderness of this CANAAN of the WEST."

Kanadesaga (now Geneva) was first settled in 1787. In 1798 the State Road, leading from Utica by way of Cayuga Ferry and Canandaigua to the Genesee River at Avon, was completed. The first stage coach passed over this road in 1779, reaching Avon on the afternoon of the third day. After the completion of this road, Geneva improved more rapidly. Still another great impulse favoring western emigration, is attributable to the construction of the Ithaca and Owego, and Ithaca and Geneva turnpikes, the former of which was completed in 1808, and the latter in 1811.

In 1799 and 1800, the Cayuga Bridge was built by the Manhattan company, at an expense of $150,000. Five years previous to the undertaking of this laudable enterprise, the surrounding country was a gloomy forest, inhabited only by Indians. The present bridge was constructed at an outlay of about $15,000.

In 1797 Albany was made the Capital of the State, and in 1809–10 the public buildings were erected ; the State House was first used by the legislature in 1811.

In 1792 Capt. Williamson, the great land Mogul of his day, settled at Bath. In 1794 he accepted the agency of the Pultney estate, and soon after erected the Geneva Hotel.

Rochester received its first white inhabitant in 1808. The Wadsworths located at Big Tree in 1790. This famous council tree is still standing near Geneseo.

The Holland Land Company purchased their immense tract of Land west of the Genesee in 1792.

Thomas Gallop was the first permanent settler at Chenango Forks. He located in 1786.

Lisle was settled in 1790. Soon after, Mr. Lampeer located seven miles up the Tioughnioga River.

The previous year (1791) Amos Todd and Joseph Beebe planted the standard of civilization within the rugged confines of Cortland county.

Thus having hastily glanced at the various early settlements, we are fully prepared to reässert the fact previously referred to, that after the bloody tide of revolution had rolled away, and the national elements of the opposing forces had subsided, giving peace to the hitherto oppressed colonies, emigration increased more rapidly, and settlements became more permanent. It will also be most readily perceived, that the pioneers penetrated central and western New York from three quarters. "Pennsylvanians, and particularly inhabitants of the region of Wyoming, pushed up the Susquehanna to Tioga point, whence diverging, some made settlements along the Chemung and Canisteo, while others established themselves on the east branch of the Susquehanna and its tributaries. Adventurers from the east, crossing from New England or the Hudson River counties to Unadilla, dropped down the river in canoes and settled along the Susquehanna or Chemung, or traveled into the upper Genesee. Yet another band took the ancient road through the Mohawk valley to Oneida lake, then on to Canadesaga," and gradually dispersed over the Genesee country. No settlement was, however, made at Buffalo until 1800.

CHAPTER VIII.

ORGANIZATION OF CORTLAND COUNTY.

"The eye explores the feats of other days."

It is a duty which we of the present generation owe to the memory of the pioneers of civilization in the region of country where we dwell, to gather up with care whatever records of the times there are left, and, studying them well, transmit them in the most enduring form to succeeding ages.

In taking a retrospective view of the past history of our country, we observe the mighty changes which have taken place since the territory of the United States was an unbroken forest, inhabited only by the rude aboriginals, who have slowly but surely yielded to the progressive march of the Europeans, whose advent into this western world "was their misfortune."

The native lords of the wilderness have disappeared. Their generations sleep in our cultivated fields; our harvests wave upon their hills, and nod like ancient plumes in their luxuriant valleys; we have robbed them of their homes and their hunting-grounds, and despoiled them of their ancient greatness—their former glory.

Nor have we stopped here; in numerous instances, the venerated names of antiquity have been chosen to take the place of the more expressive titles by which they knew hill and valley, lake and stream ; and which, in most respects, are certainly less euphonious, and wanting in agreeable taste. How illy do the appellations of Spring Mills, Harloe's Corners, Middletown, Port Royal, Geneva, Rochester, Detroit, and Sleepy Hollow, compare with the sweet, musical, and ever-classic names of Unadilla, Wyalusing, Susquehanna, Cayuga, Tuscarora, or Canisteo ? We are far from favoring the custom which has so eagerly sought out and applied to our cities and smaller towns the names of heroes, novelists, and poets. What knew Homer, Virgil, Scott, or Solon, about the trials, sufferings, and toilsome pursuits of the progressive spirits of go-ahead pioneers ? It may be questionable as to their ever having seen a stump, raft, or side-hill plow ! They dreamed mostly of castles of ivory and columns of glass. Hector, Hannibal, and the Grecian conqueror, thought but of crowns, sceptres, helmets, and glittering plumes. The idea of borrowing names from the ancient republics, merely on account of their bearing a classical character, is a most perfect absurdity. If republican freemen cherish the habits and customs of former ages, why not reverence with peculiar devotion the ancient Indian custom of arraying themselves in fantastic costumes, and dancing a grand war-dance around a stump, in a manner at once ludicrous, and which would naturally lead the uninitiated spectator to doubt the sanity of the grandiloquent centre of attraction ? True, we would not desire to see the American people achieving laurels by the tomahawk, scalping knife, or deadly arrow. We certainly may with perfect safety banish from among us their ancient relics ; yet, regarding them as the original proprietors of this western continent, we think it highly proper to preserve the more elegant appellations of the Indians, and would certainly "approve the taste that would restore the aboriginal names of places," in all cases consistent with association, and which would favorably characterize the ancestry of the red men of America.

Scarce seventy years have passed away since the territory embraced within the boundary of Cortland county was only traversed by the rude Indian hunters—warriors of proud and lofty bearing—chieftains who were quietly borne upon the bosom of the limpid waters of the Tioughnioga, and with far more pleasurable emotions than were the Goths or Vandals, in their memorable passage down the Hellespont. Nearly seventy years have passed away since the aboriginal lords of the wilderness—the Romans of the West—here pursued with stealthy step and faithful quiver, the panther, the wolf, and the bear, as they ranged o'er

"Rocky dens and wooded glens."

Then they cautiously trapped the moose, the otter, the fox, the catamount, and the lynx ; and the rapacious French and English traders received their pelts and furs in exchange for powder, lead, tomahawks, scalping knives and blankets, with an occasional supply of very poor rum. Nearly seventy years have rolled away since the first echo of the axe of civilization was heard in Cortland valley, or the Yankee rifle laid open the skull of old Grizzler, as he sat crouched behind his rocky rampart in the gloomy mountain gorge, grinning a look of defiance at his unwelcome intruder. Nearly seventy years have passed away since the footprints of civilization first appeared in the Tioughnioga valley. Nearly seventy years have winged their rapid flight since, in this wild of forest trees,

> "Art built her dome in Nature's silent bowers,
> And peace and gladness crowned the pilgrim's hours."

The long, deep silence which had for ages pervaded these luxuriant valleys and rugged hills was at length broken, for the " woodman's axe" was making war with the stern old monarchs o'er whom for centuries the thunders had rolled and the lightnings wheeled in awful grandeur. For ages back, the wild men had wandered o'er them in the pursuit of forest game, or as they defiled along upon the war path. Battles waged for power and conquest within the borders of our county, are neither recorded upon the historic page, nor treasured up in our county archives. There are, however, some interesting traditionary relics preserved among the aged chieftains of the *Leni-Lenape* tribe, which, though not conclusive evidence of fact, yet they measurably establish the probability of there having been, during the Sixteenth century, wars of the most cruel and unrelenting character waged in our valley. We have seen many curiously-wrought implements of Indian warfare, now in preservation, which have from time to time been turned up by the plough of the progressive agriculturist. We have seen spear heads, chisels, pestles, arrow points, and pipes of great antiquity—leaden crosses of Maltese shape, referring to the missions of the Jesuits—beads, necklaces, and rings, of very ancient origin

—the section of a circle, perforated near the rim, with very small holes,—and last, though not least, of ingenious construction, is a bone charger, in perfect preservation, and the same as was used by the Senecas at the tragical conflict in 1687, with Marquis De Nonville, in the Genesee valley.

As we can neither give record to the bloody acts of crowned heads begirt with royal gems, or describe in glowing colors enormous battlements from which emerged warriors clad in iron mail, with bristling bayonets and brazen armor, as they met some formidable foe ready to contest the right of soil on which they walked, we shall have to content ourselves with recording events of an entirely dissimilar character. True, the swarthy savages were occasionally seen ascending the Tioughnioga, or trailing along the war-path, with a frightful-looking lot of scalps, fresh from the brows of the "pale faces," dangling at their belts.

The history of Cortland county is therefore of a pacific character. It was the remark of a celebrated author, that "that country is the happiest which furnishes the fewest materials for history." Assuming the truth of this position, we shall be led to believe that a cultivation of the arts of peace are certainly more conducive to happiness, than a recurrence to the arbitrary acts and influences of war.

Tryon county, as we have already remarked, was organized in 1772.

In 1784, Tryon was changed to Montgomery, in order to gratify the many patriotic citizens who were thoroughly opposed to longer retaining the name of a tory governor.

The territory at this time embraced within its boundaries the five districts known by the names of Mohawk, Canajoharie, Palatine, German Flats, and Kingsland.

Herkimer county was organised from territory taken from Montgomery, in 1791.

Onondaga county was organized in 1794. It was taken from the western part of Herkimer, and embraced within its limits that portion of the Military Tract, which at present comprises the counties of Seneca, Cayuga, Cortland, and Onondaga, with portions of Tompkins and Oswego.

Cayuga	was organized	from	Onondaga in 1799.
Seneca	"	"	Cayuga in 1804.
Cortland	"	"	Onondaga in 1808.
Oswego	"	"	Oneida and Onondaga in 1816.
Tompkins	"	"	Cayuga and Seneca in 1817.
Wayne	"	"	Ontario and Seneca in 1823.

The principal causes which led to the organization of Cortland county, will be found in the following interesting document,—the original petition for its erection,—and which we procured through the politeness of Hon. G. W. Bradford, from the archives of our State.

The petition was originally written in an easy and graceful hand, and in almost every instance the signatures were the autographs of the signers.

To the Honorable the Legislature of the State of New York in Senate and Assembly convened: The Petition of the subscribers, inhabitants of the towns of Fabius, Tully, Solon, Homer, Virgil, and Cincinnatus, humbly sheweth :—

That the county of Onondaga is ninety-six miles in length, and at an average breadth about twenty-five miles; that from the extreme of the southern boundary of the said county to the court-house is sixty miles,—which operates greatly to the inconvenience of many of your petitioners in giving their attendance at court. That the population of said county is now very great, and is daily increasing, which renders it impossible for our Court of Common Pleas and General Sessions of the Peace to transact with due expediency the legal business of said county; whereby the suitors of the said courts experience great delay of justice, which, in the opinion of your petitioners, is equivalent to a denial of justice. That your petitioners humbly conceive that a division of the said county will be of signal advantage to the inhabitants of the said towns of Solon, Fabius, Tully, Homer, Virgil, and Cincinnatus, and also to the inhabitants of the northern part of the said county.

Your Petitioners, therefore, humbly pray that the before-mentioned towns be erected into a new county by the name of Courtlandt, and that there be three Courts of Common Pleas and General Sessions of the Peace held in the said county as follows, viz: on the second Tuesday of April, and the first Tuesday of September and December, in every year, after the due organization of the said county.

And your Petitioners as in duty bound will ever pray.

Appended to the petition were the names of seven hundred and forty-seven of the most prominent citizens of the [then] southern portion of Onondaga county, who were desirous of securing a division of the same.

The petition was, on the 4th day of February following, introduced into the Senate by Hon. John Ballard, a member from the western district, then a resident of the town of Homer, and was referred to a committee consisting of Mr. Ballard, Mr. Buel, and Mr. Yates.

The next day, (Feb. 5th,) Mr. Ballard reported in favor of the petitioners, and presented a bill to that effect, which was read the first and second time, and referred to a Committee of the Whole.

It was again called up in Committee of the Whole on the 8th, and ordered to be engrossed.

On the 10th it was read the third time, and passed; and on the same day was sent to the Assembly and read the first time, and referred to the Committee of the Whole.

Several of the northern towns of Onondaga remonstrated against the measure. The spirit of opposition was cherished and cultivated with the most assiduous care. Disunion was a monster of hideous form. He was a creator of discord, and aimed at dividing members of the social compact. He was a political tyrant,—an admirer of crowns, sceptres and chains.

But remonstrances, in all their multifarious forms, could not save the county from being divided. Even the eloquence and profound logic of the gifted member, the Hon. Joshua Forman, failed to prevent its dismemberment. The bill finally passed the Assembly, and became a law on the 8th day of April, 1808.

We select such portions of the act as will be of interest to the general reader:—

An Act to Divide the County of Onondaga, passed April 8, 1808.

1. *Be it enacted by the people of the State of New York, represented in Senate and Assembly,* That all that part of the county of Onondaga, to wit: Beginning at the south corner of the town of Cincinnatus, and thence running north along the east line of the towns of Cincinnatus, Solon and Fabius, to the north-east corner of lot No. 60, in said town of Fabius, thence running west along the north line of that tier of lots through the towns of Fabius and Tully, to the north-west corner of lot No. 51 in said town of Tully; thence south along the east line of the county of Cayuga, to the south-east corner of the towns of Virgil and Cincinnatus to the place of beginning, shall be one separate and distinct county, and shall be called and known by the name of Cortland.

2. *And be it further enacted,* That the Courts in and for the said county, shall be held at the school-house on lot No. 45, in the town of Homer.

3. *And be it further enacted,* That all that part of the town of Fabius, situated in the county of Cortland, shall be called Truxton; and all that part of the town of Tully, in said county of Cortland, shall be called Preble.

Additional sections provide that Cortland shall have one member of Assembly, and that it shall form part of the Western Senatorial District, and part of the Thirteenth Congressional District.

CHAPTER IX.

MILITARY TRACT.

"It was a gloomy wild where Indian warriors trod,
Where savage minds in solitude looked up to Nature's God."

Cortland county was named in honor of General Peter Van Cortlandt, a gentleman who was extensively engaged in the purchase and sale of land. It is bounded on the north by Onondaga county; east by Madison and Chenango; south by Broome and Tioga; and west by Tompkins and Cayuga.

Its area is a fraction over 500 square miles, and contains about 320,000 acres, forming a portion of the high "central section of the State." Its northern boundary lies on the dividing ridge which separates the waters flowing into Lake Ontario and the tributaries of the Susquehanna river. The surface of this county is much diversified, and may be appropriately divided into rich valleys and fertile hills.

The territory comprised within the boundaries of Cortland county, is composed of four whole and two half townships of the Military Tract, or lands granted by the State of New York to the soldiers of the revolution.

The bloody enormities and cruel massacres perpetrated along the frontier of New York, by the tories and Indian allies, during the stormy period of our country's history, and more particularly, of the years 1779 and 1780, and the neglect of several other States to furnish their proportion of troops for the protection of the lives and property of the people, caused the legislature of 1781 to enact a law requiring the enlistment of "two regiments for the defence of the frontier of New York." All necessary expenses incurred were to be canceled by the United States, and the troops were to be employed in the actual service of the country for the "term of three years, unless sooner discharged." The faith of the State was held in pledge for the positive payment for such services. "The council of appointment of the State of New York was to commission the field-officers, and the Governor of the State, the captains and subalterns."

The non-commissioned officers and privates were each to receive in land, as soon as surveyed by the Surveyor General, 500 acres,

Major General,	5,500	"
Brigadier General,	4,500	"
Colonel,	2,500	"
Lieut. Colonel,	2,000	"
Major,	2,000	"
Captain,	1,500	"
Regimental Surgeon,	1,500	"
Chaplain,	2,000	"
Subaltern,	1,000	"
Surgeon's Mate,	1.000	"

The act above referred to contained a clause making

an absolute settlement "on these lands" within three years from the close of the war necessary, otherwise they were forfeited, and reverted back to the State.

The United States Congress also granted one hundred acres of land to each of these soldiers as an additional compensation for their valuable services in their country's defence. Officers of the different grades received larger amounts, according to their commission or rank.

Major General,	1,000 acres
Brigadier General,	900 "
Colonel,	500 "
Lieut. Colonel,	450 "
Major,	400 "
Captain,	300 "
Lieutenant,	200 "
Ensign,	150 "

The land granted, or set apart, for the payment of revolutionary claims in accordance with the act of Congress, was located in the State of Ohio. Arrangements were however made which enabled the soldier to draw his whole quota of 600 acres in one body in New York, on condition of his having first legally relinquished his claim to the 100 acres in Ohio; but if he neglected, or otherwise felt inclined, the sixth part, which his patent called for, reverted to the State of New York, and hence originated the term of "State's Hundred." If notice was given, $8 was taxed the patentee as a fee for surveying, and in case of failure in paying that amount, fifty acres reverted to the State, and hence again arose the term of "Survey Fifty." Commissioners were appointed in 1784 to grant bounty land, "and settle individual claims." They consisted of the Governor and Lieutenant Governor, Speaker of Assembly, Secretary of State, Attorney General, Treasurer and Auditor.

The Military Tract was especially set apart by the legislature of 1782, as bounty lands to be given to the soldiers of the revolution. The tract contained 1,680-000 acres, and embraced within its boundaries the counties of Onondaga, Cortland, Cayuga, Tompkins and Seneca, with parts of Oswego and Wayne.

The Indian title was extinguished by Treaty of Fort Stanwix, Sept. 12th, 1788.

The tract was surveyed by act of Legislature of 1789 into twenty-six townships of one square mile, and each to contain one hundred lots of 600 acres. General Simeon Dewitt, assisted by Moses Dewitt and Abram Hardenburgh, "laid out the whole tract," the former "plotting, and mapping the boundaries, and calculating its area."

We annex a table of the townships as originally named, though previously known only by the number.

TOWNSHIPS.

No.	1.	Lysander.	No.	10.	Pompey.	No.	19.	Homer.
"	2.	Hannibal.	"	11.	Romulus.	"	20.	Solon.
"	3.	Cato.	"	12.	Scipio.	"	21.	Hector.
"	4.	Brutus.	"	13.	Sempronius.	"	22.	Ulysses.
"	5.	Camillus.	"	14.	Tully.	"	23.	Dryden.
"	6.	Cicero.	"	15.	Fabius.	"	24.	Virgil.
"	7.	Manlius.	"	16.	Ovid.	"	25.	Cincinnatus.
"	8.	Aurelius.	"	17.	Milton.	"	26.	Junius.
"	9.	Marcellus.	"	18.	Locke.			

In 1791, the commissioners decided by ballot who

were the claimants to these bounty lands. "Ninety-four persons drew lots in each township." One lot was especially set apart for the promotion of literature, and another for the support of the Gospel and common schools. There still remained four lots in each township to be disposed of. These were appropriated to the benefit of certain officers, and to such as had drawn lots which were measurably covered with water.

In 1792 township number twenty-seven was surveyed and known by the name of *Galen*. This grant was made, in accordance with law, to the Hospital department.

In 1796 it was found that there were yet many unsatisfied claims for bounty lands, and consequently another township was laid out, and numbered "twenty-eight," which satisfied all legal claimants. To this was appropriated the name of *Sterling*.

The act relative to a positive settlement in three years was annulled, and the time extended from 1792 to 1799.

The State, in disposing of its bounty lands, conveyed them by an instrument called a Patent, to which was attached a large waxen disc, with paper on each side, bearing the arms of the State on the face, and an impression on the back, called the "reverse."

It is, perhaps, well known to the general reader, that a town frequently embraced a number of townships. Ulysses originally included the townships of Ulysses, Ithaca, Enfield and Dryden. Pompey contained the townships of Pompey, Fabius and Tully. Homer embraced that of Homer and Cortland. Virgil embraced Virgil, Harford and Lapeer. Cincinnatus contained

Cincinnatus, Marathon, Freetown and Willet. Solon embraced Solon and Taylor. Preble contained Preble and Scott.

A township embraced one hundred lots, though, for lack of a proper understanding, many have confounded the terms of town and township ; and we notice instances where authors have substituted the one for the other.

Previous to 1792, the revolutionary claimants suffered materially on account of the many frauds committed by a lawless band of land pirates, who, in order to rob the HERO and PATRIOT of his inheritance, hesitated not to commit the most open and glaring forgeries. Numerous fraudulent conveyances bore anterior dates, and consequently gave rise to many unpleasant contests, as well as bitter recriminations. In some instances, four and even five forged conveyances were held by as many different individuals for the same lot of land.

In some cases the legal claimants were deprived of their rights. But these land-sharks were not always aware of the material with which they had to contend, and occasionally met with a rebuke and discomfiture from which they did not soon recover. Among those gallant spirits who braved the danger of revolution, and who were unappalled by the roar of British cannon, and the menace of hostile armies, were men who were not easily forced or ejected from their possessions. In the eastern part of Cortland lived one who was an associate with the chivalrous sons who marched to Quebec when winter's awful tempest opposed their progress, and who crossed the ice-choked Delaware, regardless of chilling winds and angry waves—again, defying the rage of battle beneath the burning sun at Monmouth—kindred spirits to those who fought at Lexington, Concord and Bunker Hill. He had made bare his bosom to the shafts of battle, and shrunk not from the horrors of a seven years' war. After locating on his lot, and at a time when hope painted to his eager vision long years of future happiness, he was called upon by one of these gentlemen Shylocks, who informed him that he held a conveyance of his lot, and that he was the only legal owner, and gave him a very polite invitation to evacuate his possessions. But the stern old patriot—the hero of many battles, and who carried on his person the certificates of his valor—was not thus hastily to be ejected from his revolutionary inheritance. The fire that once glowed so brightly in the old man's eyes on the field of battle was rekindled, and he would sooner have fallen a martyr to justice and right than have obsequiously acquiesced in the mandate of his ungallant oppressor. The conveyance was at length laid open and examined, and was found to bear a date prior to that of his own. In short, it was a forgery.

When the defrauder found that the stern, heroic warrior would not yield to his demand, he threatened him with the terrors of law, and the cost of an ejectment suit. This, however, only caused a smile to play over the face of the worthy pioneer of civilization. He knew that he had fought and bled upon the gory plain; that he had sacrificed the soft endearments of home, discarded honors, and rushed to the "tented field," to strike for liberty and universal freedom; that his possessions were legally bequeathed him, as a comparatively small gift for the sacrifices he had made in the cause of human emancipation; and to be thus deprived of a home which he had purchased with sacrifices and blood, would not comport with the principle for which he had contended, and he spurned the intruder from his presence.

Instances of a like character were of frequent occurrence. Some yielded without making scarcely an effort at resistance.

But the soldiers suffered from other circumstances, and from causes over which they had no control. The long *interim* of time which intervened between the day of promise and the time of legal assignment of bounty lands, and the coldness with which their appeals were received by the State government, caused many to doubt the propriety of urging their claims, and in numerous instances parted with their patents for a mere nominal sum, and in some cases for an amount varying from three to eight dollars.

The act of '94 was intended to prevent future frauds, and unquestionably had the desired effect. "All deeds and conveyances executed before that time, or pretending to be so, were to be deposited with the clerk of the county of Albany, for the time being, and all such as were not so deposited should be considered fraudulent." This put a stop to further forgeries ; yet the courts were pressed with suits in regard to contesting claimants. Very few lots were quietly settled upon, there being two or more pretended owners. Squatters had to be ejected, and often exorbitant sums paid for the mere shadow of an improvement. The disputes became so frequent, so unpleasant, and withal so injurious to the peace and comfort of the Military Tract, that, in 1797, they united in a general and urgent petition for the passage of an act whereby all difficulties might be settled, and the controversial war ended. The petition was heard and answered. Commissioners were appointed, "with full powers to hear, examine, award, and determine all disputes respecting the titles of any and all the military bounty lands." Wrongs of long standing were redressed, and justice equitably distributed.

The termination of these vexed questions of right gave rise to a more liberal and happy feeling among the pioneers, and resulted in a more speedy settlement of the territory, and consequently in a rapid increase of population.

Cortland county is at present divided into fifteen towns, which were organized as follows:

Homer,	1794	Marathon,	1818
Solon,	1798	Willet,	1818
Virgil,	1804	Cortlandville,	1829
Cincinnatus,	1804	Harford,	1845
Preble,	1808	Lapeer,	1845
Truxton,	1808	Taylor,	1849
Scott,	1815	Cuyler,	1858
Freetown,	1818		

CHAPTER X.

GEOLOGY, MINERALOGY AND METEOROLOGY.

"Nor gold nor jeweled gems were there,
Yet 'neath the turf were mines of richest store."

To THOSE who read the book of Nature with due attention, and who are conversant with the laws of cause and effect, the study of Geology, Mineralogy and Meteorology will prove not only interesting, but instructive, and they will necessarily be led to inquire into those causes and influences which may have operated at a very remote period of time in giving an almost entire change to the general appearance of the earth's surface. In our mind there is no question as to the fact of the ancient ocean having, far back in the dim distance of the past, overspread our hills and valleys, ebbing and flowing in obedience to physical laws, and, as now, sending her storm-beaten surf against the huge rocks that line the mountain gorge. Then, as now, it was dotted with isles and sand-bars. Then, as now, there were calms, when the sun, the moon, the stars, looked down in beauty upon its glassy surface. Then, as now, the rainbow clasped the wide expanse, while its ever-varied hues were reflected far beneath the gentle wavelets. Then, as now, the zephyrs played o'er its unfathomed waters, sending its undulating swells to ripple along the beachen shore, "recording its history in the sands beneath."

The Tioughnioga river has its source near the southern line of Onondaga, and flows southward, with its tributaries watering nearly the whole of Cortland county. The Otselic is its main branch.

Geologically, Cortland does not present as great a variety of specimens as some of the other counties in the district.*

Slate is the basis-rock of the county. The Hamilton group, extending from Onondaga, enters the northern part of the town of Truxton, and terminates some distance east of Tinker's Falls.

In Preble, Truxton, and parts of Homer, are found quantities of Genesee slate. These generally project from the hills which form the barriers of the valley.

The Portage and Ithaca groups extend over the towns of Cortland and Solon, the larger portion of Homer and Scott, "and the terrace between Truxton and Solon." They are found on either side of the Tioughnioga, but become more narrow as they "increase in thickness going south." Some fine specimens are also found along the borders of the Otselic in Willet and Cincinnatus.

These groups form a number of valuable quarries, and from which have been taken large quantities of stone

* This (the third) Geological district is composed of the counties of Montgomery, Fulton, Otsego, Herkimer, Oneida, Lewis, Oswego, Madison, Onondaga, Cayuga, Cortland, Chenango, Broome, Tioga, and the eastern half of Tompkins.

for building and flagging purposes. A short distance above Port Watson are the quarries of Messrs. Miller & Derby. To the south are those of Messrs. Stephens, Rose and Betts. Between Homer and Cortland are Pierce and Rood's quarries. These are of great value, "and furnish nearly all the flag-stones used in Homer." The lower part of the quarries consists of flags from one to six inches in thickness; not so smooth or straight as those of Sherburne, but waved like the slight movements which water produces upon a sandy bottom. The flags contain fucoids, large and small, some of which anastomose and are smooth. Above these layers there is a line of concretion, about a foot or more in diameter, with shale. On the top of these are slaty, broken up, and decomposed layers of shale and sandstone, forming the refuse of the quarry. Some of the lower layers of sandstone contain vegetable impressions, and show small accumulations of coal, owing to the alteration which the material of the plants has undergone."* This quarry is a most valuable acquisition to the mineral wealth of Homer.

Those citizens of Homer who are observant of objects about them, will find many interesting confirmations in the flag-stones upon which they walk, of the truth of the above observations. The beautiful ripple marks, everywhere seen, carry us back to the time when these same rocks formed the soft floors of shallow Silurian seas.

North and west of Homer, are other valuable quarries, in one of which a variety of vegetable impressions

* See State Geological Report, 1842, to which we are indebted for many interesting facts.

are discernible—none, however, which resemble those noticed by us in the quarry above referred to.

The Chemung group covers the southwest part of Virgil. This is the highest elevation in the county. The same group is perceptible on the lines of Freetown, Cincinnatus, Willet and Marathon.

There are three marl lakes or ponds a few miles south west of Cortland village. The larger one covers an area of fifteen acres, the second in size, six, and the third, four. When freed from the particles of vegetable matter, it presents a very light appearance, and is without doubt a fair species of carbonate of lime. Large quantities of lime are annually burnt and disposed of at the kilns.

Marl is also found in smaller deposits in Tully, Preble, and the northern part of Homer. It will at some future time prove to be of great importance to the county, especially as a manure.

Bog ore, it is believed, does not exist in this county to any great extent, though small specimens have been found in some of the swamps.

Albite, or white feld-spar, exists in small quantities in Scott, Fabius and Solon.

We have two or three specimens of amphibole, or basaltic hornblende, gathered from the northern part of the county. The crystals are well-formed, but so firmly imbedded in the rock as to render it difficult to detach them without marring their beauty.

Calcareous tufa is common in some of the eastern localities of the county.

On the west branch of the Otselic river is a small

calcareo-sulphurous spring, the water of which is strongly impregnated with the mixed ingredients of sulphur and lime.

In the county are several sulphur springs, some emitting very pure particles of sulphur. Little York, or Sulphur lake, a few miles north of Homer, is slightly tinctured with sulphur.

Tornadoes are classed among the more prominent meteorological phenomena. Their course is invariably in an eastward direction, and, unlike that of a whirlwind, moving "in a circuit round its axis," their whirl is always to the left. They frequently travel at the rate of a hundred miles per hour, leaving the marks of devastation behind.

On the 13th day of August, 1804, a tornado swept over the northern part of this county, and in its maddened course tore up trees, demolished buildings, and blasted the pioneer's hopes of a plentiful crop.

Just a half century after, Cortland county was again visited by a tornado. Its path was narrow, yet alarmingly destructive. Its course was east south-east, and its ravages were traceable for a distance exceeding 250 miles. A little previous to its appearance, cloud after cloud of awful blackness rolled up in the west, and gradually spread over the sky, until finally the whole firmament became enveloped in almost *tartarean* darkness. Forked lightnings flashed athwart the sky, or, zig-zag, leaped from apparent spiral columns of red-hot wreathing flames. The rain poured down in torrents. It was not like one of those ever-drizzling rains so common among the tropics, but more like a perfect avalanche. The rain was succeeded by a violent hail-storm, which tended greatly to cool the overheated atmosphere, the mercury having ascended to a point unusual for this latitude.

The tornado entered this county from Locke, and passed, in its desolating and destructive course, within two miles of Homer. Having gathered fresh strength in crossing the valley, it rose the eastern hills—those ancient battlements where the shadows of ages have fallen and which fearful convulsions have shaken—with a spirit unawed and unbroken, and then waged war with the hitherto unconquered monarchs of 400 years' standing, tearing them up by the roots, or twisting them into splinters as Sampson did a green twig, and whirling their shattered fragments in almost every conceivable direction. Indeed, sad havoc was made with the forest trees. But the ancient dwellers offered no opposition, for the storm-god did not even presume upon a contest for the right of way. His course was onward, and woe to the giant oak that came within the whirling folds of the destroyer.

A gentleman, crossing Cayuga lake in a small boat at the time of this occurrence, describes the scene as one of terrific grandeur. As it approached the water, it leveled every impeding obstacle. The roaring of the tornado, the sharp, vivid flashes of lightning, and the deafening thunder, were to him really alarming. The water, for the space of several rods, extending across the lake, suddenly became elevated a number of feet, very much in the form of a pier, and for an hour or more ebbed and flowed with the same regularity as is observed in the ocean's tide. On, on sped the storm-god, raving and howling as if forced forward on the very wings of despair.

There were several remarkable incidents connected with this singularly strange and destructive visitor. In the town of Locke, Cayuga county, a brass kettle was caught up in its terrible folds, and lodged, some forty rods distant, in the top of a graceful poplar. A wagon-seat was carried across the Tioughnioga river, and dashed to atoms. A barn roof was divided, and one-third carried away without materially injuring the remaining two-thirds. In Chenango, a little boy, five or six years old, was caught up and carried upwards of thirty rods, and safely deposited by the side of a hay-stack, having escaped with only a rude shaking. An aged matron, stepping to the door to shake the crumbs from her table-cloth, had it rather unceremoniously taken from her, and the last she saw of her favorite linen, it was at a great distance, cutting fantastic capers in "mid air," being under the immediate control of the storm-spirit.

On the 30th day of September, 1858, another tornado visited our county. Its course, from Lake Erie to the Atlantic, was wide and fearfully marked with its desolating effects. In various places its strength was divided, and it traveled in different lines for miles, and when again united, raved and roared with redoubled fury.

The sky was shrouded with thick and sulphury clouds, increasing to almost pitchy blackness. Forked lightnings flashed athwart the sky, and deafening thunders rolled and reverberated amid the contending elements. The damage to property was immense. Orchards and forest trees were alike prostrated; fences were blown down, houses and barns unroofed, and in some instances entirely destroyed. We visited one sugar-orchard of two thousand trees, all of which, save forty-nine, were leveled to the ground. On another lot we saw sixty acres of forest trees lying in every conceivable direction. But the damage was so great, and so generally felt, that we deem an extended notice unnecessary. In the evening the sky was almost constantly lit up with spiral streaks of lightning, accompanied with deafening thunder, inconceivably grand and awe-inspiring.

The data we possess relative to our climate is limited to the results of a few observations. We have been favored with the reading of a valuable and interesting Report on Vital Statistics, made to the Medical Association of Southern Central New York, by Doctor C. Green, from which we make the following brief outline of interesting facts:

The climate of Cortland county is characterized, in common with that of southern central New York, by great variability. The region of the State, south and south-west of the Mohawk valley, including Onondaga and Cortland counties, shows, according to the report of Dr. Emmons, a lower reduction of temperature by four degrees to eleven degrees than the average of the State, and autumnal frosts occur earlier by four to thirteen days. The physical features of the county would indicate that our climate would at least be colder than the western portion of the State in the same latitude. The geological features of our county are interesting in relation to the succession of hill and dale, their relative elevation, and the elevation above tide water. These valleys are cut through the Portage and Chemung group of rocks. The hills bounding these valleys are generally of such shape that they can be cultivated to their summits, and vary in height above the valleys from two hundred to six hundred feet. The valleys, geologically speaking, are those of *denudation*, being scooped out of the rocks above mentioned. The bottoms are filled to an unknown depth with drift made up of the detritus and boulders of the northern rocks, as well as of the rocks in which they are situated. These valleys are of moderate width, and have no inconsiderable elevation above the ocean. The valley in which Homer is situated is at that place 1096 feet above tide water. This elevation will account in a measure for the difference in the climate between this and the western portion of the State, especially from Cayuga lake westward. While Homer has the elevation just noticed, Ithaca is situated only four hundred and seventeen feet above tide—a difference in altitude of six hundred and seventy-nine feet. The mean temperature of Homer is forty-four degrees seventeen minutes, while that of Ithaca, with a difference in latitude of only eleven minutes of a degree, is forty-seven degrees eighty-eight minutes, thereby giving a difference in mean temperature of three degrees seventy-one minutes. The annual range of the thermometer in Homer, for 1845, was one hundred and four degrees, while that of Ithaca was ninety-two.

The daily range of temperature is one of the most marked characteristics of our climate, and this is especially true of the late summer and early autumnal months. The vicissitudes of weather are very sudden and extreme, but the change in the daily temperature which exerts the most striking influence on the health of community, in our summer and autumnal months, is, the rapid depression of the mercury on the approach of night-fall. There is often, in August and September, a change, from two o'clock to ten o'clock P. M., of from twenty to thirty-five degrees. It will be readily seen that if the body is not prepared to resist the influence of these changes, disease must result. The following table, prepared from observations taken in Homer in 1851, shows the monthly mean of the daily range of the thermometer :

Jan.	Feb.	March.	April.	May.	June.
13.35	11.42	15.06	13.43	17.77	16.40
July.	August.	Sept.	Oct.	Nov.	Dec.
17.12	20.33	20.23	15.09	8.53	10.[illegible]3

In order to maintain an equable condition of the system, it becomes necessary to change clothing as often as the weather changes, or at least wear next to the surface of the body those materials which do not conduct heat rapidly.

The following table will give some idea of the climate of our county. The table was compiled from the records made by E. C. Reed, Esq., the Meteorological observer of the Smithsonian institute, of Homer :

1853.	No. inches rain and melted snow.	Highest p't of ther.	Lowest p't of ther.	Range.	Highest point of barometer.	Lowest point of barometer.	Range.	Direct'n wind.	Cloudiness.
May,	4.69	80	33	47	29.132	28.408	.724	N. W.	5
June,	4.00	88	47	41	29.121	28.517	.604	N. W.	4
July,	2.28	83	47	36	29.046	28.555	.491	S.	4
Aug.,	3.59	89	43	46	29.007	28.405	.602	S.	4
Sept.,	4.72	83	32	51	29.085	28.278	.807	S.	4
Oct.,	4.56	68	24	44	29.191	28.336	.855	S.	4
Nov.,	3.15	63	6	57	29.333	28.347	.986	S.	7
Dec.,	1.76	44	-2	46	29.042	27.974	1.068	S.	7
1854.									
Jan.,	2.60	54	-5	59	29.268	28.039	1.229	S.	7
Feb.,	4.46	48	-2	50	29.275	28.202	1.073	S. E.	6
March,	3.34	60	3	57	29.094	27.997	1.097	N. W.	7
April,	5.84	69	16	53	29.312	28.271	1.041	N. W.	6

CHAPTER XI.

LEGEND OF TIOUGHNIOGA VALLEY.

"Can you tell me a tale or some legend old,
Of the forest wild or the streamlet cold,
Where the Indian, hound, or the arrow flew,
Or the true hearts pledged their love anew?"

THERE are many interesting and instructive legendary reminiscences treasured in the memory of the young braves and chieftains of the scattered remnants of the Delaware tribe. They are particularly fond of rehearsing the unwritten incidents which form the only perfect memorial of the ancient history of their nation. The one which we are about to narrate was gathered from a source which entitles it to a place in our history, and the various corroborating facts derived from the traditions of the early Indian occupants of the Wyoming valley, clothe it with a garb of undoubted reality.

At a period far back in the annals of the heroic past, there were numerous Indian settlements clustered along the banks of the classic Wyoming, the majestic Susquehanna, the serpentine Chenango, and the ever to be admired Tioughnioga. Near the mouth of Cold Brook, a small tributary of the Tioughnioga, the Indians had established a small settlement. The wigwams were rudely constructed, yet sufficiently comfortable to answer the requirements of these red dwellers of the forest. They belonged to the Leni-Lenape or Delaware tribe, which originally came from the eastern shores of the North American continent. They were a warlike people, proud and ambitious, bold and resolute. Early in the sixteenth century, they separated by common consent from a branch of the parent tribe, which had previously settled in the Wyoming valley. Here they came seeking repose by the side of the beautiful stream that flowed through the picturesque Tioughnioga. They were superior hunters, and lived chiefly by fishing or upon the success of the chase. As their numbers increased and their hopes brightened, the Mingoes, who were scattered along the shores of the great northern chain of lakes, became more or less jealous of the surrounding tribes, whom they endeavored to bring under their subjection, while they extended their jurisdiction over the hunting-grounds of their more feeble neighbors.

The impulses of the Lenapes were warm and ardent—their enthusiasm extravagant, usually leading to laudable ends. They frequently suffered from the incursions of predatory parties of Mingoes, who sought by stealth to lessen their means of enjoyment, or, if possible, arouse in them a spirit of revenge, that they might find in it a pretext for making war against them, and thereby exterminate or make them yield to their dictatorial notions of right. The aggressions of the Mingoes were carried on to the last point of forbearance, adding insult to insult, until finally the cry for revenge was only to be appeased by blood. The old chief was disabled by various infirmities from directing or taking part in the inevitable struggle for which the Lenapes were preparing. He had fought in many a severe battle, and had particularly distinguished himself in the fierce and bloody wars waged against the Alligewi on the Mississippi, as well as in the devastating incursions against the Mengwes. The scars upon his person were so many certificates of his valor ; and when he saw the storm rising and heard the elements muttering, his soul went up to the abode of the Great Spirit, invoking the assistance of the strong arm of Right in behalf of the oppressed. He called to his presence Ke-no-tah, a young and aspiring brave, and thus addressed him :

"I am an old warrior, but can no more go out to battle. When the moon went down, crimsoned with the blood of my people who fell on the shores of the Great Waters, I was borne from the victorious battle-ground covered with my blood. My father and brothers were among the slain, and I wept that my pierced limbs would no longer sustain this now withered and decaying body, for my heart thirsted for blood. I was then young and strong, and could strike for the hearth-stone of my cabin. A few moons more, and this branchless tree will have fallen to the ground. The night is dark and the wind rages—a storm is gathering about the Great Lakes. Our enemies will soon be upon us, and Ke-no-tah must nerve his right arm to crush the destroyer."

The dark eyes of the young brave flashed a falcon glance upon the venerable chieftain, as his tall and manly form assumed a still more noble and dignified appearance. "Give me," said he, "command of the braves, and we will go out to battle—we will consume our enemies—we will drink their blood and devastate their homes."

A council of warriors was convened, before whom the powerful eloquence of Ke-no-tah was poured out like a wild gushing torrent, and he was at once chosen chief to lead the young and impetuous braves to battle. He had on several occasions evinced the true, native war spirit, having never faltered, not even when surrounded with darkness and danger, and, if the safety of his people required it, his blood should be poured out upon the red altar which the Mingoes had erected.

The sun had appeared in the orient sky, and his chariot wheels were fast approaching the zenith of the heavens. The dark green foliage clothed the ancient forest trees, the sweetest incense rose from the dewy flowers and was borne upon the balmy zephyrs, hill and dale were made vocal with the native songsters of the woods, the water of the beautiful river lay calm and smooth, and pure as a transparent sheet of glass, the antlered deer bounded over the hills, while at various intervals the scream of the wild bird was heard in the distance. All was peace and quietness in the little settlement. Suddenly, however, "the scene was changed." Three painted savages from the northern lakes appeared at the wigwam of the aged Sachem Conduca, demanding a surrender of their cabins, their arms of defence, and their hunting-grounds. Altahalah, the youngest daughter of Conduca, unnoticed by the invaders of her quiet home, silently withdrew from their presence, and hastily throwing her blanket over her shoulders, she bounded with the speed of a youg nfawn to the home of Ke-no-tah, to whom she had been promised in marriage.

"Brother! brother! they have come!—Fly! fly to the home of Conduca!" It was enough; the young brave, snatching his tomahawk and war-club, hastened to the relief of the worthy and much-loved chieftain. When he entered the cabin he found the Mingoes making loud threats against the peaceful settlement, and intimating that unless a general surrender was made blood would be spilt. This brought Ke-no-tah to his feet. The muscles of his face became suddenly swollen with passion, and his eyes flashed defiance as he thus addressed himself to the foremost speaker:

"Talk not to me of blood; it is my delight. It is the element upon which I live. I was not born like other warriors. I was never dandled upon the lap of a mother. A dark cloud came over the high hills, and from that cloud a thunderbolt was hurled against a large pine tree, shivering it to the stump, and from that stump I sprung up completely equipped for war. Blood is my delight! Vengeance is mine!" Such was the effect of his eloquence and manner that the Mingoes absolutely quailed before him. Thus finding all attempts at bringing the *Lenapes* to their desired terms, they left muttering curses upon the heads of Conduca and Ke-no-tah.

The day declined. The sable shades of night had curtained the earth, and the hollow murmurs of the storm-beaten tempest were heard advancing; anon the muttering thunder told the name of God, and the lightning's flaming wing pointed to his dwelling-place. But hark! what wild scream was borne upon the midnight air? It was the Indian war-whoop, and it fell like a death knell upon the ear of Altahalah. The Mingoes had suddenly fallen upon the little settlement, and though but partially prepared to make a resolute resistance, were not to be defeated without one gallant effort forcountry and home,—aye, for their lives. The far-seeing eye of Ke-no-tah had watched their approach, and he had already gathered the young braves, as well as many of th e old scarred warriors, around,him. At the first shrill whoop of the invaders, Ke-no-tah and his brave warriors rushed like fierce blood-hounds from their retreat, and fell like a thundering avalanche upon the Mingoes,—whose spring was like the hungry panther as he leaps upon his prey, and whose deafening war-whoop was death ! The contest was short but terrible. The two forces fought with the fierceness of tigers, and when the battle-cry had ceased, and all was still save the low wailing of the wounded and dying, it was found that the Mingoes had fled, leaving the greater number of their well-trained warriors locked in the icy hue of death. The Lenapes had suffered severely, as but few remained to tell the tale of the horrid butchery. The banner of Ke-no-tah had triumphed.

The full-orbed moon rent her mantle of darkness and looked down upon the work of carnage, where many a brave and ardent defender of his rights had fallen. At this moment Altahalah was discovered, clasping in her arms the lifeless form of Conduca, and silently wiping the congealed blood from his wounds. Her face was deadly pale, and a cold tremor ran over her whole frame.

Relaxing her hold on Conduca, and looking down upon his livid features, she exclaimed, " Oh ! my father, my father, has the Great Spirit called thee hence to his fairer hunting-ground in the brighter land of promise? or, hast thou fallen by the hand of the usurper, whose pointed arrow cleft thy warm heart?"

"Calm thyself," said Ke-no-tah; "the great Spirit has smiled upon the soul of the brave Conduca, and the strong arm of thy friend will protect thee."

A shriek burst from Altahalah, for at that moment a powerful, athletic savage, who had secretly stolen to her side, had seized her and was fast disappearing in the deep, dark wilds. Pursuit was immediately made, but the almost impenetrable thicket into which he had darted with the seeming celerity of a winged spirit, very greatly impeded their progress, and it was only occasionally that they were revealed to their pursuers by the sudden flashes of lightning that glared through the trees. The pursuit was continued until nearly morning, when all signs and traces of their flight were entirely lost. Returning to the place of massacre, what a heart-rending scene met their sight! Many of the dead and dying were still lying where they fell, pierced by the fatal arrow, or the hunting-knife, or still more murderous tomahawk.

> "The gaunt wolf,
> Scenting the place of slaughter, with his long
> And most offensive howl did ask for blood,"

for they had come howling like so many demons to feast and surfeit upon the remains of the slain. It was with difficulty that they were driven back to the hills, or destroyed, that the wounded might be protected and the dead removed for sepulchre.

The last mournful rites having been paid to the dead,

and such protection prepared for the few remaining disabled and infirm warriors, with their wives and children, as the limited means allowed, Ke-no-tah gathered his bold and intrepid warriors who had escaped in the sanguinary conflict, and, putting himself at their head, again sallied forth into the unbroken wilderness to seek and recover the fair captive. Days, weeks and months were spent, but without avail. Once, however, Ke-no-tah supposed that Altahalah was almost within his outstretched arms. Descending a deep ravine, just as night had curtained the earth, a sudden flash of lightning gleamed across the dark mountain pass, and exhibited to view the reclining fugitives. Slowly, but silently, they pursued their way until they had approached within a few yards of the hated foes. Presently another flash of lightning glared fully upon them. There they were, sleeping upon the green verdure of the hill-side; but Altahalah was not there. Was she dead, or had she flown as the young dove wings its way from the talons of the eagle? These were questions which their unlettered minds could not solve. But they resolved that the score of usurpers should die at their hands, and they were true to their determination,—for when the next flash of lightning sent its livid glare over their dark features, they were cold, ghastly, dead!

Ke-no-tah called Altahalah, but he heard no responsive answer; and the horrid thought that she might be dead, or dying by starvation in the wild wilderness, came rushing upon his bewildered and maddened brain, and in his frenzied moments he smote his forehead in agony.

The Tioughnioga valley was deserted, for the red

men had abandoned their homes made desolate by the ruthless barbarity of the unfriendly Mingoes, and had joined the Monceys whose council-fires burned at Minisink on the Makerisk-kiskon, or Delaware river.

The evening shades were gathering their misty folds over the earth. The orient moonbeams sent a golden hue through the tall tree-tops, and the dark shadows of the gnarled oaks looked like huge monsters, as they loomed over the calm, still water. A dusky maiden reclined by the side of her native river, which lay as a polished mirror upon the wild bosom of nature. Her sweet voice, like an æolian harp, chanted the favorite air of her noble brave. She heard the tramp of the fleet-bounding deer, the hoot of the old gray owl, and the sharp, terrific scream of the panther. She saw their eyes glaring like fiery meteors in the thick underbrush near where she had selected for the night her moss-covered couch. Her hair hung in long dark braids over her uncovered shoulders; her eyes were black as the raven's plumage; her complexion of the purest olive, and her whole form of the most perfect beauty and symmetry.

Now she gazes upon a little cloud that is peering o'er yonder misty peak. A gentle breeze ripples the glassy waters; the cloud increases with terrific blackness; the wind sweeps by with tempestuous force; the moon is veiled from sight; one-half of the blue expanse is palled in the tapestry of gloom, and the other half exhibits clouds of every shape, now piled like Alps on Alps in snow-white purity, now bathed in purple, pink and gold; afar, the rumbling thunder is heard, and sharp flashes of lightning leap like tongues of fire athwart the darkened sky : the rain pours down in torrents. But 'tis passed ; delightful coolness fills the air, and all nature is refreshed. She gazed down the river, and her quick ear caught the sound of oars, for at that moment a canoe was gliding through the gentle wavelets. Her eagle eye discerned at a glance the richly ornamented crest and white plume of her favorite chief. Nearer and nearer it approached the shore—a stroke more—the young and devoted sachem leaped upon the shore, and ALTAHALAH was in the arms of KE-NO-TAH, her lover.

CHAPTER XII.

EARLY SETTLEMENTS AND ORGANIZATION OF TOWNS.

"Their fortress was the good greenwood,
Their tent the cypress tree;
They knew the forest 'round them,
As seamen know the sea."

It is a characteristic principle of the correct historian, to describe with the most perfect minuteness, the origin, or first feeble beginnings of a new settlement. These are usually read with more than ordinary interest, and especially if the pioneers suffered many and great inconveniences. In most instances, those progressive spirits possessed many of the self-sacrificing traits of character, kindred to those which contributed most essentially in providing the blessings of freedom which we now enjoy. They labored not alone for themselves, but for their children, friends, and country. It was no easy task to abandon the hearth-stone of their boyish days, the endearments of social ties, cultivated associations and the many luxuries common to settlements that have long prospered under the progressive spirit of civilization. It required something more than mere passive beings to convert these valleys into fruitful fields, or cause these rugged hills to yield forth the rich products of a virgin soil.

The early pioneers possessed something more than mere negative characters. They were bold, enterprising men, well suited to the task of preparing a lodgment in the wilderness. Nay, they were stern realities. The law of progress was most legibly stamped upon their characters. They exerted all their energies to the furtherance of the general improvements of the age in which they lived — whose forward movements were steady and firm as

> "The eternal step of progress beats
> To the great anthem, calm and slow,
> Which God repeats."

We love to study and contemplate the attributes of character which so peculiarly distinguished these brave and devoted pioneers, for great achievements succeeded their bold efforts for the extension of civilization. We delight in recurring to their history, for their good deeds and noble enterprises should forever live fresh and green in our memories, and stimulate us to deeds of patriotism, philanthropy, and a devotional fellow feeling worthy the descendants of those who warred with the mountain oak, when they struck their tents in the wilderness and grappled with stern adversity for the mastery. Their triumphs were of the noblest character, achieved by men whose native dignity and determined will made them what they really were—Nature's true noblemen. They were kind and courteous, possessing none of that apish pride so common among those of more refined regions. Their law of courtesy consisted of justice and equal rights. They loved truth, took pleasure in assisting each other, laboring to increase the happiness of those around them. They lived not merely for the sake of living, but that good might result from their labors in the field of enterprise. To slumber on in undisturbed repose, or waste their time forgetful of the object of their creation, or the duties of active men — to live, breathe and move as though the world's prosperity and adversity to them were alike—to stand as marble statues in the great waste of time, or voluptuous monuments of ease and indifference, they regarded with the most utter abhorrence. Such men have been the forlorn hope of marching armies and tottering empires. Such were the ever-conquering spirits whom Napoleon held in reserve to strike the blow that should send consternation and death through the ranks of his iron-clad opponents. Such were the resistless and stern actors who, in the bloody conflict which gave an immortality to Wellington for his heroism upon the field of Waterloo, hewed their way to victory or death. Such were the champions of heroic valor, who left the sunny plains of Italy, camped along the banks of the noble Tiber, and finally put forth an impulse that gave a historic immortality to the seven-hilled city, over which was reared the standard of ancient Rome. Such were the daring men of our country's Revolution, who, amid death and desolation, strove to erect the temple of Liberty and Independence. Such were the men who converted our hills and valleys into green pastures and fruitful fields.

The hardy adventurers who first struck their tents along the banks of the Tioughnioga, or reared their rustic cabins on our hill-sides, were subject to incidents common to all pioneers, and which, to them, were full of point and interest. Many of them suffered severely during their long and weary journey to their forest home. Looking back through the dim distance of the past, we behold a little company of bold spirits slowly winding along the banks of the majestic Hudson. Day after day they toil onward: night after night they sleep in a Connecticut covered wagon, or retire to rest beneath the branches of some huge umbrageous tree, or near by some sparkling fount or limpid rill. They have left home and friends behind, and, like the pilgrims who braved the dangers of the stormy ocean, have resolved to seek a home in the new land of promise. Some of the number, having never seen an Indian, and being unacquainted with their pacific character, were constantly tortured with the idea of being massacred, or perhaps carried away into hopeless captivity. They had read the murderous tales drawn from the bloody scenes of the border wars of New York and Pennsylvania, and had listened to the startling incidents connected with the heroic struggles of King Philip—scenes of devastation and blood, the bare recital of which sends the blood curdling to the heart. As they approached the Mohawk valley, they were met by half a dozen Oneidas, who, in a most decorous and courteous manner, inquired with regard to their health and destination. Their manner, at once so agreeable, struck the ladies with astonishment. The warm shake of the red man's hand became in after time associated with some of the most interesting incidents connected with their adventurous wanderings.

'Tis night. They have paused for repose in a dense wilderness, and their camp fire is already blazing by the side of a majestic old oak. The last quart of Indian meal is hastily converted into journey cake, the time-worn tea-pot is replenished with a few leaves of old hyson, and the only remaining venison shank assists in the preparation of a plain, but wholesome dish of soup. The end board of a wagon serves for a table, being elevated on a little hillock, around which the company gather to partake of the simple repast. The hoot of the old gray owl is heard in the distance, while the howl of the wolf and the scream of the panther mingle their discordant notes in the mountain gorge. Vapory clouds had o'erspread the face of heaven and shut out from view night's diadem. Far to the northward was heard the rumbling thunder, and anon the forked lightnings dashed athwart the aërial sky. But look ! the electric fluid has descended and shattered a sycamore of three centuries' growth into a thousand fragments ; suddenly the little band grouped about the table are startled by the well-known bark of the old house-dog. At a few rods distant are seen two globes, of fire-like brilliancy. The unerring gun is seized, and quick is heard the sharp report of the Yankee rifle, succeeded by death-like screeches, as some unknown form bounded away in the thicket. But hark ! the death-struggles of the huge monster are heard. A torch is snatched from the camp fire. The Yankee rifle is reloaded with a double charge, and three of the adventurers go in pursuit of the wounded animal. They had not proceeded over ten or fifteen rods, before they came upon an enormous panther weltering in his blood. The shot had taken fatal effect. Another report of the rifle was heard, and all was still. A quarter of an hour after, the animal lay stretched out before the camp fire, and was found by measurement to exceed nine feet in length.

An hour after, the clouds had disappeared, and the stars

> "That point with radiant fingers
> Thro' each dark greenwood bough,"

looked out in beauty from the vaulted sky,

> "Girt with Omnipotence, with radiance crowned
> Of majesty Divine."

Before the sun had flung forth his flaming beams along the orient sky, the little band of brave pioneers were toiling onward, having disrobed the panther, and left his skinless form to the protecting care of the hungry hyena and rapacious vulture. They passed with entire safety through Indian settlements, receiving the frank expressions of friendship whenever met by any of the roving natives, who, although unwilling to give up their hunting-grounds without a satisfactory equivalent, would not condescend to offer insult, or treat with contempt or indifference their more powerful rivals. They subsisted for several days almost entirely on the wild game of the woods. An old lady, relating to us the hardships through which they passed, remarked, that "had it not been for the deer that roamed at large, they should have suffered still more severely, and perhaps even unto death, as roots and venison were their only food for many a long and gloomy day." And the tears came in the eyes of this sainted mother of Israel, as she told her tale of privation, suffering and sorrow.

There were several families that came in during the

winter season, and were consequently subjected to unusual hardships. The great depth of snow that frequently fell impeded their progress. The Indian trails were often entirely hidden from sight. Then again, another great difficulty interposed almost insurmountable barriers. Many miles had to be traversed, without roads, and in a dense unbroken wilderness. Much of the country through which the pioneers passed presented a very level surface, which, when covered with forest trees, was wet and swampy, and from which arose the foul miasma which not unfrequently generated disease,—if not fevers of a malignant cast, at least those horrid ague chills, which often undermine the strongest constitution, and lead the unhappy victim to prostrate the system still lower with the thousand nostrums and humbug panaceas of the day. There were numerous instances where their progress was obstructed by various obstacles, and to an extent to preclude their making over five or six miles per day; and we have been informed of an instance, where the company, for several successive days, did not exceed three. To us, in these days of progress and steam, it seems like making slow headway if we do not exceed twenty-five miles per hour.

But the idea of being in a dense forest, with little suffering children pleading for food, without having the power to satisfy those wants, is most horrible. And yet such occurrences were experienced by some of the first settlers of this county. What mighty changes have been wrought by the finger of time! What stupendous obstacles have been overcome. The heavy forest trees, over which for centuries the lurid lightning wheeled in awful grandeur, and through which the untamed whirlwind swept—those mighty forest oaks which defied the the blast and the storm, have been removed. The rock-ribbed ridges have been converted into productive pastures, and the pestiferous marshes of the Mohawk now form one of the finest and most valuable agricultural districts in that region of country. The Indian trails have disappeared, and in their places have been substituted excellent roads. The terrific howl of the wolf has given place to the sharp, shrill scream of the locomotive whistle. An enterprising population is located in the valleys and scattered over the hills. Wealth has sprung up in almost every department of business, and Mammon stands, with brazen front, contending for power and place.

A New Englander, on his way to this land of promise, who had passed in safety through the northern wilderness, undismayed at the growl of the bear, the howl of the wolf, or the frightful scream of the great northern panther, had arrived within a few miles of Manlius, when suddenly his dream was changed to positive reality. A man of surly, dark features, tall, erect and commanding figure, presented himself before the astonished New Englander, and very politely demanded his money. To this unexpected appeal the Yankee demurred. He did not discover the means by which he was to receive any benefit from such a kind of procedure, and frankly told the supposed wild man of the woods that he had no money for him, and threatened him with a severe caning if he did not depart and leave him to proceed on his journey. But the French trader (for such he undoubtedly was) was not so easily to be put off. Summoning all his commanding powers, he, in a tone the most authoritative, again demanded the granite rocks. But the reply was equally authoritative, that he could have none. Then said the highwayman, "give me the hand of your beautiful daughter—*amor vincit omnia.*"* But the stern old man thundered in his ear in tones the most indignant, "avaunt! scoundrel, avaunt!" Still the higwayman persisted in his unjust demands, brandishing a large hunting-knife over the head of the unarmed pioneer. Suddenly, however, the scene changed, for the invincible New Englander siezed a bludgeon of wood, and in an attitude at once threatening and alarming, made for the wretch who hoped to wrest from the worthy man, not only his treasure of gold, but the idol of his heart; but his shadow was fast disappearing in the thicket before him, from which he did not again venture for the purpose of molesting the stern old man of the granite hills of New England.

The timber was generally of heavy growth, a fact going far to sustain the generally conceived opinion, that the Indians had not for at least two centuries made any very successful attempt at cultivating any portion of the Homer flats. True, we have the opinion of an aged Oneida sachem, and also some traditionary evidence, which go far towards establishing the fact of there having been, anterior to the sixteenth century, a race of red men located along the western shore of the Tioughnioga river, and that by intestine broils and internal commotions they were entirely destroyed. There have been instances in which arrow points have been found imbedded in the hearts of trees of great age,—at least the

* Love constraineth all things.

concentric circles would indicate that they were of more than four hundred years' growth.

During the spring of 1855, while engaged in excavating a mound of earth, we were surprised on finding that it contained specimens of charcoal, in a perfectly sound state. There were also fragments of mouldering bones, and singularly wrought impressions on the surface of dark, slatish-colored stones. How, when, or by whom these deposits were made, are questions which we leave for geologists to solve.

The heavy growth of forest trees was a great drawback to the more rapid improvement of this section of country. At the time the first permanent settler located in the county of Cortland, the Phelps and Ghoram tract was being rapidly settled. The Indian title to the Genesee country had been extinguished prior to that of the Military Tract. And the inducements to settle on the former were much greater than those held out in behalf of the latter. Individuals, natives of Massachusetts and Connecticut, were personally interested in the Phelps and Ghoram purchase, and consequently possessed considerable influence over the greater proportion of those who migrated from the New England States; and in 1790 about fifty townships had been sold. A monster, hideous to the sight of the Six Nations, sat in his den of unhewn logs at Canandaigua, cutting up the rich hunting-grounds of the Senecas into gores and townships, and disposing of them at a mere nominal price, which of course had a strong tendency to facilitate the more rapid settlement of the Genesee country. Many of the original claimants to military lands were dead; others had disposed of their right, which, perhaps in turn, had been transferred to a third, fourth, or fifth purchaser, which in the end gave rise to many litigated contests before the titles were permanently settled.

Aside from the many privations and hardships endured by the early adventurers in reaching their various points of destination, they were subjected to many and great inconveniences after they had arrived at their new homes,—having no floors to their dwellings, save such as were constructed from split logs ; using blocks for chairs, poles tied at the ends with bark for bedsteads, and bark for bedcords ; chips for plates, paper for windows, sap troughs for cradles, and so on to the end of the chapter.

The first crop of grain grown by the primitive settlers was a half acre of corn, one third of which was eaten while green. The small amount of meal brought with them at the time of moving had already been consumed, and of necessity they had to resort to various expedients to sustain life and drive away hunger, and as a substitute for the more favorite and substantial food, they dug ground nuts, and many nutritious roots, and after boiling them for a length of time, ate them with a relish quite unknown to that class of "upper tens" of the present day who are living in castles of ivory, or mammoth structures which have been reared by the productive labor of others. In the settlement of western, or central southern New York, we have heard of but a single instance in which this mode of living was surpassed, and that was by Oliver Crocker, who in an early day came into Broome county with a pack on his back, and, while engaged in "clearing his land, lived for some time on roots and beech leaves." He was at this time only eighteen years of age—had been for two years in the employment of Elder Joshua Whitney, when he found himself able to purchase four hundred acres of land. He became a very enterprising and wealthy man, yet held a most perfect abhorrence of that species of popularity which is purchased at the shrine of gold. His property did not lift him above the common level of humanity.

As soon as the corn had become partially ripe, a quantity was gathered, and after drying, was, by means of a stump hollowed out for a mortar, and a pestle hung to a well-sweep, pounded into coarse meal, which by boiling was coverted into samp or hominy—a most excellent and healthy dish.

The family of Mr. Morse, the pioneer of Cuyler, lived the greater part of one summer, on greens, and yet did not repine, but looked forward for better days.

There were resolute, determined actors, with strong arms, at war with the ancient forest trees. The wilderness was doomed to disappear. Migrators were launching their frail crafts upon the Hudson, forcing their canoes along the Mohawk, Unadilla, and Susquehanna, eagerly pushing forward, with a longing wish for a glimpse of the Onondaga, Chenango, and Tioughnioga. The panther, the wolf, the bear, the deer, and the thousand homogeneous tribes of fur and bristles, were retreating to the swamps and miniature mountain passes with a present prospect of safety from the leaden missiles of New England rifles. The proud old Romans, the native dwellers of the woods, began to exhibit strong symptoms of jealousy towards the "pale faces," who were thus encroaching on their rights ; and even "barbarism drew its fantastic blanket over its shoulders, and, clutching its curiously-wrought tomahawk," was seen "withdrawing to other solitudes, jingling its brazen ornaments and whooping as it went." Improvements rapidly increased, and settlements multiplied. The soil being rich and productive, other crops came in, were harvested, and converted into wholesome food. At this time there were no roads, save such as were made by following the Indian trails, removing the larger logs, cutting away saplings and under-brush barely sufficient to admit of the passage of a team. Eight to ten days were required to effect a commercial intercourse with Chenango Forks, forty miles south; six to eight with Ludlowville, twenty-five miles west; and about an equal number with Manlius square, thirty miles north, at which place they procured salt and grinding. At the former and latter, they purchased tobacco, and linsey-woolsey, while for axes they went to Cazenovia. Tea was an unbearable extravagance. True, a few of the more thoughtful had laid in a small quantity, before leaving the "land of steady habits," and this was resorted to only on extra occasions. An elderly lady told us of a long expedition made by her husband to Ithaca, and how her heart was gladdened on his return, on learning that he had purchased a whole half pound of *Bohea*. It was indeed a luxury.

But now that the delicious article was obtained, its stimulating and soul-cheering effects must be enjoyed. The whole neighborhood received an invitation to come in and spend the afternoon in a social chat, and testify to its merits. The afternoon came, and with it the company. The daughter, a flaxen-haired girl of sixteen summers, not forgetful of the generous sympathies that prevailed among the primitive settlers, had, in the meantime, contrived to despatch a special messenger, bearing an affectionate billet-doux, to her dear devoted friend John,—a very worthy young man of another settlement,—requesting his presence, inasmuch as they were intending to have a kind of glorification over the choice beverage. She was entirely free from deceit, dishonesty, haughty pride and fashionable idleness, and frankly told her friend that her mother was in want of a tea-pot, and hoped, inasmuch as his mother had one of revolutionary memory, and which had been used by his grandfather in the camp, that he would do her the favor to bring the article with him. John came, and, true to the desired courtesy, brought along the old war relic, and placing it on the slab table, very coolly remarked that he was somewhat given to dreaming, and that in one of his favorite reveries he had dreamed that a party of friends were to be convened at the double log house ; and presuming that the olden trophy of a passing age might be serviceable, had, at the risk of being laughed at, obeyed the direction given him in his nocturnal visitation.

The explanation of John was received with a hearty laugh, and a grateful expression of remembrance on the part of the mother. Not one of the company ventured to whisper a suspicious thought. They could not be so unkind. The visit was really enjoyed, and the *Bohea* proved a most valuable auxiliary in giving life and spirit to the frequent interchange of sentiments.

We were told by Mr. Lilly, that at a later day, himself and brother went on foot to Genoa and Scipio, to reap wheat. They labored five and a half days each, and earned eleven bushels ; threshed and carried it to mill, one mile east of Moravia.

We have been told of numerous instances of a like persevering industry and kindly attention to the wants of the dear devoted ones at home—of the father or eldest son setting out with a sack of grain on his shoulder, for a journey of twenty-five, and even forty miles, to a mill, in order to secure the wherewith to supply the place of the fast disappearing loaf. It was, however, a prevailing custom, when necessity did not demand more immediate attention, for one who was blessed with a team to take the grists for a whole neighborhood—an act evincing a generosity of sympathy peculiar to new settlements.

A grist-mill at a distance of twenty-five miles was of valuable consideration, when compared with a mortar and pestle.

Linsey-woolsey was a great achievement when allowed to take the place of buckskin pants and jacket coats. Glass windows were regarded as a very great improvement over those fashioned from paper. A service of earthen ware, when allowed to supplant the place of chips and wooden trenchers, was a luxury most ardently desired; and when a cherry table graced the kitchen, it was looked upon as a mark of increasing prosperity. A wagon with wooden springs attached to the seat, was procured at a most exorbitant price, and was regarded as a luxury to be enjoyed only by the few. A horse was almost deified. They had but few barns, and these were rude huts, their grain being stacked out door, winnowed by the breeze of heaven, placed into sacks and swung across the beams of the kitchen. Stairs were not yet thought of, and a garret floor was shrouded in their undreamed of philosophy. If they were not the days of gentility and refinement, they were at least the days of lustihood, generosity, and good fellowship. Respectability did not then consist in wealth alone, and a mean and beastly selfishness would have been despised, even though clothed in "silk and faring sumptuously." Indeed, greatness of character did not consist in fine houses and broad acres. Forced smiles and hypocritical pretensions, were reserved for older, and perchance, more refined regions. Land sharks, money shavers, and political gamblers, were not of their order. They possessed not only muscles, sinews and bones, but a fleshy form, containing a human soul. They were not automatons—they could appreciate a good act, and return a favor without accompanying it with a grudge.

Previous to 1791, the territory now comprised within the county of Cortland was known to the whites only by charts and maps, and though forming a constituent portion of the State of New York, was regarded, on account of its location, of but minor importance.

HOMER.—In 1789, Amos Todd and Joseph Beebe migrated from New Haven, Conn., and located at Windsor, Broome co., N.Y. In 1791 they removed from Windsor, and were the first of the noble pioneers who planted the standard of civilization in the Tioughnioga Valley.

These enterprising spirits were accompanied by only one lady,—the sister of Mr. Todd, and wife of Mr. Beebe.

We shall not stop here to recount the various degrees

of unremitting toil, privation and effort through which they passed in their journey to their new and uninviting home.

Mr. Beebe erected his house north of Homer village, near the upper bridge, on ground now occupied by the residence of Joseph Burt. In our mind there is no doubt existing with reference to the locality of Mr. Beebe's house. His son Spencer, who, in 1852, died in a prayer meeting at Harrison Valley, Pa., has left some early reminiscences and data, together with a map, which accurately describes the Tioughnioga, and marks the location of the first four dwellings erected west of the river. These are now in the hands of the writer. The edifice would illy compare with those now occupying the adjacent grounds. It was in the main composed of poles, twelve by fifteen feet. Before this temporary abode had been completed, their team strayed away in the woods. Leaving Mrs. Beebe alone, they set out in its pursuit. She had no protection except the four walls of poles, without floor or roof, and simply a blanket stuck up with forks to cover the space intended for a door. The husband and brother were absent three days and nights, and during the long and lonely hours, Mrs. Beebe maintained a tranquil mind and received no annoyance, save such as was caused by the howling wolf and screaming panther, of whose rapacity for blood she had often heard, and whose terrible yells made night hideous and tenfold more alarming to the tender feelings of a sensitive female. She received but one call, and that was from a wolf, who, being rather timid, only displaced the blanket sufficient to introduce his phiz and take a look at her ladyship.

During the following winter, Messrs. Beebe and Todd returned to Windsor for their effects, and were snow-bound for six weeks. Mrs. Beebe remained at home, the sole occupant of her palace of poles. She must have been blessed with more than ordinary courage and fortitude. Probably but few women in these days of modern refinement, similarly situated, would exhibit an equal amount of patience and force of character. Let us not be understood as wishing to speak disparagingly of the females of the present day : far from it. Circumstances give an entire change to human character. The elements of which it is composed, are variously operated upon. Other circumstances might have made Lord Byron a Washington, or Washington a Byron. Education, properly considered, is everything.

It was a cold day in the middle of winter. Their goods were closely stowed away in their little craft, and as they "pulled away from the shore," and bent their course homeward, a farewell shout echoed from shore to shore.

Arriving at Binghamton, they were joined by John Miller, Esq., father of deacon Daniel Miller, whose company was very acceptable to these half land, half water craftsmen.* The men took turns in directing the course of the boat, while the others followed on foot along the shore of the river, removing obstructions, and driving the cattle. When the stream was too shallow, the boat was drawn across the rifts with their oxen, and then

* Mr. Miller was a native of New Jersey. He lies entombed a short distance south-east of the County House, where four generations of the Millers "sleep."

again set afloat upon the watery element. Then the facilities for moving goods were in wide contrast with those of the present day. Then they were not even favored with a common highway over which to transport their property, but were gratified in having the power to lend a strong arm in propelling a common Indian canoe. Now, in addition to the various other facilities, we have the powerful aid of the Iron horse, whose limbs are steel and whose lungs are fire, and by whose generous assistance the rich treasures of the East and the valuable products of the West are unladen in the very lap of the fertile valley through which he passes, belching fire and smoke.

The brave and hardy pioneers are approaching their new home. There stands the humble cabin, containing the soul and centre of Mr. Beebe's felicity. In the door appears the young and cherished wife of fond affection, ready to greet her more than "noble lord"—her generous hearted husband. She is a high-souled, noble-hearted woman, worth more than gaudy gems or golden crowns. For six long weeks she has been a lonely inhabitant of the valley, and during the stormy days and darksome nights, she was truly "monarch of all" she "surveyed." And now she rushes from her forest palace, with heart all kind, and eyes all bright, with form and mien glowing in the sunlight of pure affection, radiant with hope and beauty, as though just baptized in the sparkling fountain of ever blooming youth.

The sable shades of night have curtained the earth. The moon rolls high in the vaulted dome—the stars look out in beauty from the radiant sky; and joy reigns in the cottager's home,—for peace and gladness dwell in the breasts of all as they gather around the social board to partake of the frugal repast prepared by the hand of her who had left the home of cherished friends to become the copartner of him who had reared the seat of his chosen empire amidst the stillness of the primeval forest.

Mr. Miller made some explorations of the country bordering East and West River, and then returned to his home near the noble Susquehanna. In the spring ('92) Mr. Miller, John House, James Matthews, James Moore, Silas and Daniel Miller, came in from Binghamton. Camping at the forks of East and West River, they built a fire against a large oak tree, a portion of which is still remaining. Here the women remained, while their husbands went forward and erected cabins for their temporary residence.

Squire Miller, located on lot 56, erected a house near the willow trees ;—almost every person has been made acquainted with their history—how the original sprout was purloined from its parent tree by Dea. Miller, when returning on horseback from a visit to his friends in New Jersey, giving great offence to its owner, and how it served its new possessor in the capacity of a riding whip—was afterwards stuck in the ground, where it took root, sent out numerous branches, some of which have grown to fine trees,—ornaments to the ground on which they stand. Mr. Matthews built on the upper end of the same lot. Mr. House about eight rods northwest of the residence of Ebenezer Cole. Mr. Moore near the bridge south of the Cotton Factory.

Darius Kinney came from Brimfield, Massachusetts, in 1793, and located on East River. About this time, Mr.

Beebe abandoned his place of poles, and settled on the premises of his brother-in-law, Mr. Todd, on lot 42, west of the village.

Roderick Owen came from Lebanon, N. Y., and located about one hundred rods south-east of the residence of Dr. Jones.

The Ballards were from Holland, Mass. John first located on the east side of the Tioughnioga ; three years after, settled on the farm at present owned by Paris Barber. It was owned at this time by Capt. David Russel, who had but recently located, and erected a double log house near the north-west corner of Mr. Barber's orchard.

Another company came in by way of Cazenovia through Truxton, in 1794, pioneered by Jonathan Hubbard, and Col. Moses Hopkins. The former of these settled on ground now covered by Cortland village, and the latter one mile west, on lot 64.

During the year 1795, several companies came in by way of Manlius and Truxton. Thomas L. and Jacob Bishop came in from Brimfield, and located on lands now owned and occupied by Noah Hitchcock. In an early day it was known by the name of the Vanderlyn farm. Lot 25.

Thomas Wilcox came from Whitestown, N. Y., and located on Lot 64, where Joshua Ballard now lives.

Zebulon Keene located on the farm now owned by Mr. Sheffield. John Stone, originally from Brimfield, settled on the Albert Barker farm, lot 25. Joshua Atwater, father of Ezra and Joseph, located on lot 13.

Libeus Andrews came from Hartford, Conn., purchased and settled on land south of Mr. Kingsbury, lot 56.

John Keep, Solomon and John Hubbard came in from Massachusetts, and selected various locations. Mr. Keep made a permanent settlement on lot 56, and built the original part of the County House. Solomon settled on lot 25, and John on lot 26, where his son Lyman now resides. His house, when originally erected, was regarded as being by far the most expensive dwelling in the county, and was denominated a "mammoth." The influence and enterprising efforts of these gentlemen, in after years, proved of valuable importance.

On rolls the tide of progress. The spirit of enterprise is awakened, and the brave pioneers come pouring in with warm hearts and strong hands, resolved to make war with the forest oak, or grapple with stern adversity in the dark hour of peril.

Thomas G. Ebenezer and Charles Alvord came in from Farmington, Conn., and settled in the north-west part of the town, on lot 13. The former drew lot 56. When he reached Manlius, he was met by a couple of land-sharks, who, on learning the lot upon which the old hero was intending to settle, very coolly informed him that they had been to Homer, and that they were well acquainted with the position of his land, and could assure him that it was an exceedingly poor, wet lot, the greater part of it being covered with water. In short, he was, by means the most deceptive, induced to part with six hundred acres of most valuable land for the trifling sum of a few dollars. Jacob B. Alvord resides on lot 13—his farm is on lot 12.

In 1797 Joshua Ballard came in from Holland, Massachusetts, and selected a location on lot 45. We shall refer to him in a subsequent chapter.

John Albright, the pioneer of East Homer, located on the lot he drew for Revolutionary services.

Asa White and Caleb Keep migrated from Monson, Mass. The former located on lot 45 ; erected his house on ground now covered by the residence of Jedediah Barber. He purchased and completed the first grist-mill in the county, in 1798. The latter bought and settled on the farm now owned and occupied by Noah Hitchcock, a grandson of Mr. Keep.

During the year 1798, a very considerable accession was made by persons settling in various parts of the town, and more especially along the borders of East and West rivers.

Stephen Knapp came in with his brother-in-law from Goshen, Orange co., N. Y., to explore the country. His father having been killed during the Revolutionary struggle by the Indians on the Delaware river, near the mouth of the Lackawaxen, left him to carve out his own fortune ; and he sought this wild region of country for that laudable purpose. His mother, having some little means, which was placed in his care, a purchase was made through Judge Thompson, of lots 55 and 84. Returning to Goshen, he early made preparations for moving to Homer ; but circumstances over which he had no control, delayed his departure until 1798. He came by the way of Poughkeepsie, Shonkunk, Kingston, head waters of Schoharie ; followed down the river to Prattsville ; thence to Harpersfield ; crossed Wattles Ferry ; thence to Oxford ; thence to Solon, afterwards called Hatheway's Corners. Here he followed the Salt Road about two miles to Squire Bingham's ; thence over the hills to Judge John Keep's ; thence to Mr. Matthews' on lot 56 ; and thence to Hon. John Ballard's. Here Mr. Knapp and his friends remained for some time, during which period his brother Daniel purchased the farm of Capt. Russell.

Soon after this sale, Mr. Ballard located in the village. Mr. Russell died with the small pox.

Mr. Knapp is still living, a venerable relic of a former age. Neither marble nor fulsome epitaph will be necessary to perpetuate his memory.

The Hobarts were from Monson, Mass. Daniel, father of Alpheus, located on lot 43 ; Samuel on 15 and 16. Gideon settled with his father, and remained on the same farm until his death, April 30th, 1857. The farm is now owned and occupied by Manly Hobart.

Titus Stebbins, from the same town, settled on lot 43.

Samuel Hotchkiss, from New Haven, Conn., located on lot 44.

Dr. Lewis S. Owen came from Albany, and after a general survey of the country, located on lot 66. Here he remained three years, when he moved to Homer village and erected a house on the ground now occupied by his son, Dr. Robert Owen, lot 45.

Deacon Noah Hitchcock came in from Brimfield, and located on lot 25. He was a kind, generous-hearted man, and in brief, a prominent and useful citizen.

The venerable Zenas Lilly came from Brimfield, and located on lot 33, where he lived about twelve years, when he sold to Messrs. Tubbs and Keep, and settled on Factory Hill. Some years after, he disposed of his property and settled in Lenox, but subsequently returned to Homer and located on lots 34–5. His history is closely identified with the history of Cortland county.

Timothy Treat, Enos Stimson, William Lucas, and Asahel Miner were from different parts, and selected various locations. Mr. Treat was from Berkshire, Mass.; he settled about eighty rods north of the former residence of John Barker, now owned by Mr. Bowen. Family consisted of parents and eight children. The third, a daughter, married Stephen Knapp. Mr. Stimson was from Monson ; he settled on the ground now occupied by the elegant residence of Jacob Schermerhorn. He reared a small house and hung out a landlord's sign. The next spring the people were greatly alarmed on account of the *small pox*, which had made its appearance in the valley. Several took it, and died. His wife and children went to Aaron Knapp's, in Cortlandville, and were vaccinated, which, as we are told, caused clear cases of small pox, but soon recovered, and were able to return home.

An incident occurred during the absence of Mrs. Stimson, showing most distinctly the influence of ardent spirits upon the Indian character. Twelve Onondaga Indians called one evening at Mr. Stimson's, drank freely, got highly exhilarated, called for more liquor in their own familiar way—" Tegoye ezeethgath" and " Negauqh,"*—were repeatedly refused, and told that more would do them injury. But no, they had got a taste, were ardently inspired, would not listen to reason. They became uncivil, deranged, and threatened Mr. Stimson with violence. Retreating as they approached him in a menacing attitude, he sought safety up stairs, cautiously pulling the stair-ladder after him. The sav-

* Have you rum and wine, or firewater?

ages were noisy and quarelsome, as might be expected, having made themselves perfectly free with the *aqua morbi et mortis** of the bar, even draining the bottles to the very dregs. But the midnight revel, the bacchanalian orgies not yet ended, for their brains had been fired until the poor degraded beings reeled with delirium. They were bound to the car of Bacchus, which for centuries back has creaked and groaned beneath its burden of blasted hopes, crushed affections, and depraved humanity ; aye, with the blood of hundreds and thousands of wasted wrecks and ghastly skeletons. Not content with emptying the rum, gin, and whiskey decanters, an old sachem seized a bottle containing *picra*, swallowed a portion of its contents, and hastily passed it to a young brave who drank its very dregs. This had a powerful and most alarming effect, for they came very near dying.

Just at this, and to them inauspicious moment, and while some were guarding the garret port-hole through which the landlord had made a hurried retreat, and others were bending over the victims of supposed poison, an aged Indian, at least half "sea over," stepped hurriedly from the door, and mistaking a well-curb for a fence, leaped over and brought suddenly up in the bottom of Mr. Stimson's well. This was rather a severe shock to his *spiritual* feelings, and though famed as a conjuror, he was too drunk to conjure up a plan by which to escape from his unpleasant quarters. His position was truly an uninteresting one. The element which surrounded him was of an entirely different char-

* Poison water of death.

acter from the one that was influencing within. And now, while whooping, yelling, cursing and swearing was going on in the house, the old Roman was alike interestingly employed in the well. At length, assistance came to his relief, and by the aid of a blanket, which was let down to the periled one, he was drawn up from the watery depths below.

The next morning, Maj. Stimson, under certain promises, was permitted to come down and take possession of his house. The Indians were not so spiritually influenced. The *medium* operating between them and the bottle had become inoperative. Spooks, hobgoblins, witches, wizards, and the whole infernal train of delirium devils had disappeared from among them. A few made attempts at cheerfulness, while others exhibited only symptoms of sullenness. The old chieftain felt mortified at his conduct, while the professed juggler had not courage enough left to enable him to attempt any more of his tricks at legerdemain.

William Lucas and Asahel Miner were from Woodbury, Conn. The former located on lot 35 ; the farm is now owned by Samuel Babcock. He erected a portion of Mr. Babcock's present residence. He was an exceedingly active, useful and prominent citizen—what a living witness has defined as one of the very best of men. His four surviving children reside in Ohio. The latter settled on the Lucas Welch farm. He was the first sheriff of Cortland county, having been appointed April 8, 1808. Martin Miner, his son, resides in the village.

Col. Benajah Tubbs came in from Washington county, and located on the ground now occupied by the Geo.

Phillips store. He early engaged in the mercantile trade, and continued the business for many years.

John and Richard Bishop were from Brimfield. The former settled south of the Vanderlyn farm, while the latter located immediately opposite Mr. Hammel Thompson. He afterwards built a one-story house, where Mr. Thompson now lives. Asaph H. Carpenter, some time after, added another story. Under the care of Mr. Thompson it has been made a very pleasant residence.

After 1800, the town began to settle more rapidly. Those who had previously located had passed the Rubicon, and with a determined will, quite superior to that which prompted Cæsar to cross the threshold of his own province for the express purpose of reducing Italy to his power, had labored nobly in the cause of human improvement, and were already in the partial enjoyment of its blessings. We regret that our limits will not allow of our recording the name and place of settlement of every pioneer. From 1800, we can only locate a few in the various sections of the town.

Ephraim P. Sumner came in from Connecticut in 1800, and located on lot 47, where his son E. P. Sumner now lives. He purchased two hundred acres ; died 1843 ; Mrs. Sumner, 1840 ; reared ten children—eight now living.

Noah Carpenter came in from Pomfret, Windham co., Conn., and located on lot 16. His son, Asaph H. Carpenter, who now resides on the original premises, had the honor of being first arrayed in *bib and tucker* while his parents were journeying to this land of promise. He was, however, more fortunate than the Saviour, for

He, being "cradled in a manger," had "not whereon to lay his head."

Peter Vanderlyn, father of Jacob, came from Ulster county, N. Y., and purchased one hundred acres. He drove in fifty head of sheep, the first in the town ; also several head of cattle, and the first lumber wagon. He built the first fanning mill that was used in the county; the wings were made of cloth, and it proved a valuable acquisition in the department of saving labor.

Thomas, Nathan, and Samuel Stone were from Brimfield. They located on lot 46.

Waterman and Levi Phillips were from Connecticut. The former located on lot 69, near where Trout creek empties into the Tioughnioga. He purchased one hundred and seven acres. He now resides in the village ; is eighty-one years old. His sons are Jefferson, Abel K., and George. The latter located on lot 16. He came in with an ox team and one horse ; purchased fifty acres, and subsequently ninety-seven more. His surviving sons are Levi, on lot 28 ; Charles, at Nanticoke ; Oren, on the homestead ; and Erastus, in the village. Mr. Phillips died in 1845, aged seventy-eight years ; and his widow in 1850, at the age of seventy-nine years.

Several additional settlements were opened during 1801. Seth Keep, originally from Massachusetts, migrated to Homer from Vermont, and located on the north-east corner of lot 33.

Gad Hitchcock came from Monson, Mass., and settled on the farm now owned by Albert Barker. His son, Horace Hitchcock, is an active and worthy citizen, residing in the village.

John Coats located within a few rods of the Congregational church, in 1802.

During the same year, Dea. Thomas Chollar came in from Windham, Conn.; remained some three years, during which time he made various explorations of the country, in order that he might judge correctly with reference to the soil, as well as the general advantages which were likely to be realized by those who thus early plunged into the wilderness, enduring privation, and struggling against forest and flood, disease and death. In the latter part of 1804 he selected a location on lot 17, and settled on it in 1809.

Asa Kendall, father of Abner N. Kendall, was a native of Massachusetts, but removed to Homer from Pompey, and located on the farm now owned by Dea. Conger. He purchased fifty acres.

In 1803, Jacob Sanders, Moses Butterfield, Levi Bowen, and Elijah Pierce, father of Justin M. Pierce, came in and located. Sanders removed from Swansey, Mass., and settled on lot 56. He reared an intelligent family of ten children, all of whom are now living, and in good circumstances. Butterfield was from Canterbury, Conn. ; he located on lot 47, where Charles Kingsbury now resides. The farm at present embraces one hundred and twenty-five acres. Mr. Butterfield died in 1820. Bowen settled on lot 7, where E. P. Stickney now resides ; he was from Woodstock, Conn. He purchased ninety-six acres ; died in 1832, leaving eight children—five now living. Pierce came from Brimfield.

Elie Sherman came from Brimfield in 1803, and settled on lot 47. He is now enjoying good health, and is in the full possession of his faculties—age, seventy-seven.

Abel Kinney, from Brimfield, settled in 1804 on lot 6.

Capt. Daniel Crandall, from Massachusetts, located in 1805 on lot 38. He died in 1857.

Capt. Zephaniah Hicks, originally of Rhode Island, migrated from Connecticut in 1805, and located on the south-east corner of State's Hundred, lot 17. His house stood on the ground now occupied by the dwelling of Norman Southworth. Capt. Hicks was an active, energetic, high-minded man; generous, humane, obliging, and courteous. His hale, prompt, manly greeting gained for him the good will of his neighbors, and gave him much influence in the occasional pioneer gatherings. The influence of Dea. Chollar was much the same. It is related of these men, that when a question of right was to be decided the appeal was usually made to them; the deacon having given an affirmative decision, the almost universal response would be, "That 's right, Deacon Chollar; ain't it so, Capt. Hicks?"

The Captain removed in 1835 to Ingham, Michigan, where he still resides, a venerable relic of the "olden time."

Jacob Hicks, his son, who at the time of his migration to Homer was but two years old, is settled on lot 27. His advent on to the Hill dates farther back than that of any remaining settler. His eldest daughter, Nancy, is the wife of Silas Elbridge Mann, a prominent citizen and hardware merchant of Jordan.

In 1806, Col. David Coye, from Royalton, Vermont, and Lemuel Bates, from Cincinnati, came in and located. The former settled on lot 45, where he now resides. He purchased the first acre sold for a village lot. He followed his trade, that of joiner. In 1815, he purchased one hundred acres on lot 44. The rear of his dwelling was erected in 1808; the front in 1826. His shop, one story and a-half, twenty by thirty-five, stood on the ground occupied by Newton's store. He has filled several prominent offices; among others, that of sheriff. He has reared a family of eleven children—seven now living. Two reside in Missouri; one in Buffalo; one in San Francisco; one married Caleb Sherman, and another Francis De Long, of Lockport; Mary, the youngest, is still at home. The latter settled on lot 26. His sons are Joseph and Ransford. The former lives in Little York; the latter on the forks of the road above Homer village.

William Shearer came from Washington county in 1807, and located on lot 36. His son Reuben lives on the original premises. Mrs. Shearer was an early schoolmate of Hon. Samuel Nelson, and remembers him as a youth of warm and generous impulses.

Stephen and Joel R. Briggs, Ariel Tickner and Erastus Hayes were originally from Otsego county. They located in 1807 on lot 50. The former died in 1844. His widow survives him at the age of seventy-six. She resides with her son, Jabez Briggs. Mr. Tickner died some years previous. Joel R. Briggs lives on lot 38, in Homer, and Mr. Hayes resides in Spafford.

Deacon Ira Brown came in from Brimfield, in 1808, and located on lot 24. He now resides in Cortlandville. He has reared a respectable family, and accumulated a good property.

Joseph Bean, father of Jeremiah, of Cincinnatus, and Samuel, of Homer, located in 1809. He purchased one hundred acres. During the same year, Noah R. Smith and Matthias Cook came in and located. The former came in from Middletown, and settled on lot 45.

He has been a prompt, active, and influential citizen; has filled several important offices by appointment and election; was appointed sheriff in 1819. The latter came from Albany, and entered into the hatting business, which he continued successfully for many years. He was at one time a copartner in trade with Col. Benajah Tubbs. He was appointed county clerk in 1821, elected a member of the legislature in 1824, and was chosen Justice of the Peace at the first election of such office by the people.

Deacon Jesse Ives, and Andrew Burr came in during the year 1810. Mr. Ives was from Litchfield, Conn. He located on lot 16, and purchased originally ninety acres of land. He was emphatically a man of progress—an industrious and enterprising farmer, and his genial and excellent qualities made him universally respected and beloved. He died Nov. 27, 1857, aged 81 years.

Mr. Burr was from Sharon, Conn. He originally located on the ground now occupied and owned by William Kingsbury. He early engaged in the manufacture of leather, but subsequently sold his tannery to Willam Kingsbury, who located in 1816, and went into the saddlery and harness business, which he carried on for thirty years. He has erected several dwellings, and otherwise labored to improve and advance the interests of the village. The rear portion of his dwelling is composed of the original or first church which was erected in Homer. The front part was erected in 1812 for a house of public entertainment, and was called the "Mansion House."

Richard Graham and Henry Corl came in and located in 1811. The former was from Herkimer county, and settled on lot 28. The latter was originally from Schenectady, but came in from Locke, Cayuga co., and settled on lot 8, where he remained one year, and then removed to the Abel Owen farm, now owned by Dr. Jones. Here he remained two years, and then settled on the Hill, which now bears his name. He purchased 120 acres. He is now 78 years old—has raised a family of nine children, all now living.

During the war of 1812–15, the progress of settlement was greatly interrupted. The settlements were, however, frequently visited by a kind of floating population, having no fixed purposes, but would come and go like the waves of the ocean.

George W. Samson, from Plympton, Mass., located in 1812 on lot 28 ; remained four years, and then settled on lot 19, being the first settler on the lot. He erected the Mt. Etam Stand in 1824, and went into it the next year ; commenced keeping a house of entertainment in 1827—in Homer village in 1839. He possesses considerable native talent, great vivacity, blended with wit and generous sympathy.

James Hull came from Norfolk, Conn., about 1815, and settled on the farm now owned by Willis Alvord. He now resides in the village. His industrious habits, and moral and social sentiments, entitle him to a just and honorable mention in the pioneer annals of Homer.

Erastus Goodell, father of C. B. and Erastus, Jr., came in from Sturbridge, Mass., in 1816, and located on State's Hundred, lot 7. He originally purchased 50 acres ; has now, with an additional purchase, owned by his son Erastus, 130 acres. His land was entirely covered with a heavy growth of timber, when he came upon it. He first erected a small house in the hollow east of his barn, but soon after put up a log house on the ground now covered by his present residence. The latter was erected in 1834. His son, C. B. Goodell, owns the Joseph Bates farm.

William Andrews came from Fabius, Onondaga co., in 1817. From 1820 to 1843 he served in the capacity of constable and under sheriff, and in 1831 was elected sheriff, on a union ticket between the liberal portion of the Jackson and Clintonian men. The opposing candidate was Martin Keep. Mr. Andrews is a prominent and influential citizen.

Daniel Josling, from Windham, Conn., located in 1818 on lot 17. Kenneth A. Scudder, from Monmouth, N. J., settled in 1813 in Herkimer county, and subsequently removed to Homer and located on lot 18. He reared a family of eight children, all of whom are living. He died in 1843, aged 77. His widow survives him at the age of 76.

Having thus presented a general outline view of the early settlement of Homer, dating from 1791 to 1818, we shall proceed to exhibit some important dates and facts connected with its history, interspersed with interesting incidents bearing upon the political, moral, social and religious character of the noble spirits of other days.

The town of Homer was organized March 5th, 1794, and, as we have previously stated, originally embraced the townships of Homer and Cortland. The town officers were not, however, limited to the town limits, but Virgil and Solon were permitted to share in their selection, and as such we give their names as though they had really belonged to Homer. The territory has a broken and diversified surface—presenting to the observer the rugged hill and fertile valley. The soil is generally good,—consisting of clay, sandy and gravelly loam, while flats of rich alluvion border East and West River.

The political temperature of the early pioneers at the time of the erection of the town, stood at about zero, as will appear evident from the perusal of the following document, which is copied from the town records.

STATE OF NEW YORK: } ss:
ONONDAGA COUNTY. }

Whereas the town of Homer, in said county, on the 5th day of April did neglect to appoint the necessary town officers for the year one thousand seven hundred and ninety-five:

And whereas, by a law passed on the 7th day of March, one thousand seven hundred and eighty-eight, directing three justices of the peace of said county, to nominate, and under their hand and seals appoint such officers as under said act is necessary, therefore, we, Asa Danforth, Hezekiah Scott and Daniel Keeler, three of the justices of the peace, appointed in and for said county, nominate and by these presents do appoint,*

For *Supervisor*,—John Miller.

Town Clerk,—Peter Ingersoll.

Assessors,—Thomas L. Bishop, Moses Hopkins, Joseph Beebe, Daniel Miner, Roderick Beebe.

Commissioners of Highways,—Samuel Benedict, David Russel, Moses Hopkins.

* At this time Justices were appointed at Albany, by the Council of appointment.

Overseers of the Poor,—Joseph Beebe, Christopher Whitney.

Constable and Collector,—John House.

Signed, ASA DANFORTH,
HEZEKIAH SCOTT.
DANIEL KEELER.

The meeting at which these appointments were made was held at Squire Miller's on the 9th of April, 1795.

The first annual town meeting for the election of officers, was held at Mr. Miller's house on the 8th of April, 1796. The following were the successful candidates.

Supervisor,—John Miller.

Town Clerk,—Peter Ingersoll.

Assessors,—Ezra Rockwell, Billy Trowbridge, Daniel Miner, Francis Strong, David Russel, Jacob Bishop.

Collectors,—Roderick Beebe, Barzilla Russel.

Overseers of the Poor,—Zera Beebe, Ozias Strong.

Com. Highways,—Zera Beebe, Thomas L. Bishop, Oliver Tuthill.

Constables,—Barzilla Russel, Roderick Beebe.

Overseers of Highways, — William Tuthill, Ebenezer Jones, Zera Beebe, Samuel C. Benedict, Joseph Beebe, Solomon Hubbard, John Morse.

Fence Viewers, — Elnathan Baker, George Strowbridge, Johnson Bingham, David Jackson, John House, Moses Hopkins.

If the officers of those days were not selected with the regularity that attends our elections at the present time, they were at least chosen with less of bitterness engendered by political knaves and unprincipled demagogues. The contests for political preferences continued to be mild and conciliatory for many years. In 1800, however, the political elements throughout the State were greatly agitated, and in that severe struggle for power, the pioneers exhibited some symptoms of excitement, and shared, to a degree, in the general fever that pervaded the country.

In 1796, it was agreed by vote, " that every man make his own pound. That hogs run at large without yokes or rings.

That fences be made four feet and one half high, and not to exceed four inches between logs or poles."

In 1797, it was agreed by a unanimous vote, "that every man in the town may provide his own pound for every creature that does him damage, and yet be entitled to damage the same as at the town pound. That hogs be free commoners.

That three feet of sound fence shall not be more than five inches between earth, logs or grass."

In 1798, it was voted, "that one inch more of space be allowed between earth and wood."

A citizen of the town was not allowed to bring in or receive cattle from another town to keep for any period of time, under penalty of one dollar.

If some of these requirements were enacted and strictly adhered to, at this time we do not question their beneficial results. At least there would be less wrangling and bitter neighborhood recriminations in consequence of poor fences and disorderly cattle.

In 1797 the town of Homer was divided into highway districts. Amos Todd and Johnson Bingham were Commissioners of highways.

1798. A wolf scalp commanded a premium of from

five to ten dollars, according to size ; bear, five dollars ; panther, ten dollars ; and foxes, fifty cents.

In 1797 Homer contained ninety-two inhabitants. Valuation of property reduced to dollars, $,6,670.

On Wednesday, the 27th of May, 1794, the first meeting of the Board of Supervisors of Onondaga county, was held at the house of Hon. Asa Danforth, in the town of Manlius. Homer had not at that time been organized, and consequently was not represented. The Board, however, made an estimate at random of the valuation of property and proportion of tax for the towns of Pompey, Ulysses, Lysander and Homer. The latter was estimated at £500, and the proportion of tax at £6, 5s.

The pioneers of Homer were a people who revered the Bible, and valued its ordinances. They brought with them corresponding habits. When six families had arrived in town, (1793,) they all convened upon the Sabbath day and commenced public religious worship. From that day to the present time, (1859,) this divine reverence has been continued on the Sabbath, and we are assured from the most positive authority that there has occurred but one omission. This is a fact of marked significance, bearing upon the character of the people and the prosperity of the settlement. It was a common saying, as emigrant families came from New England on to the Military Tract, if you wish to settle among "religionists," go to Homer. The first sermon in the town was pronounced by a missionary, who in a later period was Rev. Dr. Hilliard, of New Jersey. This discourse was delivered in the open air under a large tree upon the Hill, about one hundred rods north-east from the present dwelling of Eleazar Kingsbury. The people were collected for the purpose of raising a building, and before the work had proceeded far, it was currently reported among the company that a missionary was lending a willing hand in the work of progress, and soon a voice was heard calling out "a sermon, a sermon." Upon which a very polite invitation was extended to the Rev. Doctor of Divinity to favor them with a discourse, and in answer to which he preached a most thrilling and heart-feeling discourse. The next sermon was preached by Elder Peter P. Roots, of the Baptist denomination, in Mr. Baker's barn, from the text, "Faith, Hope and Charity."

The present generation in Homer will do well to pause and look in upon these six families, on this memorable day of their first worship, and intelligently meditate upon the results of this movement, and gratefully embalm their names as the benefactors of the township. The standard then erected has not yet been taken down. The banner then unfurled still waves, bearing on its ample folds, GRACE AND GLORY. The incense of prayer from this little band was an offering accepted of God. The communication then and thus opened between Him and the people has not since been closed. Our God will keep his covenant forever.

The varying views of these pioneers, touching religious doctrine and practice, delayed for several years the formation of a Church. But their frequent consultations and protracted discussions were in good feeling, and they could all happily meet for worship on common ground. But a church organization was a necessity that would not stand in waiting without jeopardy to the spiritual welfare of the community. At length relief came through the sagacity of a WOMAN. The WIFE of Lieutenant Hobart, and the MOTHER of Deacon Jacob Hobart, of undying memory in the annals of Homer, with deep feeling intelligently weighed her responsibility in this matter. But as the custom then was, and still is, that females must be silent partners in business matters, she earnestly pressed upon her husband that delay should terminate, and procured from him a pledge that a meeting for consultation should be called, and that he should move that those who were so far agreed that they could walk together in church order, should at once unite in the organization of a Church. It is not known whom she prevailed upon to second the movement. This done, she waited before God for the result.

This movement was sustained, and on the 12th day of October, 1801, the Congregational church of Homer was organized by the Rev. Hugh Wallace, of Solon, and the members resolved to maintain a Monthly Church Conference. Thus early, on the banks of the Tioughnioga, and in the centre of Homer, was kindled a beacon light, to reveal to the teeming population in a wide circuit, danger and duty in reference to their religious, intellectual and social interests.

In February, 1803, Rev. Nathan B. Darrow became the pastor of this church, and this connection closed in October, 1808. In October, 1809, Rev. Elnathan Walker became the pastor. He was removed by death in June, 1820. His remains were entombed in the public cemetery, and the hallowed spot was subsequently marked by an appropriate marble monument, bearing the following inscription :

This Monument

IS ERECTED BY AN AFFECTIONATE PEOPLE, AS

THE LAST

TESTIMONY OF RESPECT TO THEIR

BELOVED PASTOR.

His daughter, Tryphena, married the Rev. C. H. Reed, of Richmond, Virginia, one of the most able and eloquent men of the age. Mr. Reed is not only a sound and really able speaker, but he is most emphatically an independent and accomplished orator. His address at the Atlantic Cable Jubilee in Homer was full of bold, pointed Southern sentiments; and yet, proclaimed as they were before a Northern audience holding in the main opposite views, were listened to with marked attention, and elicited, at the conclusion, spontaneous applause.

But to return from the digression. In June, 1821, Rev. John Keep was called to perform pastoral labors for this church, and, like a pious herald of the cross, continued ministering to the spiritual wants of the people until 1833, when he removed to the city of Cleveland, Ohio.

The harmony and enterprise of the Congregational Church and Society happily resulted in the dedication of a spacious and commodious house for public religious worship by the Middle Association of Ministers. Sermon by Rev. Mr. Darrow, June, 1807. During 1824, this "Meeting House" received the addition of an ornamental front, a convenient vestibule, and extensive interior improvements. Its completion was commemorated by public religious exercises on the 23d day of

December. Sermon by the pastor, Rev. John Keep, from the text, "Rejoice with trembling." This was one of his most happy and brilliant efforts. Strong, argumentative, yet touchingly eloquent. When the reasons given for rejoicing had nearly reached their culmination, the large, well-trained choir, accompanied by a full-toned organ, interrupted the speaker by the anthem chorus—

"Oh, be joyful in God, all ye lands."

The early pioneers brought with them the religious sentiments of the New England people, and early engaged in public religious worship. Their meetings were without "denominational distinction," being attended by the religionists without regard to order or sect. Those holding to the Congregational sentiments were most numerous, and put forth the first active efforts for the formation of a church, and although they succeeded in forming the first "Religious Society in the town of Homer, in 1799," they were nine days later in the organization of the Congregational Church, than the Baptists were in the organization of their church, which was formed October 3d, 1801. For a number of years the Baptists were not favored with regular or stated preaching. There were, however, occasional sermons pronounced by Rev. Joseph Cornell, James Bacon, Peter P. Roots, and Rufus Freeman. Rev. Alfred Bennett, became the first permanent pastor.

The Methodist Episcopal Church was organized in 1833. Nelson Rounds was the first preacher. The Calvary Church in 1831.

The Universalist Church was formed in 1839.

The Advent Church was organized December, 1848. John Smith and Joseph L. Clapp, deacons.

The officiating clergymen are Albert Bigelow, of the Congregational ; C. A. Clark, of the Baptist ; and Hiram Gee, of the Methodist.

In 1810	the population of	Homer was	2,975
1814	"	"	4,046
1820	"	"	5,504
1825	"	"	6,128
1830	"	"	3,307
1835	"	"	3,584
1840	"	"	3,572
1845	"	"	3,602
1850	"	"	3,836
1855	"	"	3,785

The early tradition of Homer, in many instances, is very obscure. In all cases we have adopted such evidence and facts as we have believed to be the most authentic, to the exclusion of every item of doubtful character. The first house was erected on the bank of the Tioughnioga, in 1791, by Joseph Bebee. The first improvements were made the same year by Amos Todd, west of Homer village. The first frame house was built for Dr. Lewis S. Owen. In 1799, the first frame barn was built for Col. Moses Hopkins, on lot 64, and is still standing. The first school-house was built in 1798, about twelve rods beyond where the railroad crosses the road leading to little York, and the second one on the north-east corner of the Green. The first grist-mill was erected by Asa White, John Hubbard, and John Keep, in 1798. Hooker Ballard was the first tailor ;

Matthias Cook, the first hatter ; Aaron Knapp, the first carpenter ; Joshua Ballard, the first school-teacher ; John Osborn, the first permanent silversmith. Eleazar Bishop, the first blacksmith ; Rev. Nathan B. Darrow, the first stated preacher ; Townsend Ross, the first attorney and post-master ; Luther Rice, the first physician ; Maj. Stimson, the first inn-keeper ; John Coates, the first merchant ; Prof. W. P. Beck, the first Daguerreian artist. He built the first Daguerreian carriage in the State ; and is an accomplished artist.

The first death was that of Mrs. Thomas Gould Alvord. She died in 1795. The first male child born in town was Homer Moore. The first female child was Betsey House. The first marriage was that of Zadock Strong and widow Russel. The parties intended to have been married by Squire Stoyell, of Moravia Flats, but being disappointed, they went to Ludlowville on horseback, and were united in the sacred bands by Squire Ludlow.

In 1798, forty dollars and seventy-eight cents were appropriated for the use of common schools in the town of Homer.

The first "burying ground" was on a little knoll, about thirty rods west of the factory.

The are but four of the old veteran pioneers now living, who came into Homer previous to 1800, viz.: widow Moses Hopkins, age seventy-nine ; Stephen Knapp, age eighty-one ; Zenas Lilly, age ninety ; Alpheus Hobart, eighty-four. The two first are in the enjoyment of their usual good health, and in the full possession of their intellectual faculties. Mr. Lilly and Mr. Hobart are slowly but surely wearing away with the infirmities of age ; and yet they are calmly and serenely awaiting the hour to depart. May they go down to the silent tomb alike honored and respected.

The venerable pioneers are fast passing away, and soon it may be said of them, " they have been, but are not."

Solon.—This town originally comprised the military township No. 20, and was organized March 9, 1798.

It was subsequently reduced by attaching the four northern tiers of lots to Truxton, and in 1849, by the erection of the town of Taylor.

The surface of the town is considerably broken and diversified. The hills are generally arable, and the valleys rich and productive. Some of the long ridges, or druidical elevations, covered with the deep, thick foliage of the olden forest trees, present a wild, picturesque and pleasing aspect. In brief, the town is well adapted to grazing. The staple products are butter and cheese.

The first permanent settlement was made in Solon in 1794, by Roderick Beebe and Johnson Bingham. The former located on lot 75, on that portion which is usually called Mount Roderick. He was originally from Massachusetts. The latter was a native of Connecticut, but came in from Vermont, and located on lot 62. He purchased 550 acres, reared eight children, seven of whom are living. He was Justice of the Peace for about twenty years, and associate Judge for a long time. Died 1842, aged 79 ; his widow survives him at the age of 95, in the enjoyment of good health.

William Galpin, from New Jersey, located in 1797, on lot 47. His stay was brief, owing to the fact of his having purchased and accepted a forged title. He subsequently settled in Pompey.

It may be well to remark here, that the early settlements were mainly made in the northern and eastern portions of the town; these are noticed in the history of Truxton and Taylor.

In 1799, John Welch came from Wyoming, and located a little to the south of Roderick Beebe. He remained a few years, and removed to Cleveland, Ohio.

Col. Elijah Wheeler, came in from New Haven, Conn., in 1801, and located on lot 100. He originally purchased 100 acres.

The venerable Capt. Stephen N. Peck, from Stanford, Dutchess co., N. Y., located in Solon, lot 62, in March, 1804. He purchased 92 acres, and subsequently, considerably increased the area of his land. He survives at the age of 80 years, more than usually exempt from the infirmities of age.

Garret Pritchard came from Litchfield county, Conn., in 1807, and located on lot 74. He came in with a pack on his back, having but $16,50 in money. He went to work with a determination to carve out a fortune, and he has most fully succeeded. His father, having come in the previous year under greatly embarrassed circumstances, found it very difficult to pay back arrearages, and yet succeed in a new country. His son, however, had the nerve and muscle to accomplish both. He earned and paid $500 for his father; after which he located where he now lives, on lot 75. He owns upwards of 500 acres of land, and is pleasantly and favorably situated.

During the same year, Richard Maybury, from Luzerne, Pa., came in and located on State's Hundred, lot 53. Purchased 100 acres. He was an industrious and worthy man, and has left several intelligent and valuable representatives. His children are Lewis, John, Josiah J., Elizabeth, Nancy, and Deacon Samuel.

Henry L. Randall, from Sharon, Conn., located in 1808, on lot 74. He moved in with a two horse team, bringing with him a few of the necessary articles for immediate use in his new home. He is now 81 years of age, enjoying in a remarkable degree his physical and intellectual faculties. He has remained for a full half century where he first settled ; has reared a family of five children—Henry, David, William, Linus and Orrin—the three former accompanied him from his New England home.

Jonathan Rundall, from Sharon, Conn., located on lot 74. Ebenezer Blake, from Stoddard, New Hampshire, settled on lot 84. He was a soldier in the American revolution, and was in the battle of Bunker Hill ; drew his land in Ohio.

In 1810, the taxable property of Solon, as returned, was $99,612, and there were 110 Senatorial electors.

In 1800	the population	of Solon was	370
1810	"	"	1,263
1814	"	"	717
1820	"	"	1,262
1825	"	"	1,781
1830	"	"	2,033
1835	"	"	2,103
1840	"	"	2,311
1845	"	"	2,426
1850	"	"	1,150
1855	"	"	1,057

VIRGIL.—The town of Virgil, named in honor of the distinguished Roman Poet, *Virgil*, and to whom many classical allusions are made, was organized April 8th, 1804. It was No. 24 of the Military townships, surveyed in 1790. The town presents a broken and diversified aspect, and to the general observer, exhibits a great variety of picturesque scenery. Much attention is being paid to the dairy business--the soil being better adapted to grass than to the growing of grain.

The citizens generally are prosperous and happy. The town, politically, morally and socially, holds an important and commanding influence in the county, and compares well with that description given in the ancient Chinese aphorism :—

> "Where spades grow bright, and idle swords grow dull,
> Where jails are empty, and where barns are full,
> Where church paths are by frequent feet outworn,
> Law court-yards weedy, silent and forlorn,
> Where doctors foot it, and where farmers ride,
> Where age abounds, and youth is multiplied,
> Where these signs are, they truly indicate
> A happy people, and well governed State."

After the tide of revolution had rolled away, and the people were becoming comparatively happy, conflicting claims and unpleasant controversies were renewed, having a strong tendency to create bitter recriminations between inhabitants of adjoining States, and especially those of New Hampshire, Connecticut, Massachusetts and New York.

The controversy pending the conflicting claims of the two latter States, grew out of an antiquated and pretended or supposed right on the part of Massachusetts to a certain portion of land lying within the boundaries of New York.

In 1786, the question at issue was finally settled by an amicable adjustment of the differences of opinion, through the united exertions of Commissioners duly appointed, and clothed with the Confederative power to arrange the matter in controversy, and thus silence the clamor which had for a long time tended to create unpleasant remarks, as well as to weaken the bonds of fraternal fellowship. The Commissioners granted to Massachusetts 6,144,000 acres of land, known as the Genesee country. This tract comprised all the land of the State west of a line beginning at the mouth of the Great Sodus Bay on Lake Ontario, and running due south, through the middle of Seneca lake, to the north line of the State of Pennsylvania, excepting one mile in width, the whole length of Niagara river, which was ceded to New York. Another tract, afterwards known as the Massachusetts Ten Townships, embracing 230,400 acres of land, lying between the Owego and Chenango rivers, was also ceded, without the least equivalent, to Massachusetts, reserving to New York barely the right of sovereignty. The former, as we have previously stated, was sold by Massachusetts to Oliver Phelps and Nathaniel Gorham, for the sum of $1,000,000. The latter was purchased by John Brown & Co., for a fraction over $3,300.

It will be observed that we have heretofore spoken of Virgil as township No. 24 of military lands, granted to the soldiers of the Revolution. It should, however, be noted in this place, that the whole of the town of Virgil did not originally belong to the military grant.

A strip of about 1½ miles in width from east to west, across its southern side, was taken from the Ten Township grant to Massachusetts.

Joseph Chaplin, the first permanent settler, (whose name has occurred in previous chapters,) located on lot No. 50, in 1792, but did not move on his family until two years later. His rude log house was erected during the time he was engaged in exploring and surveying the route for the Oxford and Cayuga lake road, preparatory to his engaging in the enterprise of constructing the work with which he had been entrusted.*

John M. Frank settled with his family on lot 43, which had been granted him for services in the American Revolution, in November, 1795.

In 1796, John Gee, from Wyoming, Pa., moved on to lot 21, having the previous year erected his dwelling, and made some other preparations for the more convenient reception of his family. He was a soldier of the Revolution, and was well worthy of the heroic title. His house was composed of logs 12 by 16. His family consisted of himself, wife, father, mother, and six children. Some of Mr. Gee's descendants still occupy the original premises.

Johe E. Roe moved in from Ulster county during the winter of 1797–8. The ground was covered with a heavy body of snow, just then dissolving beneath the warm rays of the sun. The journey from the old hearthstone was made in a sleigh, which contained a few of the more costly effects for the new house. Among these were a few fancy, or flag-bottomed chairs, which, unfor-

* This road was sixty miles in length.

tunately, were greatly lessened in value as well as for service, on account of the bottoms holding out a strong temptation to the horses, which were tied to the sleigh, without food, while the family were resting for the night at Mr. Chaplin's, then within a few miles of their destined place of abode. The temptation was too strong, and consequently the chairs were freed of their flags, though a rather poor substitute for hay.

A bridge had not yet been erected, consequently the few that crossed the river were in the habit of using a small canoe belonging to Mr. Chaplin. The high water, which had suddenly risen from the effects of the dissolving snow, to their great surprise had carried away their little water craft. The horses could swim the stream, but as for Mrs. Roe, her case was one of doubtful result. But the pioneers were full of expedients. They were men of enterprise ; and when they formed a plan, or resolved upon a measure, they usually had the will and the power to carry those plans into practical operation. The residence of Mr. Chaplin was on the opposite side of the river, and they must either secure shelter as best they could, where they were, for it was near sunset, or manage some way to get over the swollen stream. As a final resort, a hog-trough belonging to Mr. Chaplin was floated over, and Mrs. Roe, with the courage of an experienced tar—a true son of the ocean, —seated herself in the frail craft, and passed over with entire safety. Mr. Roe and his team next made an effort at crossing, and though it was hard swimming, the horses succeeded in reaching the opposite shore without injury. A three year old heifer, the only cow they possessed, and which had followed the sleigh from

Ulster, was still behind. But she had no notion of being left, and after making a few flourishes with her head, leaped into the water, and after a powerful effort, stood on *terra firma,* on the other side of the river.

The next morning they set out for their intended home ; the weather was unpleasant, and the snow still quite deep ; and besides this, there was no track to follow, and in truth, we might as well say, no road. It was a long and tedious day, for the sun was just disappearing behind the ancient hills as they drew near their uninviting house, the body of which had been put up by Mr. Roe the previous spring. He had hewed and put down a plank floor, and prepared bark for the roof, which, according to an arrangement, was to have been put on by an individual who resided in Homer. But, contrary to his expectation, Mr. Roe found his house in the precise state of completion in which he had left it. He had triumphed over every other obstacle, and was not now to be disheartened, though greatly disappointed. The snow was full two feet deep in the house ; this, however, was soon shoveled out, or at least a portion of it. A fire was built against the logs, and thus commenced their first unpropitious attempts at housekeeping in their long looked for, and at length inauspicious achievement, in their forest home.

The next year, (1798,) there were a number of additional families who came in and settled in different parts of the town. Among these were James Bright, James Knapp, Bailey, John and James Glenny, and Wait Ball.

In 1799, Enos Bouton, Dana Miles, John Lucas, Henry Wells, Jared Thorn, and Primus Gault came in and selected locations.

During the year 1800, James Wright, John Calvert, James Sherwood, Peter Jones, Seth Larabee, John Ellis, Oren Jones, Moses Rice, Abial Brown, Jason Crawford and Moses Stevens were added to the new settlements.

In 1801, Daniel Edwards, Nathaniel Bouton, Prince Freeman and James Clark came in and settled in various parts of the town.

In 1802 the settlement was increased by Jonathan Edwards, Samuel Carson, Alexander Hunter, George Wright, Abner and Ezra Bruce, William Lincoln, and Peter Gray ; and in 1803, Moses Olmstead, Peter Powers, John I. Gee, Andrew Van Buskirk and Dorastus DeWolf.

In 1804, Silas Lincoln, Alexander M'Nist, Obadiah Gilbert, Lemuel Barnes, Peter Tanner and Jeremiah Shevalier came in, selecting locations in different parts of the town.

In 1805, Isaac Barton, Jotham Glazier, Simeon Luce, Zophar Moore, Oliver Ball and Isaac Elwell became resident settlers ; and the next year John Hill, John Green, Zachariah Squires and others came in and located.

From this time the settlements increased more rapidly. The soil, though not of the very best quality, was not of the most inferior kind. Perseverance and a strictly economical mode of living produced wonderful results. It required active and laborious exertions to subdue the wild forest and convert the wilderness into fruitful and productive fields. Had the virgin soil yielded various valuable productions like many portions of the sunny South, without any effort on the part of the proprietors of the soil, and where indolence is most proverbial among the people, the inhabitants of the new settlements would undoubtedly have exhibited less energy, less enterprise, and would, as a natural result, have been indolent and imbecile. The case was, however, quite the contrary. The pioneers of that early period, and those who warred with the old forest monarchs who had reigned from three to five and even six hundred years on the Virgil hills and valleys, were composed of materials that could brook misfortune, discouragement, and the numerous trials and hardships, the natural results of the first attempts of planting new settlements in a wild and almost unbroken wilderness, swarming with voracious animals, eager, anxious to lap their tongues in the warm blood of some unfortunate victim.

The word "discouragement" did not belong to their vocabulary. What know we of the present day of the toils, privations, and sufferings, through which our fathers and mothers passed, when they thus early struck their tents in the forest, deprived of the many luxuries and conveniences which we so freely and fully enjoy! They did not repine, though they of necessity were compelled to erect their houses of logs, cover them with bark, split logs for their rude floors, using paper windows, wooden trenchers, pine slab tables, crack their grain in a mortar, or journey forty or fifty miles to a grist-mill; and then, perhaps, if not fortunate enough to have a span of horses, which few did, trail along with a yoke of oxen, attached to a dray, loaded with a small quantity of corn or wheat, winding by way of an Indian footpath around the sedgy marsh, fording streams, ascending the hill-side, and again descending into the valley, camping out night after night; or, peradventure, if still less fortunate, impelled by the wants of the dear ones at home, with three pecks of corn thrown over his shoulder, and a cold lunch in his pocket, he starts off on a wandering tour to a mill at Chenango Point, Ludlowville, or Manlius Square.

When Mr. Agar came into the town and located near the little streamlet that runs gurgling through the rocky ledge, leaping the cascade, and dancing in the sunlight as it enters the Tioughnioga, he had but a cow, an axe and an auger to help himself with. Mrs. Agar was, if possible, quite as poorly provided with articles for housekeeping. Instead of marble tables, foreign sofas, rosewood chairs, Brussels carpets, etc., Mrs. Agar's furniture consisted of a hewed slab elevated on four legs for a table, square blocks for chairs, and a corn husk rug in lieu of an elegant carpet. Chips served the purpose of plates, and a bake kettle for an oven, dish kettle, water and milk-pail, as well as for soup-dish, a frying-pan and a coffee-pot. And yet we are told that they enjoyed life and finally became wealthy. While reflecting on the inventive power of this self-sacrificing woman, we cannot help comparing her genius with that of Joseph Chamberlain, who emigrated from Herkimer county in 1806, and located in Steuben. He was the owner of a dog, a cow, and an axe. He did not possess a single article generally used about the kitchen, or upon the most common table. But he had both tact and genius ; and these were speedily brought into requisition. His cow must be milked, but into what kind of a vessel was a problem which he alone seemed prepared to solve. Near his cabin might have been seen the trunk of a common-sized tree. Into this he had cut a small notch, or basin. Morning and night he would drive his cow astride of this log and milk her into this rudely constructed vessel. Standing at a little distance, the observer might see him crumb his roasted bread into the milk, which he ate with a wooden spoon.

There are many touching incidents connected with the early history of Virgil, which might be both interesting and instructive, as they exhibit most fully the noble independence and moral greatness of the early pioneers, and evince most evidently the necessity for decisive action in all great enterprises, whether moral, social, or political. We regret that our limits will not allow of extended comments.

The first town meeting after Virgil was organized (1804), was held at the house of James Knapp, on the 2d of April, 1805, when the following officers were duly elected :

Supervisor,—Moses Rice.

Town Clerk,—Gideon Messenger.

Assessors,—Abner Bruce, John Gee, Joseph Chaplin.

Commissioners of Highways—John Glenny, George Wigant, John I. Gee.

Poor Masters,—Jonathan Edwards, Peter Powers.

Constable and Collector,—Shubel S. Marsh.

Fence Viewers,—Moses Olmstead, Abial Brown.

The first *Justice of the Peace* was James Glenny. He was appointed in 1802 by the Commissioners of appointment at Albany.

The first post-office was established in 1808, and Zophar Moore appointed post-master.

The first school-house was erected in 1799, near the

present residence of J. C. Hutchings. Charles Joyce was the first teacher.

The first merchant was Daniel Shelden. When the news of the arrival of his goods spread through the settlement, it was received with great interest, and considered as an important event in the annals of Virgil.

The first saw-mill was built by Daniel Edwards, in 1801.

The first grist-mill was erected in 1805, by Peter Vanderlyn and Nathaniel Knapp. The erection of this mill was regarded as a work of valuable importance. The inhabitants had previously been compelled to procure the grinding of their grain at Chenango Point, (now Binghamton,) or Ludlowville, near the east shore of the Cayuga lake. We have heard of numerous instances of individuals carrying the grain upon their backs to the latter place, a distance of twenty-four miles.

The first carding machine was put in operation by a Mr. Baker, in the latter part of the year 1814.

The first public burying ground was deeded to the town in 1806, by George Wigant. The first tombstone was erected in 1823, to the memory of an esteemed and worthy citizen, James Roe.

The first cider was made by Enos Bouton in 1819. It commanded four dollars per barrel. The apples were bruised by a pestle hung to a "spring sweep;" and the juice was extracted by means of a very simple lever press.

The inhabitants seem to have taken considerable interest in elevating the standard of education. There were gentlemen with warm hearts and active minds laboring to advance the interests of the school-room. A grammar school was first taught in 1819, by Henry J. Hall.

In 1837 the "Literary Institute" was organized. It continued until 1845, having been successfully taught by N. Bouton and William E. Gee. Various other schools flourished from time to time.

The "Virgil Library" was established in 1807, and another, with a capital of two hundred dollars, was organized under the name of the "Virgil Union Library," in 1814.

The first Sabbath school was organized in 1822.

The first religious meeting was held in 1802.

The Congregational organization was completed Feb. 28, 1805. There were then eight members. Rev. Seth Williston presided.

The Baptist Church was organized in 1807.

The Free or Open Communion Baptist in the south-east part of the town, was constituted in 1820 ; and that of the Free Baptist Church in the west part, was organized in 1822.

The Methodist organization took place in 1826 or 1827. Their church was built in 1831.

The Universalists organized into an Association in 1831.

The Christian Church was formed in 1828.

The first physician was Elijah Hartson.

The first child born in town was a son of Mr. Chaplin.

The first death was that of a stranger, Charles Huffman, who died in April, 1798, in the woods, while attempting to travel from Ebenezer Brown's, in Lansing, (then Milton,) to Mr. Chaplin's.

The first death of a resident settler was that of Mrs. Derosel Gee, in March, 1802. She was the wife of one of the heroic soldiers of the French Revolution of 1754–63. He was a man of iron frame and active mind, and could repeat tales of the tented field, of blood and carnage, that would never fail to send the blood curdling to the heart.

The first marriage occurred in 1800. The parties were Ruluff Whitney, of Dryden, and Susan Glenny, of Virgil. The event was regarded with more than usual interest, and formed an era, or starting point, from which future events were to be dated. And it is worthy of remark, that when we were collecting our historical materials, we frequently met with individuals, who, when interrogated with reference to certain points, would immediately refer to the marriage of Miss Glenny in 1800, and then figure backward or forward, as the case might be, and thus arrive at what they concluded to be positive periods of time, or certain points of fact.

In the autumn of 1853 a Town Agricultural Society was organized, and held its first annual Fair in 1854. The result was commensurate with its importance. In 1857 it was reörganized, according to the act of 1855, passed to facilitate and encourage the formation of Agricultural Societies. During that year a beautiful piece of ground was obtained on a lease, and a fence, enclosing upwards of four acres in a square form, was erected; as also, a building for the exhibition of dairy products, home manufactures, and needle-work. The building has since been enlarged and improved. A spirit of enterprise has been awakened in the town, and its example has been followed by some surrounding towns and localities, in the formation of similar societies.

In 1846 Virgil was divided into three towns; the north half constituted one, and retained the original name. The south half was formed into two; the west received the name of Harford, and the east that of Lapeer. Since that time a part of Virgil has been set to Cortlandville, and another part, consisting of lot No. 20, has been attached to Freetown.*

In 1810, six years after its organization, the population numbered 913. There were seventy-seven Senatorial electors, and the whole amount of taxable property was $84,351.

In 1798 the population of Vigil was			30
1810	"	"	906
1814	"	"	1,437
1820	"	"	2,411
1825	"	"	3,317
1830	"	"	3,912
1835	"	"	4,291
1840	"	"	4,502
1845	"	"	4,541
1850	"	"	2,410
1855	"	"	2,231

CINCINNATUS was one of the original townships (No. 25,) of the Military Tract; located by act of Legislature of New York, in 1786, to which reference was made in a previous chapter. It originally contained 100 lots, or 64,000 acres of land. It was organized April

* See Festive Gathering of Early Settlers, by Hon. Nathan Bouton, the able and popular pioneer annalist of Virgil—page 31.

8th, 1804, and retained its original limits until April 21st, 1818, when it was reduced by the erection of Freetown, Willet and Marathon. Freetown was taken from the north-west quarter, Willet from the south-east, and Marathon from the western portion of the township.

The settlement of Cincinnatus commenced in 1795. The inducements were not of that flattering character which were calculated to attract the earlier attention of intelligent and enterprising pioneers. The lands were not regarded as being of the most productive character. In this respect, however, great changes have resulted from the labors of industrious agriculturists. And although the general quality of the soil does not equal the rich flats washed by the glassy waters of the Tioughnioga, or surpass the more elevated lands of Homer, Preble, or Scott; yet it is quite certain that great improvements have been made, and that farmers are reaping the rich rewards that spring from the industrious pursuits of life. Much of the surface of this town is hilly, though by no means mountainous. The soil is of various qualities, generally better adapted to grass than grain, a fact which appears to be well understood by the dairymen, for we have the most positive authority for asserting that some of the very best specimens of butter, which find their way into Washington Market, New-York, are made in Cincinnatus.

Previous to 1798, when a grist-mill was erected at Homer, the citizens of Cincinnatus were in the habit of going to Chenango Forks, Ludlowville, or Manlius Square, with drays loaded with wheat and corn, drawn by oxen, to get their grinding done. If the reader desires to understand how these drays were constructed, it will only be necessary for us to state that they were made from the crotches of trees, having a few boards or cross pieces attached to them by means of pins. They were usually from six to eight feet in length, and, as we are informed, from eight to ten bushels made a very respectable load. In more modern times, the drags, and even stone-boats, were similarly constructed.

The settlement of Cincinnatus commenced in 1795, under the auspices of John Kingman, Thadeus Rockwell, Zurial Raymond, Dr. John McWhorter, Ezra Rockwell, and Samuel Vining. Mr. Kingman was a native of Massachusetts, born in Wethersfield, October 5, 1770. With an ordinary education, he left home at the age of sixteen, and learned the shoemaker's trade with Mr. McGee, an Irishman, who carried on the business in Sheffield. At the age of twenty-five he came to Cincinnatus, and located where he now lives, on lot 19. He had never worked at farming, and consequently purchased originally only fifteen acres. He possessed a strong physical frame, and was an active and energetic man. He busied himself in clearing his land in the daytime, and in making shoes and boots during the early portion of the night; in this way he paid for much of his hired help. He subsequently made different purchases, until he had secured 150 acres—which is now owned by his sons Charles, George, and John. In a military capacity, he rose from 2nd Corporal in a company of infantry to Colonel. He was supervisor of Cincinnatus for eleven successive years; and held numerous other town offices. He has reared a very intelligent family of children: Leroy W. resides in Owego, Tioga county; Lyman, in Groton, Tompkins county; and Oliver, Charles, and George I., at Cincinnatus. All have been merchants; and it is worthy of remark, that neither of them ever failed in business, and are therefore enjoying the well-earned fruits of their own industry. Oliver, John and George have been members of the Legislature; the former was an associate Judge from 1828 to 1846. Leroy, at the time of writing, is the popular county clerk of Tioga county. The Rockwells were from Lenox, Massachusetts. Ezra first located in Solon, now Taylor, in 1793, but in '95 removed to Cincinnatus and settled on lot 19—purchased 100 acres. Thadeus settled on lot 9. Mr. Raymond was from Williamstown, Massachusetts. He located on lot 29, on a revolutionary claim, which he had the fortune to secure through his wife, Widow Young. Dr. McWhorter came in from Oxford, Chenango county. He married the step-daughter of Mr. Raymond, a very interesting and accomplished lady. This was the first wedding that occurred in Cincinnatus. Thomas Rockwell told us that at the time referred to, there was no person there authorized to marry, and consequently a clergyman was employed to come from Oxford and officiate. This done, another difficulty arose, but was easily overcome. The clergyman had no authority to marry out of the county of Chenango; and hence the company, pioneered by Thos. Rockwell, marched out and as they supposed crossed over the border line into Chenango, but, in reality, had not reached the then limits of Onondaga. They had, however, approached a romantic spot, such as the marvellous would presume to be the retreat of sylphs and nymphs; and there, beneath the pavilioned sky, in the midst of the unbroken forest, on a beautiful moss-covered heath, the happy couple were duly and appropriately married. Dr. McWhorter was a man of more than ordinary ability ; was an active and prominent politician, and was at different periods elevated to responsible positions. From 1804 to November 8, 1808, he was a member of the New York Assembly. He also held, by appointment, the office of surrogate. He reared a large family of children ; three are now living. One is the wife of Burton Wakeman, son of Judge Wakeman, of Pitcher,—a gentleman of respectability and fortune. Another daughter resides on the Genesee Flats, and a son, Zurial McWhorter, near Buffalo.

Phineas Sergeant, from Oxford, in 1796 came to Cincinnatus, and was employed as a kind of general job ber.

Charles De Belle was from Berkshire, Massachusetts. He located in 1797, on lot 9. He died in 1854. Mrs. De Belle is still living, and is remarkably active and healthy. She is eighty-three years old, yet frequently walks upwards of a mile—not of necessity, but from preference—to visit her brother, Thomas Rockwell, of Taylor. Mr. De Belle left five children, all in good circumstances. Their names are Truman, Polly, Sophronia, Francis, and John.

Jesse Locke, from Oxford, settled about 1800, on lot 19. Of his family or fortune in life, we have no particulars.

The Wyoming Indians occasionally visited the valley, (Otselic,) during the few first years after the settlement commenced. The Onondagas and Oneidas, also, made periodical visits. In 1796, forty of the Oneidas camped on the ground occupied by the Brick store ; and during the fall and winter they killed forty-two bears. The oil they preserved in some of the larger intestines, and used it in cooking their meats. Soon after Col. Kingman began to improve his land they erected their cabins farther down the river. He informed us that they were very peaceable, and well disposed towards their white neighbors.

The inhabitants exhibited considerable public spirit in their efforts to establish and render beneficial the common schools, which claimed their early attention. Public religious worship did not commence at as early a period as in many of the sister towns. This, however, was not owing to any lack of moral culture or religious belief on the part of the people, but should be ascribed to circumstances beyond their control.

The Union Congregational Society of Cincinnatus and Solon was organized November 18th, 1822. The trustees were John L. Boyd, Barak Niles, John Covert. Clerk, Barak Niles. Presiding officers, Oliver Kingman, Barak Niles.

The first sermon ever preached within the original limits of Cincinnatus, was pronounced by Dr. Williston, of the Congregational order. It was delivered in a log barn, from the text, " Hear ye."

James Tanner was the first merchant. The first miller, Benjamin Wilson. The first store was erected by Col. John Kingman, on ground now covered by the Brick store. The first school-house was built by Mr. Kingman, and stood a short distance south of his house. The first frame house was erected for Dr. John M'Whorter, about 1802. The first school was taught by Miss Hepsy Beebe.

In 1810 the population of	Cincinnatus	was	1,525
1814	"	"	1,614
1820	"	"	885
1825	"	"	1,057
1830	"	"	1,308
1835	"	"	1,018
1840	"	"	1,301
1845	"	"	1,195
1850	"	"	1,206
1855	"	"	1,119

Much of the matter rightfully belonging to Cincinnatus, will be found in our sketches of Freetown, Willet, and Marathon.

Preble was organized April 8, 1808, from the original south half of the old military township of Tully. In 1815 it was reduced to its present limits by the erection of the town of Scott.

The standard of civilization was first erected in the town of Preble, in 1796, by James Cravat and John Gill. The former was a native of Connecticut, but migrated from Pompey Hill, and located on lot 68. The latter located on lot 76. Samuel and Robert Cravath came from Norfolk, Conn, in 1797, and settled on lot 68. Harry Hill and Elijah Mason came in during the year 1798. The former was from Montgomery co., N. Y., and located on lot 87, which he drew for Revolutionary services. The latter settled on lot 78. Seth Trowbridge, from Montgomery county, located in the early part of 1799 on lot 59 ; and during the next year, Samuel Trowbridge, Minnah Hyatt, and Samuel Orvis settled on the same lot. Trowbridge served in the Revolution and drew the lot. Widow Trowbridge, of Homer, mother of Mrs. Oliver Glover, was a daughter of Mr. Hyatt. Mr. Orvis was from Norfolk, Conn. He subsequently removed to Prattsburg, Steuben county, where he died in 1851, at the advanced age of ninety-eight years. His surviving children are Reuben S., now living in Hastings, Oswego county. Phebe, (Lee,) Clarissa and Eliza reside at Prattsburg.

In 1801, Augustus Thorp located on lot 78. In 1802 Jabez B. Phelps, John Osgood, Silas Topping, and Samuel C. Buckelow came in and selected various locations. Judge Phelps was originally from Hebron, Conn., but came to Preble from Cazenovia. He located on lot 88. For the first few years he practised medicine, and was honored with the title of Doctor, but he subsequently turned his attention to politics, and was at different periods elevated to important positions, and creditably filled the office of Associate Judge, Surrogate, and member of Assembly. He died December 20th, 1850, aged seventy-four years. His widow is seventy-eight years of age, and is in the enjoyment of excellent health. Mr. Phelps reared ten children, seven of whom are now living—three in Ohio. Sophronia is the wife of Charles Clark of Groton; Laura Jane is Mrs. Dr. Burdick; Augusta is Mrs. Harry Hobart, of Truxton; Lydia married Dr. Alfred Hall, of Navarino, Onondaga county; Amanda is the wife of Hon. Ezekiel Chew, of Richland, Ohio; Abram J., of Newark, in the same State; Lydia, wife of Dr. Hall, of Onondaga; and Calvin B., of Chrysoline, Ohio.

Osgood settled on lot 77, Buckelow on 67, and Topping on 96. In 1802, Lytle Ferguson, from Montgomery county, located on lot 65. He purchased one hundred and nineteen acres; reared seven children—six of whom survive him. His sons are Michael, William, Thomas, Elias, and Lytle.

In 1803, Amos Skeel and Jason Comstock came in from Schenectady county, and selected locations. The former settled on lot 59. He was an industrious and valuable citizen. He died in 1842, at the age of seventy-five years. His widow survived him eleven years, and died at the advanced age of eighty-eight. He was the father of Hon. Ira Skeel, as also of William W. The former lives in Preble; the latter has but recently removed to Homer. His son William is at present a prominent citizen and public officer of Jefferson county, Missouri. Mr. Comstock located on lot 58. His daughter Saloma is the wife of D. G. Duncan. In 1804, John Callyer, Dr. Robert D. Taggart, and Edward Cummings, selected locations. Callyer, father of Casper Callyer, came from Greene county, and settled on lot 58. Taggart came from Colerain, and located on lot 59. He was an exceedingly active and prominent man. Cummings, came in from Peterboro, N. H., and settled on lot 59. He purchased one hundred acres, and reared a respectable family of thirteen children—eleven of which are now living—seven of whom are sons residing in Preble.

In 1806 several additional settlements were made. Garret Van Hoesen and his sons--Garret, Francis and Albert—came in from Greene county and located on lot 68. He purchased of James Cravat, the original settler of the lot, three hundred and fifty acres at twelve dollars and fifty cents per acre. Garret and Francis are still living on the lot; the former at the advanced age of ninety, and the latter at eighty-two years. William Vandenburgh, from the same county, located on lot 77. He was the father of Lambert and Richard: the latter lives on lot 85 in Scott. John C. Hollenbeck and Richard Egbertson, also from Greene county, located about the same time on lot 58. Mr. Hollenbeck left two sons, —Abram and John,—and one daughter. John occupies the homestead. The daughter, Mary, is now widow Beeman, of Tully. A daughter of Mr. Egbertson is the wife of David Beeman. Tunis Van Camp, from Schoharie county, located on lot 69. The farm is now owned by Frederick Poor. His son John lives in Tully.

In 1807, Rier Van Patten, from Schenectady, located on lot 56. His children are Mrs. Martin Vanderwarker, Mrs. Mary Ann Hobart, Asenath, now widow Egbertson, John K. and James S. The latter lives in St. Charles, Illinois.

The town of Preble presents a broken and diversified aspect. The western portion exhibits several abrupt and high elevations, the highest point of which is Mount Topping. There are numerous legendary reminiscences treasured up in the minds of some of the old sachems of the Iroquois tribe, which give a somewhat prominent feature to this rugged miniature mountain. Here the bear, the wolf, and the panther were driven from their strongholds, or made to pay a forfeiture of their lives for their unbecoming temerity. An old scarred warrior, of the seventeenth century, having pitched his hunting camp at the eastern base of this high point of land, was suddenly aroused from a sound sleep, about the middle of a cold December night, by the scream of an enormous panther, which had been attacked by a drove of hungry wolves. Springing from his pallet of dried skins, and seizing his French rifle, which had been given him by a young Adirondack chieftain, and which had often before done him good service, and creeping stealthily to the door, which he opened with the utmost care, to his surprise he beheld the fiery orbs of three ferocious animals. Levelling Long Tom, a leaden missile made a death lodgment in the brain of the panther. The wolves retreated a few rods, and as hastily returned, for they had already got a scent of the fresh blood that freely flowed from the dead animal, now secured within the unadorned walls of the hunter's tent. The purple current was soon lapped up, and then the midnight air resounded with the discordant howls of the more than half enraged wolves.

But hark! the terrific howl is answered from Mount Topping, and reëchoed in mournful expression as it dies away on the other side of the Tioughnioga. And now, while the hungry pack are hurrying down the mountain glade, the unterrified red man sits smoking his pipe, with all the coolness of a Roman knight. A few moments elapse, and they have snuffed the scent of blood, and are yelling around the pent-up confines of the stern old man. The muzzle of Long Tom presently appears emerging from the port hole, belching fire and lead; and though he spoke in an authoritative tone, and silenced forever the voice of one, he did not frighten away the voracious clan. But Long Tom continued to emerge at various intervals from the unnoticed embrasures, until seven wolves were weltering in their blood. A few escaped with broken limbs to the mountain gorge.

The first school which had any important bearing on

the moral habits and intellectual training of the children, was taught by Miss Ruth Thorp, in 1801. Under the old organization, when Preble was a part of Tully, Moses Nash furnished the settlers with goods from his little store, established at Tully Village in 1803. Two years after, he was succeeded by John Meeker, who greatly extended the limits of commercial intercourse with the hardy pioneers of the country. A public house was opened in 1802.. In 1803, when Tully was orga ized, several of the early settlers of that portion of the town of Tully, afterwards comprised in the town of Preble, were elected to responsible town offices. Among these were the Cravaths. Mr. Nash, after disposing of his mercantile interest, located in Indiana, and at a later period came within one vote of an election to the gubernatorial chair of that State.

Previous to the establishment of a post-office at Preble Corners, about 1812, the then central point of Tully, the settlers received their letters, papers, &c., from Pompey Hill. The first dwelling-house was erected by James Cravath, in 1798.

In 1804, public religious worship was commenced by the organization of the Congregational church in Tully, and consisted of eleven members. It was organized through the active and zealous efforts of the Reverends Theodore Hinsdale and Joel Hale, who were missionaries from Connecticut. This association, at a subsequent period, assumed the name of the First Presbyterian Church of Preble. In its infancy it was connected with the Middle Association; but, on the dissolution of that organization, it was assigned to the Presbytery of Onondaga, and at a still later period, to that of Cortland.

Rev. Matthew Harrison, its first pastor, entered upon his labors in 1812. Reverends Enoch Bouton, L. Weld, A. P. Clark, G. K. Clark, W. Jones, B. F. Foltse, E. H. Payson, and W. W. Collins, severally ministered to the spiritual wants of the people up to 1825, when there were seventy-seven members. Three years after, the number had increased to one hundred and nineteen. Twelve years later, there were two hundred and ten members. The next year (1841) eighty of its members withdrew and finally organized themselves under the appellation of the "First Free Church" in Preble, and might properly be termed *Unionists.*

The Baptist Association, organized at an early period with but fourteen members, owes its origin to Elder Abbott, the first spiritual teacher of that order, who labored ardently in his efforts to impart public religious instruction. The church is now under the charge of Elder Capron.

The Methodist organization dates back to 1827, and was formed by Calvin Winslow. Elder Sayers was the first stated preacher. He was followed by the ever to be remembered Elder Puffer, who was appropriately termed "Old Chapter and Verse." It was a custom of his to omit naming any chapter or verse upon which his public discourses were based. We recollect of his telling us, in our earlier days, that, if the Bible, through some unexpected revolution, should be destroyed, he could re-write every chapter, verse, and even word, in their appropriate order and place.

The dairy business is being regarded with much more attention than in former years; and consequently, the high lands are greatly improved, not only in value, but in their general appearance. The rich Preble Flats are hardly surpassed, for fertility and beauty, by any in the county.

From the highest elevation of Mount Topping, portions of Onondaga, Cayuga, and Tompkins may be seen, with their varying scenery, blending the beauties of rich productive fields with the more rugged features of nature. Standing on that lofty point, the observer may have a fine view of Homer, Preble, and Tully Flats—lands that will compare favorably with any in the State. And there, too, he may view with admiration and wonder the work of Deity, as exhibited in the numerous ridges and long sloping valleys, the rounded knolls and picturesque dales, all richly diversified, and producing in abundance the various crops common to the country. Indeed, there are many magnificent views to be taken from this rugged point, as it looms up in all its ancient grandeur. We were most agreeably surprised with our visit to this olden spot of Indian warfare, where the red man contested the right of inheritance with the wild beasts of the mountain glen, or forest glade. Had we, in our childhood, given a willing ear to the marvellous, when one of our far-famed orators endeavored to instil into our mind the fanciful stories of fairy lore, we should, we opine, not hesitate to imagine that the retreat of sylphs and nymphs was somewhere about this romantic mount.

Amos Skeel was the first supervisor and justice of the peace ; Garret Van Hoesen, the first town clerk ; Samuel Taggart, the first constable.

The first marriage was that of Amos Bull to Sally Mason, in 1799. The first birth, Nancy Gill, October

25, 1796. The first death was that of John Patterson, 1798. The first permanent merchant was Noah Parsons, at Preble Centre, 1817. The first grist-mill was erected in 1806, by Samuel C. Woolston, a native of Montgomery county. In 1827 the building was taken down, and the main part of the present mill erected on the original site. In 1853, the mill property and farm, comprising two hundred acres of valuable land, were purchased by W. E. Tallman, formerly an enterprising citizen of Tully. The mill was thoroughly renovated and improved by the replacing of new bolts and an additional run of stone. He has extended a line of shafting to his barn, a distance of three hundred and sixty feet, where the power is used for threshing, separating grain, elevating straw, shelling corn, and sawing wood, requiring less than half the usual number of hands to do the same amount of work. What a vast amount of hard labor is thus saved! What an improvement is thus suggested to other mill proprietors! Mr. Tallman has also recently purchased a water-power about thirty-eight rods below the mill; and he is new engaged in running a shaft back to his mill (six hundred and twenty-seven feet), where it will be connected with an extra run of stone, thus enabling him to use a portion of the water a second time,—another important suggestion to mill-owners; and it is with this view that we have thus freely spoken with reference to this valuable mill property, as well as to the enterprising efforts of Mr. Tallman.

In 1810 the population of Preble was			1,179
1814	"	"	1,311
1820	"	"	1,257
1825	"	"	1,327
1830	"	"	1,435
1835	"	"	1,408
1840	"	"	1,247
1845	"	"	1,325
1850	"	"	1,312
1855	"	"	1,219

In 1810 there were in Preble ninety-four Senatorial electors ; the taxable property $54,710.

TRUXTON.—The town of Truxton was organized from the south half of the military town of Fabius, April 8, 1808. It also embraces four tiers of lots taken from the north part of Solon.

As we look back over the dim vestiges of the past, and behold the hardy pioneer of civilization penetrating the boundary line which now marks the northern limits of Cortland county, we feel that his was a hazardous effort, and that a great amount of energy must have been embraced in his enterprising and wild, romantic character. Doubts and fears had little or no influence upon his mind, for he was one of those energetic characters of quick and discerning mind,—and bold, resolute actors who, when having resolved upon a purpose, allow no mere probable contingency to deter them from the accomplishment of the enterprise. The footprints of civilization had not then penetrated into this then dense wilderness. True, the French traders had visited the Indians in their rude cabins, and even established trading-posts ; but these had disappeared with time and change, and the confines of the now county of Cortland were invaded only by the red man in his hunting garb, or as he went forth upon some stealthy march. The panther, the wolf, the bear, and the deer, roamed free as the mountain bird, without dreaming of the horrid crusade that was about to be waged against them. Yet through the deep, thick forest of hemlock, maple, elm, and basswood, wandered the bold, resolute pioneer, Samuel C. Benedict, who, in the fall of 1793, located on lot 12. He erected a log-citadel, and christened it—"Home."

In 1794 Nathaniel Potter, Jonah Stiles, Christopher Whitney, David Morse and Benjamin Brown came in and selected various locations. Potter was from Saratoga county, New York. He purchased lots 77, 86, and 96. He erected a small house on lot 96, near the State bridge. In July, 1798, he was suddenly killed by the fall of a tree. Stiles came from Ruport, Vermont, and located on lot 4. He purchased one hundred acres, now owned and occupied by Samuel Freeman. He died in 1840. His daughter Julia married John Wicks ; Sophia, Alexander Forbes, of Litchfield, Ohio ; Jonah lives at Seville, in the same State ; Samuel, at Franklin, in Delaware county, New York ; and Otis, near Almiron W. Crain's Wool Exchange, at Stilesville. Whitney migrated from the east, and located on lot 3. One of his daughters is widow Moses Hopkins. Morse came from New Jersey, and settled on lot 87. He served his country in the revolution, and drew the lot where he settled, now in part covered by the village of Cuyler, where his two surviving sons, David and Joseph, now reside. Brown was from Connecticut. He located on lot 57. His surviving children are Abner, Alvin, and Wesley.

John Shedd located early in 1797 on lot 63. During the same year Nathaniel E. James and Charles Stewart, came in. The former located on lot 63; and the latter, from Colerain, Massachusetts, drew and settled on State's Hundred, lot 93.

In 1798 a number of additional settlers came in and located. Robert McNight and John Jeffrey were from Monmouth, New Jersey, and settled on lot 2; Charles McNight, a son, lives on the homestead. Billy Trowbridge, from Westchester county, New York, settled on lot 5. He filled several respectable county offices; was twice elected to the State Assembly, and for one term held the office of sheriff. His sons John, Levi, and Hubbard, reside at Detroit, and Smith, in Syracuse. Stephen Hedges, from Troy, located on lot 93. Increase M. Hooker was a native of Bennington, Vermont. He was with Ethan Allen during a portion of the Revolution, and witnessed the terrible conflict at Bennington, August 16, 1777. He married in Litchfield, Conn., and some years after moved to Greene county, N. Y. In 1797, removed to Solon, on lot 88; and the next year came to Truxton, and settled on lot 94. Soon after, he purchased a grist-mill of Joseph Sweetland. It was covered with elm bark, and contained one run of stone. It was rebuilt in 1816 by his sons. In 1842 he removed to New Jersey. In 1848 he visited his son in Illinois, and on his return died at Onondaga Hollow. He reared five children: two now living, John H., and Harley; the former lives in Newbrunswick, N. J., and the latter

10*

in Rockton, Ill. John H. Hooker recently told us that he visited Onondaga county when there was but one house at Manlius, one at Pompey, and one at Onondaga Hollow.

John Miller, from Amenia, Dutchess county, located in 1801 on lot 93.

Hugh and William Stewart, from Colerain, Mass., settled in 1803 on lot 4.

Lewis Wicks came from Saratoga county, in 1804, and located on lot 13.

The Pierces were from Colerain. Zebulon migrated in 1805, and located on lot 34. He reared a family of eleven children—four now living.

Judah settled in 1806 on lot 12. He left eight children—three reside at the West. Ethan lives on the homestead. Mr. Pierce accumulated a large property; was an influential citizen. He died at the age of seventy.

Dea. James Bell was from Ruport, Vt. He migrated to Truxton in the winter of 1812, and located on lot 95. In 1821 he removed to Medina county, Ohio. He was a most excellent citizen, and reared an interesting family. His sons, James and Jacob, are active and prominent politicians; the former has occupied a seat in the Ohio Legislature.

In 1814 Asa Babcock, originally from Rhode Island, came in from Madison county, N. Y., and went into the mercantile trade, which he continued for a period of forty-three years. With the sands of life running low, he calmly awaits his summons to depart.

Asa Campbell was a native of Hampden county, Mass. He came in and settled (1816) on the farm now owned by Jennings Bennett. The widow and daughter reside in the village.

Stephen Ambler came in from New Berlin in 1818, and located on lot 83. He purchased one hundred and twelve acres; reared nine children—four now living; two sons in Cuba.

The settlement was visited quite early by itinerant missionaries, and public religious worship was instituted in 1801, through the laudable exertions of Rev. Hugh Wallis.

The first post-office was established in 1799, and Stephen Hedges appointed post-master; he was also the first merchant. John Miller, the first physician. The first miller was Joseph Sweetland. The first child born was Stephen Potter, in 1794. The first death was that of the father, Nathaniel Potter, already referred to.

In the earlier town organization, this town belonged to Pompey, which was organized in 1794, and included the townships of Pompey, Fabius, and Tully; and also, "part of the Onondaga Reservation, lying south of the great Genesee Road, and east of Onondaga Creek." Fabius was erected from Pompey in 1798, and at that time included two military townships,—Fabius and Tully,—and comprised the present towns of Fabius, Tully, Truxton, Preble and Scott, with portions of Spafford and Otisco.

The pioneers of the town of Truxton labored early and late to procure a support for themselves and families. The luxuries they enjoyed were the real necessaries of subsistence. They dealt only with the stern realities of life. The follies and fooleries of our times were unknown to the primitive settlers. They studied nature as she really was, rather than in what they would have her to be. When success had so far crowned their laborious efforts as to enable them to spare a portion of their products, they did not deem it a hard task to place the scanty surplus on an ox sled, and, taking an Indian trail, or such road as had been cut through the wilderness by wandering emigrants, thus trudge on from day to day, until they reached Utica, Whitestown or Herkimer, where they exchanged them for the substantials of the farm and the kitchen. The exchange did not then, as in these days of refinement, consist of satins, silks and lawns for their daughters, but in a few yards of linsey-woolsey ; an axe, bush-hook, grub-hoe, and last, though perhaps not least thought of, a half-pound of *old Bohea*, which was always received by the happy matron with a smile as sweet as the lively lay she sang.

The surface of the town of Truxton presents a broken and diversified aspect. The Truxton Flats are, however, very beautiful, rich, and abundant in agricultural elements ; yet they are unquestionably better adapted to the growing of the coarser grains, though wheat is produced to a limited extent.

In 1810	the population	of Truxton was	1,031
1814	"	"	1,768
1820	"	"	2,956
1825	"	"	3,325
1830	"	"	3,885
1835	"	"	3,712
1840	"	"	3,658
1845	"	"	3,587
1850	"	"	3,623
1855	"	"	3,444

In 1810 there were one hundred and twenty-nine Senatorial electors ; and the taxable property was assessed at $47,673. The village contained twenty houses. The town is well watered, and especially by branches of the Tioughnioga, which have their origin in the town.

The streams of Truxton afford many excellent mill-seats, which in most instances are used to good advantage, placing her in the front rank of manufacturing towns in the county. There are five grist-mills, several saw-mills, a large sash and blind factory, a firkin and tub factory, and a Wool Exchange. The latter we propose to briefly notice. In 1809 Jonah Stiles and Alvin Pease erected a grist-mill, the second one in the town. In 1810 they erected a carding machine. These subsequently passed into the hands of Otis and Jonas Stiles ; the latter, however, soon sold out to Samuel Stiles ; and finally, the latter interest was purchased by Otis, who, in 1814, added to his business another branch, —that of cloth dressing. A few years previous, Jacob Otis commenced cloth dressing, but he discontinued it in 1820. In 1826, Mr. Stiles rebuilt, and engaged more largely in the manufacture of cloth. In 1837, he added the improved machinery. In 1838, Almiron W. Crain became an active partner, and in 1848 sole proprietor. In 1854 Perry P. Crain became a partner. In 1826 the business of exchanging cloth for wool was commenced, and has been gradually increasing until the present time. The sum total of exchange during the year 1858, amounted to 25,000 pounds of wool. We re-

NOTE.—Since the main portion of our history was placed in the hands of the publisher, the recently organized town of Cuyler has been formed from the east half of Truxton.

gard the wool exchange business as one of great practical importance to the wool-growers of Cortland county, for while they get their cloth at a reduced price, they receive an advance profit on their wool, making the exchange a profitable investment.

SCOTT.—The town of Scott was erected from the west part of Preble, April 14, 1815.

The first permanent settlement was made in this town in 1799. There had, however, been a rude hunter within its boundaries as early as 1795. He erected a bark shanty, and lived by hunting,—a kind of employment for which he seemed peculiarly fitted, and to which he was greatly attached. He spent about one year and a half in the deep solitude of that unbroken wilderness, when he was joined by a half-breed Indian, originally from Three River Point, Canada; and in a few months after, they gathered up their peltry and furs, and made their way to a French trading post, then established near Whitestown, where they made a profitable disposition of their effects, and then sought, if possible, a still more gloomy retreat in the wilds of the far West. He was an eccentric and original genius, constitutionally fitted for the rude life he lived. His birth-place is not known, though it is evident from certain excentricities of character that he was of French extraction. An Indian of the *Leni* tribe, from whom we gather these facts, and who occasionally visits the Oneidas, relates many characteristic anecdotes touching this singularly strange, yet interesting original. Years after, he was seen standing upon the bank of the great Father of Waters,—the majestic Mississippi. There was heard a shriek, a plunge,—the waves closed over the lone hunter, and all that was mortal had disappeared forever. And when the horror-stricken Indian, who had watched his movements, called for the white man of the woods, the evil genius that had wrecked his hopes in early life and made him a wanderer, answered :—

" Where the dark tide runs strongest,
The cliff rises steep ;
Where the wild waters eddy,
I have rocked him to sleep.

" His sleep is so strong,
That the rush of the stream,
When the wild winds are abroad,
Cannot waken his dream."

During the year 1799, several settlements were made. Peleg Babcock, accompanied by his brothers Solomon and Asa Howard, came in from Leyden, Massachusetts, and selected locations. Peleg settled on the south part of lot 82. Solomon located on the north-west part of the same lot, while Howard stuck his post a little to the east of Solomon. About the same time George Dennison, from Vermont, pitched his tent on the west part of the lot, making the fourth settler on No. 82. Cornish Messenger and Daniel Jakeway came in from De Ruyter in 1800, and settled on lot 92. In 1801 Maxon Babcock came in from Leyden, and located on the north-east corner of lot 82. Ghershon Richardson, and his two sons-in-law by the name of Clark, came from Pompey, Onondaga co., and located on lot 71. In 1802, Henry Burdick, a native of Rhode Island, migrated from Colerain, Massachusetts, and located on lot 72. He purchased originally, in company with John Babcock, 109 acres. He was an active and prominent pioneer in his locality, and now, at the venerable age of 78 years, lives retired from the toil and bustle of life. His youngest son, A. B. Burdick, of New York, is the enterprising publisher of this work.

Jared Babcock came in during the year 1804, and spent some three or four years. In 1809 he was enlisted in the mercantile trade in Spafford, being the first merchant in that place. He subsequently moved to Homer, where he still resides.

John Gillet, from Norfolk, Connecticut, located during the same year (1805), but did not purchase until 1807 or '8, when he selected 100 acres on lot 84. The farm has been increased at different periods, and at the present time embraces nearly 300 acres. He has already passed through a long, busy and prosperous life—a life of activity, of public employment, and of private enterprise. He filled the office of Justice of the Peace for a period of twenty years; that of supervisor and other town offices, at various times; was associate judge of the county court for fifteen successive years, and also member of the legislature, and presidential elector.

Jacob Smith, from Delphi, located in 1806, on lot 84. His original purchase was 50 acres : he, however, made subsequent additions until he had secured 105 acres, which he has but recently disposed of with a view of locating at Little York.

In 1806 Daniel Doubleday migrated from Lebanon, Connecticut, and located in the town of Homer. In 1809 he removed to Scott, and settled on lot 85. He has reared a respectable family, accumulated a good property, and now, at the advanced age of seventy-two, rejoices in having spent a long life in an honored and productive employment. Mr. Doubleday is in the enjoyment of remarkable health, and in the full possession of his mental and physical faculties.

During 1805, Elisha Sabins and John Babcock cut and cleared a road from Scott Corners (then called Babcock's Corners,) to Spafford Corners. They transported their goods to their new home on sleds, and found it a rather difficult task. The next year, Isaac Hall, of the latter place, passed over the road with a wagon, and after purchasing a load of lumber at Babcock's settlement, placed it on his wagon and conveyed it to his home in Spafford.

In the summer of '99, Solomon Babcock tells us that he was in the habit of making frequent visits to his brother's cornfield, accompanied by a small dog, for the purpose of frightening away the bears, they being very troublesome and destructive to the corn crop. It was a common occurrence to find a half dozen in at a time, and to him it was rather amusing to see how they would hurry away at the mere sight or bark of the little fellow.

Early in the month of March, he went into the woods for the purpose of obtaining a birch broom-stick. The snow was some three feet deep, and the crust sufficiently strong to bear up a man. A strong, active, fierce and well-trained dog, belonging to his brother Peleg, bore him company, and before the trunk of the little sapling was secured he had actually killed seven deer.

The first ordained preacher was Elder Town. The first persons baptized were Mr. and Mrs. Solomon Babcock—the former in Homer, and the latter in Scott. The first merchant was Nathan Babcock. The first inn-keeper was James Babcock. The first post-master, John Gillett. The first marriage, Solomon Babcock to Amy Morgan. This occurred in the Fall of 1802. There being no authorized person at hand to marry, the parties came to Homer on horseback, and after attending church, went to Squire Bishop's on East Hill, where they were appropriately married. The first child born in town was Harriet Babcock. The first death was an infant daughter of Peleg Babcock.

Public religious worship commenced about the year 1806 or '7.

The Close Communion Baptists, the Seventh Day Baptists, the Presbyterians, and the Methodists, have each a convenient house for religious worship.

The first post-master of East Scott was Alvin Kellogg. It was with this gentleman that Ex-President Fillmore learned his trade,—that of clothier.

The town of Scott, though containing much broken land, is favored with many most excellent farms. It is not, however, a grain growing town. The land being generally better adapted to grazing, the agriculturists are found adopting the more reasonable and productive pursuit of increasing their means in the dairy business.

In 1820	the population	of Scott	was	775
1825	"	"	"	1,006
1830	"	"	"	1,452
1835	"	"	"	1,504
1840	"	"	"	1,332
1845	"	"	"	1,368
1850	"	"	"	1,290
1855	"	"	"	1,293

FREETOWN was organized April 21st, 1818. It comprises the north-western quarter of the old military township of Cincinnatus, and lot No. 20 from the eastern part of Virgil. The soil is a clay loam, better adapted to grazing than grain growing ; but more recently has produced good crops of corn, oats, barley, flax, and potatoes ; wheat not being grown here to any considerable extent. Freetown is situated on a ridge between the Tioughnioga and Otselic rivers, and was settled principally by emigrants from the north and eastern portions of the State. The inhabitants are an honest, industrious, hardy race of men. The early settlement of this town was attended with deprivations, hardships and discouragements that required the energies and fortitude of a class which none but pioneers in a new country are capable of exercising and enduring.

The early pioneers, in preference to going to Ludlowville or Chenango Forks, to mill, usually went to Onondaga Hollow, or Manlius Square, a distance of forty miles, fording creeks and rivers, exposing themselves to cold and storms by night and day, being obliged to camp out two or three nights during their journey to and from the mill, through an almost entire wilderness, filled with wolves, panthers, and other ravenous beasts of prey. As there were then no roads, they traveled by marked trees, whiling away the dull hours of time by whistling or singing some merry tune, or in telling some legendary tale which may have been preserved for centuries by Indian tradition. At night, tired and hungry, the jaded horses were tied to a tree, and, by the roots of some enormous oak or hemlock, the pioneers would find a resting-place, with the bags for pillows and an Indian blanket for a covering ; and there, in the deep forest, surrounded with gaunt, howling wolves, and poisonous reptiles, with the "deep blue sky above," all radiant with night's diadems, or perchance o'erspread with tartarean blackness, while the harsh, hoarse thunders rolled and reverberated through the wide expanse ; now startled by a vivid flash of forked lightning as it leaps athwart the darkened sky, or shatters a proud old relic of the ancient wilderness into a thousand pieces, would await the return of day to resume their journey. And thus they endured these attendant privations until 1798, when a mill was erected at Homer,—or a year later, when Mr. Hubbard, of Cortlandville, built the old Red Mill, now owned by Mr. Mudge.

Robert Smith, a Revolutionary soldier, was the first settler. He drew lot No. 2, and moved on to it with his family in 1800, having only previously prepared a mere cabin of logs for their reception. He was originally from one of the New England States. He made a small improvement on his lot, and after struggling through many severe hardships, and enduring the privations incident to most new settlements, sold to Samuel G. Hatheway. Some of Mr. Smith's descendants are now living in Marathon.

Soon after Mr. Smith located on his lot, Caleb Sheopard and David H. Monrose moved from the eastern part of the State, and settled with their families on lot 22. Mr. Sheopard, several years since, removed to Michigan. Mr. Monrose remained on his farm until his death, which occurred in 1837. His son Daniel occupies the old homestead.

William Smith, a native of Vermont, migrated from

Great Bend, Pa., to Freetown in 1802, and located on lot 25. He made various small purchases of land until his farm numbered some one hundred and sixty-five acres. In 1835 he disposed of his property and settled in the town of Cortlandville, where he now resides. His step-mother, Eunice Smith, lives with him, at the advanced age of 95. Mr. Smith has held most of the town offices, besides several military positions. Of his nine children eight are living.

In 1804 Gideon Chapin located on lot 42, and erected soon after the first saw-mill in the town. There is at present one of a larger size covering the same ground.

In 1805 Gen. Samuel G. Hatheway, originally from Freetown, Mass., removed from Chenango county and located on lot 2, having purchased the Robert Smith farm, which consisted of about three hundred acres. The General was a man of energy and enterprise, as was evidenced in the rapid improvement of his farm. He can now relate many interesting anecdotes touching his early life. Soon after he came into Freetown, he desired to make some addition to his stock of cattle, and hearing that Caleb Sheopard, near the Salt Road, about five miles distant, had a calf to sell, made arrangements to procure it. He started from home near evening, having previously completed his day's work, for Mr. Sheopard's, with a rope halter in his hand with which he intended to lead his calf, if successful in a purchase ; and thus equipped, without coat or stockings, he plodded his course through the woods, by way of marked trees, there being no road. He succeeded in obtaining the calf, and started for home ; but night coming on, and it being much darker than he anticipated, and carelessly hurrying along with his treasure by his side, he soon found himself unable to distinguish the glazed trees, but still persevered, hoping to come out right. It was not long, however, before he found he was out of the right course, and concluding that for the present he was lost, very calmly set about camping out for the night. He fastened the calf to a tree, and, reposing by its side, was delighted through the long and darksome night by the hooting of owls, howling of wolves, screaming of panthers, and other music of a like interesting character. At length morning dawned, and, as Aurora flung her gorgeous rays over the dense forest, revealed to his eager gaze his position on the Pine Ridge, one or two miles out of his way. His calf was hastily detached from the tree, and he again set out for home, which he reached at an early hour, having a sharp appetite for his breakfast, and much to the gratification of his anxiously awaiting mother.

Eleazer Fuller came from Northampton, Mass., in 1806, and settled on lot 12. He purchased one hundred acres. He reared a family of four children ; a daughter, with whom he lives, is the wife of William Mantanye. His son, Austin Fuller, is Auditor of Indiana, residing at Springfield. Mr. Fuller is seventy-five years old, and is, at the time of writing, greatly afflicted with a cancerous ulcer, which must eventually terminate his life.

In 1808, Rockwell Wildman and Isaac Robertson came in and selected locations. The former migrated from the north, and settled on lot 15. He died in 1855. His children occupy the original premises. The latter came from Connecticut, but was not permitted to enjoy for more than a few brief seasons the fruits of his labor ;

he died in 1811 ; his wife in 1815. He left eleven children—three are now living.

In 1809, John Aker, father of Abram, came from Albany county and selected a location.

Henry Gardner, from Plainfield, N. Y., came in during the same year and settled on lot 32. He purchased one hundred acres ; died in Illinois in 1858 ; age eighty years ; left seven children—all now living. Mrs. Gardner died in 1852.

At about this time, or perhaps a little subsequent, Charles and Curtiss Richardson, William Tuthill, Jacob Hicks, Isaac Doty, John Backus and Aruna Eaton came in and selected various locations. Curtiss Richardson lives with his son William, in Canandaigua.

John Conger migrated from Granville, Washington county, in 1812, and located on lot 12. He purchased one hundred and five acres. Fifty acres have been added to the farm, which is now owned by Hugh M'Kevitt.

Mr. Conger was an enterprising, public-spirited man, and creditably discharged the duties of several town offices. He died in 1836, aged 55. Mrs. Conger, at the advanced age of seventy-five, is remarkably healthy and active. Mr. Conger was the father of five sons and four daughters—Joseph, Samuel, Harmon S., Bemon S., and Damon. Malina married David Gardner, of Harvors, Illinois ; Mary is now widow Crosby ; Esther is the wife of Ransford Palmer, of Cortland ; and Rhoda is Mrs. J. M. Barclay, of La Cross, Minesota.

In 1813, Austin Waters removed from Saybrook, Conn., and located on the same lot. He purchased one hundred and five acres, which was entirely covered with a heavy growth of timber. Having but limited means, and indeed nothing but his ambitious desire to achieve something in the way of human progress, he perserved in his toilsome efforts, and kept from yielding to the numerous discouragements with which he was surrounded. He resolved to succeed, and he triumphed over all difficulties ; and he lives, at the venerable age of eighty years, to see Freetown one of the most productive dairy towns in the county.

Walton Swetland, a native of Conn., migrated from Granville in 1814, and settled on the Trip farm, on lot 22. He made several purchases, until he had secured a farm of one hundred and thirty acres. He attended to the clearing and cultivating his land until 1838, when he disposed of it with a view of entering into another branch of business. In 1846 he engaged in the mercantile trade, and up to the present time has continued the business with general success. He has filled various town offices, among which are those of School Inspector, Superintendent, and Justice of the Peace. The latter office he has held for twenty-eight years, and still continues to officiate in that position. He was appointed an Associate Judge in 1844, and held the office for a number of years. From a corporal in a company of infantry, he rose to the rank of major.

Judge Swetland resides at Freetown Corners; is about sixty-five years old ; and is still an active, useful and prominent citizen.

Geo. I. Wavle, from Montgomery county, N. Y., located in 1814 on lot 4, where his son James now resides. He purchased four hundred and fifty acres. He was an industrious and honorable citizen. He died in 1825, leaving a respectable family of children.

During the early period of settlement, Freetown was regarded as being rather cold and sterile, and frequently the prospects of the settler were blasted by early frosts, which cut down the crops before they came to maturity; but more recently, frosts have not been as frequent, and for several years past, as good crops of corn have been raised as in most other towns of the county. But the attention of agriculturists is being more generally turned to dairying, in which they succeed much better than in their laborious efforts to grow grain, the soil being better adapted to this department of productive employment than to any other branch of industry.

The first clergyman who statedly preached in Freetown, was Elder Sheopard ; he was of the Baptist order, and resided in the town of Lisle, Broome county. Elder Benjamin W. Capron was the first preacher who made a permanent residence in this town. Don A. Robertson was the first school teacher ; his father came into town soon after General Hatheway, and reared a large family of sons. Peter McVean was the first merchant. He located at what is now called Freetown Corners, continued in the business a short time, and was succeeded by John M. and Sylvester M. Roe from the town of Virgil.

In 1820	the population of	Freetown was	663
1825	"	"	877
1830	"	"	1,051
1835	"	"	962
1840	"	"	950
1845	"	"	925
1850	"	"	1,035
1855	"	"	955

Perhaps no town in the county was settled under more discouraging circumstances than Freetown. It was decidedly "a hard town," the citizens were generally poor, and were necessarily subjected to more hardships and privations than under other circumstances would have been endured. Settlers came in slowly, and at no time made very rapid progress; even as late as 1828, when Reuben Northrop came in from Washington county and located on lot 20, what now constitutes his valuable farm was an entire wilderness. But the industrious and persevering habits of the citizens have wrought a most favorable change; and Freetown has become prosperous and influential. The inhabitants are intelligent, affable, and courteous.

MARATHON.—The territory embraced within the boundaries of Marathon,* was set off from the south-west quarter of Cincinnatus, April 21, 1818, and organized into a town under the name of Harrison, in honor of Gen. Harrison, of the late war, but was subsequently changed to Marathon, on account of there being another town of the same name in the State. The first actual settlers of this town were Dr. Japheth Hunt and wife, both aged people, two sons, James and William, and three daughters, Betsey, Nancy, and Hannah. The advanced age of the parents disqualified them as pioneers of a new country, and unfitted them to encounter the hardships and privations incident to such an enterprise. Their children, however, were of mature age, of robust constitutions, and possessed energy of character, which

* Communicated by Dr. S. M. Hunt.

enabled them to accomplish the laborious duties which now devolved upon them. They entered the valley of the Tioughnioga from the south, in canoes, in the year 1794, and located on a piece of land on the east side of the river, about a mile south of the present village of Marathon, since known as the Comstock farm and now owned by Edward Moore. Their log house was erected a few miles north of Mr. Moore's barn, on a knoll, or rolling piece of ground, immediately west, and near the present highway. Upon this rising ground were discovered a great number of excavations or depressions, of a circular form, in close proximity, rendering the surface of the ground uneven. Each of these depressions, upon examination, was found to contain human bones, which had, apparently, been deposited there for several preceding centuries. Upon removing the road a few years since, from the top to the base of this hill, some of these depressions were opened by the plough, and were found to contain not only human bones, but several curiously carved vessels or pots, of a substance resembling clay, probably wrought by the Indians to contain succotash, or boiled corn and beans,—deposited in the grave, as is their custom, to supply their departed friends in their journey to the world of spirits.

About the time that Dr. Hunt's family settled here, a road was surveyed and partially cut through the wilderness from the south, near the river, until passing their land, when diverging from the stream, it crossed the south line of lot number 72, about three-fourths of a mile east of the village of Marathon, and continuing in a northerly direction, intersected the State road at the farm recently owned by Mr. Charles Richardson, of Freetown, and extending north to its terminus at the salt works, which gave it the name of the Salt Road.

Another road, about this period, was surveyed and partially opened as a State road, by the way of Oxford westerly through the centre of the town subsequently organized as Cincinnatus, and consequently on the north line of the present town of Marathon, and crossing the river at Chaplin's ford, now known as State Bridge, and thence westerly through the county by Virgil Corners.

Dr. Hunt was an emigrant from one of the New England States, and had served his country in the Revolutionary war, in the capacity of surgeon. He died March 7th, 1808, at the advanced age of 97, and was the first person buried in the east burying ground of Marathon. His son William married Anna, daughter of Matthew Cole, an early settler on a farm south, adjoining the county line, being the present residence of Col. Lucian E. Crain. His son James was never married, and died at Genoa, Cayuga county. His daughter, Nancy, married Abram Smith, and died about forty-five years since, leaving three children, who are yet living in the town of Virgil. Betsey Hunt married Oliver Mack, of Genoa, and Hannah, the youngest daughter, married Nathan Thorp, of the same place. Wm. Hunt, some time after the death of his father, sold the farm and located again two miles north of Marathon village, where Stephen Johnson now resides, but finally emigrated with his sisters from Genoa to the "Far West," to some part of Indiana. In the latter part of the winter of 1796, John, the eldest son of Dr. Hunt, who had married Lydia, the daughter of Major Samuel Mallory, of Hillsdale, Columbia county, N. Y., was induced to move from that place into the new country in the vicinity of his father's residence. A man with horses and sleigh was employed to bring his effects, and family, which then comprised himself and wife, one daughter three years of age, and a son of six months. After several days' travel over the rough roads, they arrived at Oxford, a new settlement on the Chenango river, where their teamster left them and turned back in consequence of poor sleighing produced by a thaw. Mr. Hunt having one horse of his own, harnessed him to a hastily constructed sled, and placing a bed and a few necessary articles of furniture and provisions, with his wife and children thereon, started westwardly by the way of the State road for the place of his destination. The first day they proceeded about seventeen miles into the wilderness on this rough road, passing over several of the smaller logs which had not yet been removed from the path, when night overtook them in a dense forest, which soon became vocal with the sounds of wild animals. Fortunately, they soon came to a log cabin, recently erected, covered with bark, and having a floor of slats split from logs, with a place for an entrance, but destitute of a door to exclude the air. By means of his gun and tinder, he kindled a fire; and, placing his horse close to the opening, with his provender in the sled, which served for a manger, and having hung up a blanket at the entrance, and placed their bed on the floor, being very weary, he retired to rest, and slept comfortably through the night. But his wife, unaccustomed to such privations, was less inclined to sleep. The howling of the wolves also annoyed her, and she wondered how her husband could sleep so composedly in such a dismal place. The next morning they resumed their journey, and before noon came to the Otselic river, and were cheered with the sight of a house on the opposite side of the stream. This proved to be the residence of Wm. Tuthill, who kindly assisted them in crossing the river, and hospitably entertained them till the next day. This was at a farm subsequently owned by Ebenezer Crittenden. From this place they traveled west, till they came to the intersection of the Salt road, when turning south along the latter path at a distance of four miles, they found the new home of his parents and family. His goods were subsequently brought in canoes from Oxford, down the Chenango river to the Forks, and then up this branch, then generally called the Onondaga, to their new location.

John Hunt purchased one hundred acres out of the south-west corner of lot No. 72, and moved his family there, being on the east side of the river, upon which land a large portion of Marathon village is located. Here his second son, Samuel M. Hunt, was born, October 30th, 1798, being the first child born in this town. When a young man, he chose the profession of medicine, and pursued that study with Dr. P. B. Brooks, now of Binghamton. He has practised medicine for thirty years, principally in Broome county; but for three years past, he has been located in Marathon village, on the same premises formerly the residence of his parents. As early as the beginning of the present century, John Hunt was appointed by the Governor and Council a justice of the peace; which office he held by successive appointments to the period of his death, which occurred August 8, 1815, at the age of fifty years. His widow is still living, in the eighty-fifth year of her age. Their eldest daughter married Mr. Charles Richardson, of Freetown, and is now residing in the village of Marathon. Two other daughters are yet living. Four others of their children lived to be married and settled in this section of country, but are now deceased. Abram Brink with his family moved into the present bounds of this village in the spring of 1800, and located a few rods south of Mr. Hunt's, on the north part of lot No. 82, then State land. He came from the present town of Union, below Binghamton, on the Susquehanna river, bringing his family and furniture in a canoe. He was a son of Captain William Brink, a patriot of the Revolution, who had suffered much by the depredations of tories in the war at Wyoming, and subsequently lost a great amount of property by the great ice-flood in that valley. Abram Brink was a robust and industrious citizen, and a valuable pioneer in clearing up the rugged wilderness, and preparing it for the residence of posterity. He kept the first tavern ever licensed in this town, from the commencement of the present century up to the time of his decease in 1824. Intoxicating liquors, as a beverage, were at that time considered as necessary as food in a tavern for the refreshment of guests. And although their deleterious effects were visible, not only in occasional carousals, but in the physical, moral and mental prostration of all who indulged in the potation, yet the traffic was for a long period sustained by public sentiment and by the laws of the State. Mr. Brink was succeeded in the tavern by his only surviving son, Chester, for a few years, when, influenced by a strong aversion to dealing in intoxicating liquors, he relinquished the business and employed himself in cultivating and improving the same farm, and some other adjoining lands, which he had acquired by purchase. A few years previous to the arrival of Mr. Brink here, a family by the name of Alford had settled about three-fourths of a mile south, on the State's lot, and some years after sold out to Daniel Huntly, a son of Deacon William Huntly, who resided for several years on the next farm south, now owned by Patrick Mallory, jr. A man by the name of Lee also lived a few years on the premises of Mr. Alford, having married his daughter. At the close of the last century, a traveler from the north, in passing down this valley, after leaving the ford-way at Chaplin's, would find the following residents on the east side of the river :—First, the family of Mr. Hunt ; 2d, Mr. Brink ; 3d, Mr. Alford and Mr. Lee ; next Dr. Hunt ; and lastly, Mr. Cole, in this county. South and near the county line on the east side of the river, was the residence of Gen. Samuel Coe, and directly opposite, on the west bank, was the house of Jonathan Cowdrey.

Soon after this period John S. Squires located on a farm south of Mr. Alford, but shortly after purchased a farm in the present town of Lapeer, and removed his family there into the forest at quite a distance from neighbors ; it being the same farm where his son, Dan C. Squires, now resides. About the year 1800, Ebenezer Carley moved into this town from Unadilla, and located on the west side of the river where his son Alanson now resides. He was commissioned Captain of

Militia company No. 1, organized in this section of the country. He had a large family of children. Ezekiel C. became a Captain of the militia, and also held the office of justice of the peace. Of this large family none are now living except two brothers, Alanson and Orin. Alanson Carley, Esq., has held the office of justice of the peace of this town for several years, has been a member of the Legislature, and has served as sheriff of this county for three years. Orin Carley is now residing in Broome county. It would be a difficult task, at this remote period, to ascertain the precise date of the arrival of each family of the first settlers here, as far back as the close of the last century, or the regular order as to the priority of time, in every case, when they entered this valley. In February of the year 1805, Patrick Mallory, (who some years after became a Captain of militia) a brother of Esq. Hunt's wife, arrived here with his wife and one child, and settled on a farm one mile north of Marathon village, now the residence of G. Pennoyer. He resided a few weeks with his sister's family, while erecting a log house for the reception of his own. This was early in the spring, when each family was actively employed in manufacturing maple sugar. To secure a supply of such an important article for domestic use, it became necessary for him to tap his trees prior to finishing his house. The farm was situated mostly on the west side of the river, and his maple trees were on the flat, directly across the stream. Being busily engaged one day, assisted by his wife, in gathering and boiling sap, they were detained till approaching darkness reminded them that it was time to start for home. They then entered their canoe, and had just reached the eastern shore and found the narrow path that led down the stream to Mr. Hunt's, when, to their surprise and consternation, their ears were saluted with the most clamorous, violent and discordant sounds, directly across the river, they had ever heard. The woods were apparently full of monsters in pursuit of them, as their intended victims, and engaged in fiendish strife respecting the several shares of the spoils. How to escape from these monstrous cannibals was the subject of anxious thought and hasty deliberation. Mrs. Mallory advised a rapid retreat; but her husband, being a very stout man, and wishing to retain his reputation for bravery, had a great aversion to "an attack in the rear." He therefore firmly grasped his axe, which he carried in his hand as an instrument of defence, and cautiously followed his wife, who alternately ran forward a few rods with speed, and then fell back again, urging him to make a more rapid progress. Notwithstanding the Captain's resolute intention, it is probable that the march was not very slow; and they soon reached the house of their friends without suffering an attack, and gave the alarm of the approaching enemy. But they were soon relieved of their fears, though somewhat mortified to learn that these savage monsters were nothing more than a class of nocturnal birds called owls, incapable of injuring either man or beast.

In 1820	the population of	Marathon was	807
1825	"	"	873
1830	"	"	895
1835	"	"	986
1840	"	"	1,063
1845	"	"	1,080
1850	"	"	1,149
1855	"	"	1,341

Thus it will be seen from the above table of census reports, that the town of Marathon has been steadily increasing in population, unlike the fluctuating or periodical changes referred to in some other towns of this county. The soil is generally productive, and when considered in connection with other facilities, natural and internal, we do not wonder at its progress.

We cheerfully give place to the following exceedingly interesting letter from Hon. Thurlow Weed. Mr. Weed resided in the western part of Cincinnatus—now Marathon :

"ALBANY, May 16th, 1858.

"H. C. GOODWIN, Esq.:

"MY DEAR SIR,—Your letter of 30th of April has remained quite too long unanswered, partly on account of severe illness in my family, but mainly because your kind and not unusual request embarasses me. Several applications similar in character, from book-makers, I have simply declined, because, first, there is nothing in my life entitled to historic attention ; and second, if any of its events were worthy such attention, it is neither proper or becoming in me to furnish the materials. So strong are my convictions of propriety in this regard, that many years ago, after declining to furnish information relating to myself, asked for by the late Jabez D. Hammond, I declined also to read in manu script what he had prepared. The consequence of that refusal is, that I go down to posterity—if Hammond's Political History outlives the present generation—as a '*drummer in the war of* 1812.' Now I am entitled to no such distinction; for I never learned and never could learn a note or stave of music. I remember to have gone, when a boy, once or twice to an evening singing-school, but after unavailing attempts at quavers and semi-quavers, the teacher snatched the gamut from my hand and turned me out of the class. I will, however, in this instance, depart so far from my usual practice as will allow me to furnish you the dates you desire—though in doing so, I feel as I suppose one should feel in robbing a henroost. I will now give you some 'reminiscences' connected with my early residence in Cortland county.

"In the winter of 1808, my father,—an honest, hard-working man,—whose industry, subject to the various draw-backs of sickness and ill-luck, which the poor only can understand, enabled him to furnish but a scanty support for his family, in the hope of 'bettering his condition,' removed to Cincinnatus, in Cortland county, where Nathan Weed, his youngest brother, resided. We were settled in a log house, upon a small clearing, about a mile from the Onondaga river—or for the purpose of fixing our locality—I had better say about that distance from 'Brink's tavern.' Cincinnatus then, whatever may be it present condition, was in its almost wilderness state. I have not been there in half a *century*, and am told that there are no forests, or land-marks, or monuments, by which I could recall or identify the localities of which my mind retains familiar and distinct impressions. Inhabitants were then 'few and far between.' Our nearest neighbor was Mr. Gridley, a farmer, rather 'well-to-do in the world,' who would work hard through 'planting,' or 'hoeing,' or 'harvesting,' and then seek indemnity in a week or ten days' 'spree' on new, raw whiskey. The most fore-handed family in the neighborhood was that of Captain Carley, (one member of which, Alanson, then a boy of my own age, was, some years since, a respected member of the Legislature,) among whose luxuries, as I remember, was a young apple orchard, and the only 'bearing' orchard within a circuit of several miles.

"My first employment was in attendance upon an ashery. The process of extracting lye from ashes, and of boiling the lye into black salts, was common-place enough; but when the melting down into potash came, all was bustle and excitement. This labor was succeeded, when the spring had advanced far enough, by the duties of the 'sap-bush.' This is a season to which the farmers' sons and daughters look forward with agreeable anticipations. In that employment, toil is more than literally *sweetened*. The occupation and its associations are healthful and beneficial. When your troughs are dug out (of bass-wood, for there were no buckets in those days) your trees tapped, your sap gathered, your wood cut, and your fires fed,—there is leisure either for reading or 'sparking.' And what youthful denizens of the sap-bush will ever forget, while 'sugaring-off,' their share in the transparent and delicious streaks of candy congealed and cooled in snow!

"Many a farmer's son has found his best opportunities for mental improvement in his intervals of leisure while 'tending sap-bush.' Such, at any rate, was my own experience. At night you had only to feed the kettles and keep up your fires—the sap having been gathered and the wood cut 'before dark.' During the day we would also lay in a good stock of 'fat pine, by the light of which, blazing brightly in front of the sugar-house, in the posture the serpent was condemned to assume as a penalty for tempting our great first grandmother, I have passed many and many a delightful night in reading. I remember in this way to have read a history of the French Revolution, and to have obtained from it a better and more enduring knowledge of its events and horrors, and of the actors in that great national tragedy, than I have received from all subsequent readings. I remember also how happy I was in being able to borrow the book of a Mr. Keyes, after a two mile tramp through the snow, shoeless, my feet swaddled in remnants of a rag-carpet.

"Though but a boy, I was large, healthy, strong, not lazy, and therefore ambitious 'to keep up my row' in planting, hilling, and hoeing potatoes and corn. The principal employment of the farmers of Cincinnatus, fifty years ago, was in clearing their land. Cattle, during the winter, for the want of 'fodder,' were turned out to 'browse' in the 'slashings.' As the work of clearing the land was too heavy for men single-handed, chopping and logging 'bees' were modes resorted to for aggregating labor. These seasons of hard work were rendered exciting and festive by the indispensable gallon bottle of whiskey. There were 'bees' also for log house raisings. After the loggings, and as the spring opened, came the burning of the log and brush-heaps, and the gathering of the ashes.

"But little wheat was grown there then, and that little was harvested with the sickle, the ground being too rough and stumpy for cradling.

"Our first acquisition in the way of 'live stock' was a rooster and four hens ; and I remember with what a gush of gladness I was awakened at break of day the next morning by the loud, defiant voice of Chanticleer ; and when, several days afterwards, I found a real hen's nest in a brush-heap, with eggs in it, I cackled almost as boisterously as the feathered mother whom I had surprised in the feat of parturition.

"The settlers employed in clearing and 'bettering' their land, raised just enough to live on 'from hand to mouth.' Their principal, and indeed only reliance for the purchase of necessaries from 'the store,' was upon their 'black salts.' For these the merchants always paid 'the highest price in cash or goods.'

"I remember the stir which a 'new store,' established in Lisle, (some seven or eight miles down the river,) by the Rathbones from Oxford, created in our neighborhood. It was 'all the talk' for several weeks, and until a party of house-wives, by clubbing with their products, fitted out an expedition. Vehicles and horses were scarce, but it was finally arranged ; A, furnishing a wagon, B, a horse, C, a mare, and D, a boy to drive. Six matrons, with a commodity of black salts, tow cloth, flax, and maple sugar, went their way rejoicing, and returned triumphantly at sun-set with fragrant Bohea for themselves, plug tobacco for their husbands, flashy calico for the children, gay ribbons for the girls, jack-knives for the boys, crockery for the cupboard, and snuff for 'Grannie.' This expedition was a theme for much gossip. The wonders of the 'new store' were described to staring eyes and open mouths. The merchant and his clerk were criticised in their deportment, manners, and dress. The former wore shiny boots with tassels,—the latter, a ruffle shirt,—and both smelt of pomatum! I do not believe that the word 'dandy' had then been invented, or it would have certainly come in play on that occasion. Thirty years afterwards I laughed over all this with my old friend, Gen. Ransom Rathbun, the veritable proprietor of that 'new store.'

"The grinding for our neighborhood was done at 'Hunt's mill,' which on one occasion was disabled by some defect in the flume or dam, and then we were compelled to go with our grists either to Homer or to 'Chenango Forks.'

"I recollect, on more than one occasion, to have seen boys riding with a bushel of corn, (bare-back, with a tow halter,) to the distillery, and returning with the gallon bottle of whiskey, balanced by a stone in the other end of the bag.

"In the autumn following our removal to Cincinnatus, I had 'worked out' and earned leather (sole and upper) enough for a pair of shoes, which were to be made by a son of Crispin, (deacon Badger, if I remember rightly,) who lived on the river a mile and a half away. The Deacon, I doubt not, has gone to his rest, and I forgive him the fibs he told, and the dozen journeys I made barefooted over the frozen and 'hubby' road in December before the shoes were done.

"I attended one regimental review, or 'general training,' as it was called. It was an eminently primitive one. Among the officers were two chapeaux, to which Capt. Carley, one of the two, added a sword and sash; four feathers standing erect upon felt hats; fifteen or twenty muskets; half-a-dozen rifles; two hoarse drums, and as many 'spirit-stirring fifes.' Of rank and file there were about two hundred and fifty. In the way of refreshments there was gingerbread, blackberry pies, and whiskey. But there were neither 'sweat-leather,' 'little jokers,' or other institutions of that character, upon the ground. Having, before leaving Catskill, seen with my own eyes a live Governor (Morgan Lewis) review a whole brigade, I regarded *that* training as a decided failure.

"There were no events at all startling, during my residence at Cincinnatus;—no murders, no suicides, no drownings, no robberies, no elopements, no 'babes lost in the woods,' occurred to astonish the natives. A recruiting sergeant came along (it was in embargo times), and three or four idle fellows (Herrings and Wilders by name, I think,) ''listed' and marched off.

"There were neither churches nor 'stated preaching' in town. A Methodist minister came occasionally and held meetings in private houses, or at the school-house. In the winter there was a school on the river; and the master, who 'boarded round,' must have 'had a good time of it' on Johnny-cake for breakfast, lean salt pork for dinner, and samp and milk for supper.

"There were but few amusements in those days, and but little of leisure or disposition to indulge in them. Those that I remember as most pleasant and exciting, were 'huskings' and 'coon-hunts.' There was fun, too, in smoking 'woodchucks' out of their holes.

"During my residence there, Mr. Wattles moved into the neighborhood. He came, I think, from what was then called 'The Triangle,' somewhere in Chenango co., and was a sub Land-agent. They were, for that region, rather 'stylish' people, and became obnoxious to a good deal of remark. One thing that excited especial indignation was, that persons going to the house were asked to clean their shoes at the door, a scraper having been placed there for that purpose. A maiden lady (Miss Theodosia Wattles) rendered herself especially obnoxious to the spinster neighbors, by 'dressing up' week-day afternoons. They all agreed in saying she was a 'proud, stuck-up thing.' In those days, 'go-to-meeting clothes' were reserved for Sundays.

"'Leeks' were the bane of my life, in Cincinnatus. They tainted everything, but especially the milk and butter. Such was my aversion to 'leeky milk,' that to this day I cannot endure milk in any form.

"In the fall and winter, corn-shelling furnished evening occupation. The ears were shelled either with a cob, or the handle of a frying-pan. There have been improvements, since, in that as in other departments of agriculture!

"Such are, in a crude form, some of my recollections of life in Cincinnatus, half a century ago. That town, then very large, has since been sub-divided into three or four towns. Upon the farm of my old friends, the Carleys, the large and flourishing village of Marathon has grown up. And then, too, a substantial bridge has taken the place of the 'dug out' in which we used to cross the river. Of the sprinkling of inhabitants who had then just commenced subduing the forests, and insinuating scanty deposits of seed between the stumps and roots, but few, of course, survive. The settlers were industrious, honest, law-abiding, and, with few exceptions, temperate citizens. The friendly neighborhood relations, so necessary in a new country, existed there. All tried not only to take care of themselves, but to help their neighbors. Farming implements and household articles were pretty much enjoyed in common. Everybody 'lent' what they possessed, and 'borrowed' whatever they wanted.

"You must judge whether these hastily written recollections of Cincinnatus would at all interest the few old inhabitants remaining there; and having so judged, you are at liberty to put them into your book, or into the fire.

"Very truly yours,

"THURLOW WEED."

WILLET.—The town of Willet was organized from the south-east quarter of Cincinnatus, April 21, 1818. The general surface of the town is broken and hilly, yet by no means mountainous. The soil is generally better adapted to grazing than the culture of grain. Its agriculture, however, is respectable. The town is watered by the Otselic, or main branch of the Tioughnioga river. It was named in honor of Col. Marinus Willett, who acquired an honorable fame while second in command at Fort Stanwix, in 1777, and who made a most gallant sally upon the forces of Sir John Johnson, capturing their stores, baggage, and ammunition. He drew lot

No. 88 of the old allotments of the town of Cincinnatus. It was located in the south-east quarter of the township, and when the original tract was carved into four towns, the hero was honored by the conferring of his name upon that portion which contained the land granted him as a partial reward for his valuable and heroic services. We cannot but respect those stern actors, who, in the early settlement of Willet, evinced a determination, worthy of being recorded in the enduring annals of our country. They warred not for fame and glory, but for the improvement of the moral and social condition of those around them. They struck their cabins in the unbroken forest, and endured privation and toil, with the hope of securing for themselves and families a home upon which they might erect their little citadels, dedicated to happiness and social enjoyment. They did not expect the huge "hemlock to snap off like icicles," or the ancient hills to become at once pleasure-gardens or fruitful fields. They did not anticipate that ease and affluence were to be achieved without effort, toil, and privation. No! no! they were men of an entirely different character; and when they determined upon a plan, or resolved to perform a duty, their *wills* became fixed facts.

Ebenezer Crittenden settled in Willet in 1797. He had married at Binghamton, and in order to get to Willet, himself, wife and one child shipped on board his little craft, and by the help of the paddle and setting-pole, at length arrived at his intended home, without shelter—the trees and elements excepted. Then with his axe he cut some crotches, and with some poles formed his tent, covering it with bed-clothes. This was his dwelling until he could build a log house, which he did in the following manner :—he cut such logs as he could handle, and enough for sides and gable ends, as he had no boards ; he then laid them up, then raised two pairs of rafters, one at each end ; then let in girts or ribs from one pair to the other, in order to hold the shingles, which he made by splitting them out with his axe and putting them on with pegs. As there was no grist-mill, he built him a little one by digging a hole in a big stump and erecting a spring pole, in order to assist his wife in making short-cakes; while his gun was his meat-barrel, and the Otselic his drink.

Benjamin Wilson was originally from Westchester, N. Y., and from Oxford ; an emigrant and pioneer to Willet, in 1806 or '7. John Fisher, from England, Jonathan Gazlay, from Dutchess co., Thomas Leach, from Madison co., all date their immigration the same year as Benjamin Wilson.

Jabez Johnson, from Vermont, and Phineas Sargent, origin unknown, both located in 1807.

Ebenezer Andrews, from Massachusetts, in 1808.

Joseph Merritt, from Westchester, N. Y., Solomon Smith, origin unknown, Daniel Roberts, from Madison co., John Covert, from Windham, Greene co., William Greene, from Kent co., R. I., Ira Burlingame, from Oxford, Chenango co., N. Y., Altitius Burlingame, from Kent co., R. I., and Edward Nickerson, from Cape Cod, Mass., all located in the year 1809. Arnold Thomas, from North Kingston, Washington co., R. I., in 1810.

Solomon Dodge, from Vermont, after resting at Oxford for a space, entered the town as a resident in 1811. In the year 1816, Samuel Dyer, from North Kingstown, R.I.

John and his brother Peter Eaton, from Cherry Valley, N. Y., Samuel and Abraham Canfield, from Orange co., N. Y., entered and located as pioneers, to battle with the dense forest and privations of the wilderness.

In the language of one whose memory is true to the events of an eventful age, "Death erected his monument of claims to all of mortality, in the newly begun settlement, in the year 1812, by taking the wife of Solomon Smith."

The first birth, in the town of Willet, was a child of Ebenezer Crittenden. The first marriage was that of Solomon Smith. This occurred in 1813.

In 1807 or '8, Benjamin Wilson built a grist-mill, and also a saw-mill.

John Fisher built a saw-mill in 1808, and about the same time Jabez Johnson built another. Wilson built his mills on the waters of the Otselic, in the north part of the town, as may well be proved by most of the learned judges, lawyers, and wearied jurors of the county; and of such importance has the building of those mills been in the legal movements of the human mind, that could they all be written as were the Acts of the Apostles, they might well be entitled the books of experiment in uncertainty. Fisher's mill was also built on the waters of the Otselic, in the south-west part of the town. And Johnson's mill, on the outlet of the Bloody-pond, so called, in the north-west part of the town.

Benjamin Wilson erected a clothing-mill near his grist-mill, in 1807, and Isaac Smith attended as the workman. He erected a blacksmith's shop in 1810 or '11. In 1808 he kept a public house.

The first school-house was erected in 1814. Thus,

from the workings of mind around the nucleus of labor, progression pushed forward, expanded, absorbed, assimilated, and increased the embryonic town of Willet, until, in 1818, legislatively speaking, it was fully born, baptised, and named, although a feeble infant town, as being regarded in the legal freehold power.

John S. Dyer, son of Samuel Dyer, built a store in 1834, a second in 1837, and a third one in 1848 ; also a public house, or inn, which has since been enlarged. Samuel Dyer was appointed the first post-master, in 1823. The Methodists formed a class, and appointed a class-leader, in 1815 or '16. The Baptists organized in 1821 ; the Congregationalists in 1852.

The first Town Meeting was held at the house of Benjamin Wilson, 1819. Altitius Burlingame officiated as Moderator ; William Throop, as Justice of the Peace. And the following persons were elected as official servants of the town for the term of one year :

Supervisor,—William Throop.

Town Clerk,—Samuel Dyer.

Assessors,—W. Throop, John Eaton, Benjamin Green.

Collector,—Joseph Nickerson.

Overseers of the Poor,—Altitius Burlingame, and Henry Sawdy.

Commissioners of Highways,—Benjamin T. Green, John Briggs, John Eaton.

Commissioners of Schools,—John Briggs, Benjamin T. Green, Abner Wilbur.

Constables,—Joseph Nickerson, John Campbell.

Commissioners of Lands,—Benjamin T. Green, Altitius Burlingame, Peter Eaton.

Inspectors of Common Schools,—W. Throop, Orlando

Salisbury, John Corbett, Anson T. Burt, Bicknell Freeman, Samuel Dyer.

Sealer of Weights and Measures,—Altitius Burlingame.*

In 1818, Arnold Thomas and his much-esteemed wife were drowned in the Otselic river, at or near the termination of the Ox-bow. Mrs. Thomas was a sister of Altitius Burlingame. They were endeavoring to cross the river, on an illy-constructed raft, with a design to attend a prayer-meeting. Miss Hannah Corpse, Nelly Miller, and Mr. Burlingame, were in company with the unfortunate couple. Mr. Burlingame, being an excellent swimmer, succeeded in saving himself and the two young ladies. The bodies were recovered from the watery element, and now repose in one grave, sacred to their memory, in Mr. Burlingame's orchard.

We have previously referred to the spirit of enterprise as exhibited by the agriculturists of Willet. A laudable attention to the improvement of stock, to agriculture and domestic manufacture, marks the efforts of the more active producers of wealth.

The increase of population, with a single exception, has been slow, yet certain.

In 1820 the population of Willet was			437
1825	"	"	508
1830	"	"	804
1835	"	"	723
1840	"	"	872
1845	"	"	921
1850	"	"	923
1855	"	"	925

* Communicated by Altitius Burlingame.

CORTLANDVILLE was organized from the southern part of the town of Homer, April 11th, 1829.

The surface of the territory is, in some parts, hilly, in others quite level, or but gently undulating. Flats of rich alluvion border the Tioughnioga river in its course through the valley. The more elevated lands are interspersed with gravelly and argillaceous loam.

Much of the early history of Cortlandville rightfully belongs to the original military town of Homer, and is, therefore, comprehended in that portion of our history.

The timber of Cortlandville was unusually heavy, and embraced the various kinds which are yet to be seen dotting the surface of hill and valley. Beech, maple, elm and hemlock were, however, the most abundant. The beautiful and tasteful grounds of the Messrs. Randall and Reynolds, were covered with a most luxuriant forest of lofty elms. Indeed, nothing in the forest line could be more enchantingly alluring. Stretching far to the south-west, these olden elms, that had for centuries towered in lofty grandeur, defying the whirlwind and the storm, are described by the western warriors as greatly rivalling in forest grandeur anything they ever saw in the wide-spread territory once claimed and ackowledged as originally belonging to the Six Nations.

The early pioneers located in the dense forests, erected their rude and unadorned cabins, hoping for the sure rewards of industry, perseverance and economy. But they were often subjected to great inconvenience and suffering, for the want of the necessary articles of husbandry, and also, those of subsistence. We have been told of instances of whole families living for successive weeks upon turnips and salt; of others who boiled roots gathered in the forest, and ate them with a relish which is unknown to the epicurean lords of the present day. To them a mess of parsley presented by a neighboring hand was regarded as an act of marked and generous attention to their wants.

Grain and potatoes were not to be had in the country. David Merrick sent his team through the woods to Geneva by a neighbor, to whom he gave five dollars, just enough to purchase two bushels of wheat. It was procured and ground; but on the return, one of the bags was torn open by coming in contact with a tree, and the flour of one bushel was lost; the remainder was emptied on its arrival by Mrs. Merrick into a four quart pan. Union and a sympathy of feeling prevailed among the settlers, which tended greatly to encourage and brace them for the coming conflicts arising from misfortune and the common ills peculiar to pioneer life. The settlers were mostly from the New England States, and brought with them their high regard for religion, morality, and common honesty of purpose. In these days of cupidity and heartless knavery, too much respect is paid to land pirates and vampyre shylocks. Not so in the early times of the pioneers. A mean act, coming from whatever source, was treated with contempt; the general desire of the people being to extend favors, and, if possible, to lighten the afflicting providences of all to whom they could possibly extend a helping hand. True, there was an occasional exception; and these were always marked by the upright and deserving.

The pioneer settler of Cortlandville was John Miller, a native of New Jersey. He moved in from Binghamton in 1792, and located on lot 56. Mr. Miller was a man of character and influence, and held several important town offices.

In 1794, Jonathan Hubbard and Col. Moses Hopkins came in and located.

The former selected a location amid the stately elms that stood on the ground now covered by Cortland Village, while the latter erected his palace of poles one mile west, on lot 64, which is at present occupied by his venerable widow, and her son Hiram Hopkins and family. They came in by way of Cazenovia and Truxton.

Thomas Wilcox, from Whitestown, located early in 1795 on lot 64. Reuben Doud, on lot 75. He was originally from New Haven, Conn. James Scott, John Morse, and Levi Lee located on the same lot. Dr. Lewis S. Owen, from Albany, on lot 66. He built the first frame house in Cortland county. It is at present occupied by widow William Mallery. It is situated a few rods west of the residence of Russel Hubbard.

During the years 1796-7, several accessions were made—located in various parts of the town. Aaron Knapp settled on the Roger farm, lot 55. Enoch Hotchkiss, on 76. The venerable Samuel Crittenden and Eber Stone, from Connecticut, located on lot 66. They purchased one hundred and sixty acres. The boundary line between them run in a direct line with Main street, Cortland Village. Mr. Crittenden was located on the east side, and erected a house on ground a little east of the post-office. He came in with an ox team, and was twenty-five days on the road. He has lived to see the surrounding country endowed with religious and literary institutions, and blessed with all the evidences of substantial wealth, intelligence and enterprise. He is now an honored citizen of Groton, Tompkins county.

In 1798, Samuel Ingles and his son Samuel, Jr., came from Columbia county, N. Y., and located on lot 75. During the year 1800, Wilmot Sperry came from Woodbridge, Conn., and located on lot 73. William Mallery, from Columbia county, settled in 1802. He was a man of substantial worth, and filled various offices in the gift of his friends. He died in 1837. John A. Freer, father of Anthony and Stephen D. Freer, came from Dutchess co., N. Y., and located on lot 74. James T. Hotchkiss, from Woodbridge, settled in 1803 on lot 54. He was an active participant in the war of 1812–15. He was one of Gen. Dearborn's Life Guards, and fell at the battle of Queenstown in 1813. Of his eight children, seven are now living—six in Cortlandville. His daughter Fanny married Daniel Hamlin, of Summer Hill.

Nathan Blodget, from Massachusetts, located in 1805; purchased on lots 65 and 66; died in 1845; left five children—Loren, Lewis, Franklin, Lydia and Elizabeth. In 1808, John Ingles located on lot 74. Lemuel and Jacob Cady were from Massachusetts, and located on lot 73. John Wicks on 72. Edmund Mallery on 74. The latter came from Dutchess county. William and Roswell Randall were natives of Connecticut, but came to Cortland from Madison county about 1812.

Samuel M'Graw, from whom M'Grawville derived its name, migrated from New Haven, Conn., to Cortlandville in 1803, and located on lot 87. He purchased 100 acres. In 1809 he removed to M'Grawville, and purchased about two hundred acres. There were at this time but three families settled within the vicinity of the present village. He reared a large and interesting family,—eight sons and four daughters,—eight of whom are now living. He died in February, 1836. His widow, at the age of eighty-four years, survives him, and is still living on the homestead, enjoying remarkably good health. His son Harry, father of Hon. P. H. M'Graw, was for many years a merchant in the village. He died in 1849.

Capt. Rufus Boies came in from Blandfort, Mass., in 1812, and located on lot 54, where Linus Stillman now lives. His original purchase was but fifty acres; he, however, increased the farm to one hundred and fifteen acres. He is now, at the advanced age of eighty-one, living in the village with his son Israel Boies. In his subsequent life, he has shown himself a man of the utmost integrity of character, kind-hearted and intelligent; and his worth as a man has been fully appreciated.

Others settled at early periods on various lots: the dates of location being doubtful, we therefore do not name them. Sylvanus Hopkins and Capt. Strong settled on lot 82. Nathan and James Knapp on 84. Eleanor Richmond, with her step-son, on the west part of the same lot. Gilbert Budd and Jeremiah Chase, on 74. John Calvert, from Washington county, on lot 82. John McFarlan, John M'Nish, and Archibald Turner are believed to have moved from the same county. John Stillman, Elisha Crosby and Lemuel Ingles settled on lot 65.

David Merrick came from Massachusetts in 1800, and located on lot 44. In the year 1797, he came to Whitestown to purchase a tavern stand and one hundred acres of land, then valued at three hundred dollars. His means being limited, he finally concluded not to purchase, and returned home. The next year he visited Whitestown again, for the express purpose of closing a bargain, but the property was then valued at ten thousand dollars, and consequently he did not secure it, and came on to Homer ; a few years after, having been ejected from his premises three times, and being threatened with a fourth, he concluded to leave, and moved to Little York. In 1810, he located in Cortlandville, on lot 65.

Danforth Merrick, son of David, informed us that he drew saw logs to Homer during the winter of 1800. There was then no road—at least only such as had been made by merely underbrushing through. The mud and snow was two feet deep, and as they had to ring the top end, around which they fastened the log chain, "noosing the logs" as they called it, he could draw but two per day.

In the dwelling where he now resides, he kept tavern for twenty years.

At this period, (1800,) a road had been cut through to Virgil Corners to intersect the State road. Another had been cut through to Locke—now Groton ; a third to M'Grawville ; a fourth to Truxton, and, as above noted, a fifth to Homer.

The first barrel of cider drank in town was brought in by Mr. Lyon, who some years after was murdered in Palmer, Mass.

The first public house was kept by Samuel Ingles, in 1810, on ground now covered by the Barnard Block.

The first school-house stood on ground now covered by the Eagle hotel.

The first grist-mill was erected by Jonathan Hubbard, in 1779.

The first merchant was Lemuel Ingles ; he sold goods in a small house near the present residence of H. P. Goodrich.

We have in another portion of our history referred to the early religious efforts of the pioneers of Cortlandville. The first church organization occurred in 1801. This may be said to have been a union effort, for the meetings were held in Homer, Cortland, Port Watson, and on the East river, near the County House. The Baptist Church was erected in 1811, and dedicated in June, 1812. It was located within the present limits of Cortlandville, about one "half mile north of the old Court House." In the autumn of 1825, efforts were made by the association to secure a more advantageous change in the location of church organizations, which happily resulted in the formation of a church in Homer and M'Grawville, "leaving the Mother Church in the centre."* Soon after, three new churches were erected, one in each of the villages referred to.

During the same year, a Presbyterian Church was organized in Cortlandville, which rapidly increased in numbers and in influence.

The first Methodist meeting occurred in 1804, at the house of Jonathan Hubbard, the former residence of Samuel Crittenden. A discourse was pronounced by Rev. Samuel Hill, of the Philadelphia Circuit, and subsequently a class was formed. It was undoubtedly small as to numbers, for at the time of which we now

* See Discourse by Rev. Alfred Bennet, 1844.

write, there were but four houses within the present limits of Cortland Village. The Universalists, or Free Thinkers, and Catholic organizations are of more recent date. The former have a large and elegant church.

In 1830 the population of Cortlandville was			3,673
1835	"	"	3,715
1840	"	"	3,799
1845	"	"	4,111
1850	"	"	4,173
1855	"	"	4,423

LAPEER was organized from the east part of Virgil, May 2, 1845.

The first settler in this town was Primus Grant, a colored man; he purchased on lot 594, and settled on it in 1799. He was a native of Guinea, and the farm has always been called Guinea. He lived a number of years on his lot, and when he died was buried on one of the high bluffs that overlook the stream known as the Big Brook.

Peter Gray, a native of Fishkill, Dutchess county, was the first white settler; he came from Ulster (now Sullivan co.) in July, 1802, and located on lot 70. His widow still survives, and is believed to be the oldest person now living in the town,—age 84 years. His son, Ogden Gray, resides on the original premises. He left a respectable family of children, the youngest of whom is the wife of Dan C. Squires.

Seth Jennings, from Connecticut, settled, in 1803, on lot 597, where he lived until his death. Harry Jennings, his son, who now resides in Harford, owns the farm.

Mr. Jennings left several children, some of whom are still living in the town.

Timothy Robertson, from the same State, came in about the same time, and lived for a brief period with Mr. Jennings. He was a soldier in the Revolutionary war; was with Montgomery at the storming of Quebec, in 1775. He fought valiantly while the brave and heroic sons, martyrs to American liberty, were falling around him. His son, Eliphalet, the only remaining descendant, is now living in Lapeer.

Thomas Kingsbury and Robert H. Wheeler settled in the south-east part of the town, in 1804. The former was a Revolutionary soldier, and drew a pension. One of his daughters married Marvin Balch, who resides on the homestead. The latter has no living representative in the town. They were natives of Connecticut.

Simeon Luce, father of Martin Luce, of Virgil, located on lot 57, in 1805; and is believed to have kept the first tavern in the town. He was an ingenious mechanic, and an industrious and valuable citizen. He died at an extreme old age, leaving a numerous posterity.

Zachariah Squires and Robert Smith settled, in 1806, on lot 70. The former was the father of Col. William Squires, now residing in the town of Marathon. The latter was an officer in the Revolutionary war, and held a commission from the Commander-in-Chief, General George Washington. He drew a pension a number of years. His children still reside in Lapeer.

John S. Squires and James Richards located in 1807. The former was a native of Connecticut, but removed from Lisle, Broome co., and settled on lot 68. The farm is now occupied by his son, Dan C. Squires. He left a numerous family, of which James S. Squires, of Cortland, is the youngest. Mr. Richards settled on lot 79, on the farm now owned by Erastus Johnson.

There were sixteen soldiers of the Revolutionary war who settled in Lapeer, and all but one died there.

A number of the soldiers of the last war with Great Britain, resided in Lapeer, and drew land-warrants, or pensions, or both. In 1813, a volunteer company was organized, of which Simeon West was captain, John S. Squires lieutenant, and William Powers ensign. The service of this company was tendered the Government, and those composing it were to be regarded as minute-men, to be mustered into active service on a day's notice; but happily their service was not needed.

Among the earliest clergymen who preached in Lapeer, were the Rev. Mr. Harrison, and Dr. Williston, of the Presbyterian; Mr. Sheopard, of the Baptist, and Mr. Densmore, of the Methodist. All of them were missionaries, or traveling preachers. The latter organized a class. Other religious associations were subsequently formed,—that of the Baptist, in 1820; the Presbyterian, in 1826 or '7; and the Christians during the latter year.

The first child born in Lapeer was John Gray, son of Peter Gray, in 1803. He died in Minesota, about two years since. The first death was that of Robert C. Squires, 9th of May, 1809, aged about two years. He was a son of John S. Squires. The first marriage is believed to have been that of James Parker to Miss Lucy Wood.

Simeon Luce erected the first grist-mill, in 1827. The first saw-mill was erected by Samuel and John Gee, in 1825. Messrs. Nickols and Turpening were the first merchants, and commenced trading about 1834 or '5.

The first post-master was Royal Johnson. He was appointed in 1849, and still continues to hold the office.

A few rods to the south of the residence of Mr. H. Genung, was, at a former period, an Indian camping-ground. This was on a bluff overlooking and close to the Big Brook. From the banks of this stream flowed beautiful rivulets of cool transparent water. Here, too, were immense forests of elms, basswood, maple, and other timber, the favorite resort of the black bear, once so plenty in Cortland county. Deers, too, roamed the hills and valleys. The wolf and panther made night hideous with their discordant notes of revelry. From the camping-ground the Indians daily radiated in quest of game and fish, and at night returned to their cabins loaded with peltry—the products of the chase.

In 1850 the population of Lapeer was 822.
1855 " " " 750.

HARFORD was organized from the west part of Virgil, May 2, 1845. The first settlement in this town was made in 1803. Dorastus De Wolf, Thomas Nichols, John Green, and Cornelius Worden, were the pioneers who first selected locations and became permanent settlers of the town of Harford. De Wolf settled in the south part of the town, then a perfect wilderness. Wolves were very plentiful, and, as a consequence, he had to protect his sheep at night for about twelve or thirteen years. Bears, also, were in abundance. Deer were frequently seen in droves. Occasionally an elk was seen in the valleys. Foxes and martins, wild-cats and opossums, were numerous, but a beaver was seldom seen.

Rev. Seth Williston was the first preacher who directed public religious worship. The first meeting occurred in 1804.

The first physician was Dr. Fox.

The first school was taught in 1807, by Miss Betsey Curran.

The first post-office was established in 1825, and at that time called Worthington, but was subsequently changed to Harford.

The first merchant was Theodore E. Hart. He commenced business in 1824.

In 1845	the population of	Harford was	921
1850	"	"	949
1855	"	"	926

Taylor was erected from Solon, December 5, 1849. The surface, soil, timber, and agricultural advantages are so similar to the adjoining towns, that we do not regard it as necessary to present any separate detail. It is watered in the south-east corner by the Otselic creek, but is in the main deficient of water power. The timber is generally maple, beach, elm, butternut, basswood and hemlock. The arable land is at least in the usual proportion of other towns; the town is however better adapted for grazing and the dairy branch of productive industry, than for the producing of grain crops.

The first permanent pioneers of the town of Taylor were Ezra Rockwell, and his sons Thomas, and Ezra, Jr. They were from Lenox, Mass. The father had served in the Revolution, and drew lot 78, on which they located in 1793.

In 1795 Thomas Rockwell went to Cincinnatus and

purchased one hundred acres on lots 9 and 19. He settled on the former, where he remained for thirty-two years, and then removed to Taylor and located on lot 100. He purchased six acres on which the village of Taylor, familiarly known as Bangall, now stands. He also purchased one hundred and seven acres on lot 99. His house originally stood on the ground now covered by the public house kept by E. W. Fish. He has cleared four farms, erected several dwellings, and, with Leonard Holmes, built the tavern, about 1818. Mr. Holmes kept the house a number of years. He now resides on lot 86. Mr. Rockwell is now eighty-one years old, straight and active as a man of thirty.

The Beebes were originally from Connecticut. Roderic located on Mt. Roderic, lot 75, in the spring of 1794. He is described as being an active, hardy and industrious man, capable of enduring great privation and fatigue. The venerable Orellana Beebe migrated from New Haven in 1796, and settled on lot 7 in Solon, now Truxton. He remained there two years, and then removed to Taylor, and located on lot 100. He survives at the advanced age of eighty-eight years, remarkably active and healthy. Mrs. Beebe is eighty-four, blind, and very infirm. Ira Rockwell married his youngest daughter.

Increase M. Hooker, a native of Vermont, located on lot 88, in 1797. He removed the next year to Truxton.

Lewis Hawley, from Huntington, Conn., located on the Howe farm in Pitcher, in 1805. He remained but a brief period, and then came to Taylor and settled on the farm now owned by Ebenezer C. Wicks. One or two years after he settled on the Orrin Randall farm, where he remained two years, when he was attacked with the Ohio fever, and started for the then Great West. But the snow having suddenly disappeared, he was unable to proceed farther than Bath. The next fall he removed to Lisle, and the spring following returned to Taylor, and settled on lot 78. He subsequently purchased one hundred acres on lot 77, where he died January 15, 1858. He was an industrious, active, and valuable citizen. He reared a family of seven children—all living. Lewis T., resides in Syracuse; James T. on lot 87. Sarah Ann is the wife of John Biger; Francis, on the homestead; Hiram L., at Liverpool, Onondaga county; Cyrus M. is an active, practising attorney in Chicago; John H., in Kansas.

John L. Boyd and John Phelps migrated from Saratoga county. The former located on lot 98, in 1811, and purchased one hundred and nineteen acres. He subsequently made an additional purchase of two hundred and fifty-one acres. The latter settled on lot 86, and purchased eighty-six acres. He now has two hundred and twelve. When Mr. Phelps located on his land, the country around him was entirely covered with timber; or to use his own language, "it was a dense will derness." By economy and persevering industry, he has accumulated a respectable competence.

In 1814, David Wire, originally of Connecticut, located on lot 100. He has reared a family of eleven children—five living. His father, Thomas Wire, was a native of England; was kidnapped in London when but seven years old, and sold in Boston, where he remained until the commencement of the French and English war. He was then impressed in the English service for a period of six years. He subsequently settled in Connecticut. When the American Revolution broke out, he entered the army by enlistment, and served throughout the war.

The early pioneers were not unfrequently subjected to hardships and privation. Provisions,—the real substantials of life,—were scarce, and the prospect of procuring them from a distance was often precarious and uncertain. Orellana Beebe told us that during one of those periods of scarcity, he and his son, Koakland, went to Genoa, Cayuga county, to purchase wheat, which he obtained, and had ground at Squire Bradley's mill. The next spring he was equally as much in want, and being very anxious to get in a small crop of corn, said to his son, then only ten years old, "Koakland, can you take the horse to-morrow and go to Genoa and get some grain or flour?" The boy's answer was, "I can try." The necessary preparations were made, and at early dawn he was on his way. He took with him three bags, each one containing eight pounds of maple sugar, with which to pay for his wheat, at the rate of one dollar, or eight pounds to the bushel. Almost the entire distance (forty miles) was traversed by marked trees. He reached his destination just at evening, and immediately inquired of Mr. Bradley if he could accommodate him with the grain. A negative answer brought tears into the lad's eyes, for he felt most keenly the disappointment. Mr. Bradley, however, quieted his feelings by generously offering to take care of him and his horse until morning free of charge, when he would open a barrel and let him have the value of the sugar in flour—one hundred and twenty pounds. Morning dawned, and the boy was duly prepared to start on his return for home. He reached Judge Bingham's, at the Salt road, just at the close of day, and, though contrary to his will, was prevailed upon to remain until morning, the Judge telling him that it would not be possible for him to continue his way by glazed trees. At about ten o'clock in the forenoon of the next day he reached home in safety, much gratified with his trip. That boy had the nerve and the muscle of a man.

William Blackman was the first blacksmith ; Hiram Rockwell, the first merchant ; Ezra Rockwell, the first post-master. The office was established in 1834. Mr. Rockwell continued in the office for fifteen successive years, and is at present the recipient of its perquisites, having recently been reäppointed. Barak Niles, the first school teacher. The first saw-mill was erected in 1812, by Thomas Rockwell. A portion of the old mill forms a part of the one now owned by Hiel Tanner. The first grist-mill, by Messrs. Wells & Lord. The first missionary was Dr. Williston. The first settled minister, Ruben Hurd. The first birth was that of Polly H. Beebe, now widow Rockwell, of Wisconsin.

In 1850 the population of Taylor was 1,232
1855 " " 1,201

There are but few who fully appreciate the beauty and loveliness of the Tioughnioga Valley. The strife for rivalry and gain hangs like a fated incubus upon the minds of the people, preventing them from viewing with admiration, hill, dale, and valley, which appear spread out like a splendid panorama. Indeed, we have often wondered how little the citizens were impressed with the natural beauties and advantages with which they are surrounded. Descending from an elevated point into the valley, we have beheld a luxuriance of unrivaled richness. Here was the green herbage—yonder the golden tinge. An occasional old monarch—a proud relic of three centuries, towered aloft in his glorious majesty, while to the westward of the glassy waters of the Tioughnioga river,* our eyes rested upon the fertile uplands, dotted with the neat white cottage residences of thriving agriculturists. The quiet rural village of Homer,† nestled in the lap of the luxuriant valley; the numerous glittering spires rearing their points towards the azure zenith, and the ever-varied beauties of the surrounding landscape, complete a view rivaled only in the more rugged and picturesque scenes of nature.

HOMER is beautifully located on the west side of the Tioughnioga river, and is regarded as being one of the handsomest villages in the State.

In 1800 there were six houses within the limits of the corporation.

Whole number of its inhabitants, June 1st, 1855—1625. Increase since 1848—225.

The various branches of business indicate a healthful progression.

The present aggregate of business transacted in the village, we have not endeavored to arrive at. It is perhaps sufficient to say that the merchants, grocers

* The Tioughnioga river, as called by the Indians O-nan-no-gi-is-ka, signified Shagbark Hickory.

† Homer, as called Te-wis-ta-no-ont-sa-ne-ha, signified the place of the silversmith.

and mechanics are doing a larger business than at any previous time.

The first merchant in Homer was John Coats. His store stood on ground near Harrop's sign-post.

The first permanent merchant was Jedediah Barber. He came into Homer in 1811, but did not engage in the mercantile trade until 1813. The original part of the Great Western store, twenty-two by thirty feet, was erected at about that period. He entered into business with exceedingly limited means, but by industry, perseverance and economy, he was eminently successful, and finally became the heaviest dealer in the Tioughnioga valley, carved his way to fortune, and established a financial reputation unrivaled in the county. He has done more to improve and beautify the village of Homer than any other man. The monuments of his memory are scattered all around the village in the numerous buildings of various classes he has caused to be erected, or contributed to rear, and they will long remain more honorable and enduring memorials than any marble column which might be erected over his final resting-place. His name is identified with the history of the Tioughnioga valley, and will only cease to be remembered when the spirit of enterprise no longer exists.

William Sherman, the second pioneer merchant, came into Homer during the summer of 1815. He located near the cooper shop. Soon after, he erected a machine shop for the manufacture of nails,—the first of the kind in the State of New York,—the machinery being so arranged as to feed, cut, head and stamp without assistance. On the head of each nail was stamped the letter S. Four-penny nails were then worth twenty-five cents per pound. Iron was exceedingly high. The manufacturing of oil was another branch of productive employment in which Mr. Sherman engaged. In 1827 he erected the "Homer Exchange" store, in which for a period of nearly thirty years he conducted a heavy mercantile trade. John Sherman, and also his son William, now deceased, were at different periods his active partners in business.

The original part of the store occupied by Geo. W. Phillips, was erected in 1819 by Benajah Tubbs. It has been successively owned by Thadeus Archer, Horace White, Marsena Ballard, Amos Graves, and at present by Giles Chittenden, Esq. The brick part is thirty-six by forty-six. Mr. White added improvements to an amount of $1,200 ; Mr. Chittenden, by an increase of land, other buildings, and improvements to the store, to an amount exceeding $1,300. The brick part cost about $4,000.

The store occupied by C. O. Newton, was erected at a later period.

The first furnace was built in 1826 ; it was of a very limited structure, the blowing done by a horse attached to a plunge bellows. It stood on the opposite side of the street, and a little to the north of the foundry of Messrs. J. W. & A. Stone, sons of Deacon Nathan Stone, of pioneer memory. It ceased to be operated in 1838. During this year Jacob Saunders erected a foundry on the west side of the street; it was destroyed by fire during the fall of 1844. Damage, $2,000. Insurance, $1,000. It was immediately rebuilt, so that in six weeks from the day of its destruction, a blast was made.

The first engine was of six-horse power. The one at present in use rates somewhat higher.

The foundry was purchased by the Messrs. Stone, March 1, 1853.

The buildings cover one acre of ground. The furnace is forty by forty feet. The machine shop is twenty-six by thirty-six.

Their business is one of increasing importance. They melt upwards of one hundred tons of iron per year.

The grist-mill of Messrs. Cogswell & Wilcox, was put up in 1834. This is located on the ground occupied by the first mill erected in the county in 1798, by John Hubbard, Asa White, and John Keep.

The Homer Cotton Mills of J. O. Pearce & Co. were erected in 1834, and put in operation in 1835. The main building is fifty by one hundred feet. The machinery is propelled by steam and water. The engine is of thirty horse power, and was manufactured in Eaton, Madison county, N. Y., by A. N. Wood & Co. Number of spindles, 2,400 ; looms, 50.

In 1836 the amount manufactured in dollars, $7,000. In 1855, $30,000.

The planing mill and carpenter shop of Mr. George W. Almy was erected in 1853. The building is thirty by sixty feet, and two stories high. The machinery is propelled by a steam engine of fifteen and a half horse power. During the past year (1855) Mr. Almy has planed two hundred thousand feet of lumber. The planing and matching is done with a correctness and smoothness which makes it a most valuable auxiliary in the department of saving labor.

In 1855, the population of Homer was 1,625.

CORTLAND.—The valley of Tioughnioga is unrivaled in beauty—in wild, picturesque scenery. The quiet vales of central New York present few, if any, more attractive scenes than are to be found in our own broad valley. These exhibit all the grand requisites for the most varied and sublime spectacles. The forest-fringed hills with their impenetrable depths, present the varied shades of green and yellow, with an occasional tinge of orange and vermillion; while the young and tender leaves glisten in the morning frost, or sparkle amid the fresh dewdrops kissed by the soft rays of the orient sun.

"Here, in this lovely valley, the quiet village of Cortland is situated, about three miles from its twin sister, Homer; and through it a beautiful stream passes with murmuring music on its journey to the Susquehanna, which adds a new charm to the romantic and sequestered spot. This beautiful village exhibits much enterprise, united with social comfort; for the undisturbed retirement of the location invites hither, during the summer, many of that class of citizens who prefer seclusion to the bustle of city life."

Cortland Village was incorporated November 5, 1853, under the act passed in 1847, providing for the procurement of village incorporations by an order from the Court of Sessions and a vote of the citizens.

Cortland contains many attractive and costly private residences, among which are those of W. R. Randall, Roswell Randall, Joseph Reynolds, W. O. Barnard and G. N. Woodward. The first mentioned was built by William Randall, now deceased, father of the present occupant of the estate. The premises upon which the building stands, comprises about six acres of land. The portion fronting Main street is beautifully laid out in flower plots, dotted here and there with evergreens and stately shade trees. There are winding graveled walks, on either side of which are beds of flowers, selected and cultivated with great care. In the rear of the elegant mansion is an extensive greenhouse filled with a superb collection of cactus-roses, and flowers of almost every variety and hue, besides orange and lemon trees. In spring time the various buds and blossoms that appear are most grateful to the eye, and impart a most healthful and cheering influence. Poetically, "myriads" of happy songsters fill the air with their melodious strains, making the delightful grounds appear like a Paradise of delight. There are very few more attractive residences in the State.

The village contains four churches, one academy, a number of first class hotels, stores, groceries, manufacturing establishments, and warehouses.

The "Randall Bank" commenced doing business December 3, 1853.

Capital, $50,000; deposits March 8, 1856, $80,718; amount of business transacted during the year 1855, $4,810,685 25. William R. Randall, President; Jonathan Hubbard, Cashier.

The large and extensive hardware, agricultural and seed store of Mr. S. D. Freer, is situated on Port Watson street. The building is appropriately divided into necessary apartments, among which are the foundry, machine, blacksmith, wood, and tin shops. It is thirty-six by one hundred and forty feet. The original portion was erected in 1836—rebuilt in 1848.

The grist-mill—the second one in the county—was erected in 1799, by Jonathan Hubbard; is at present owned by Ebenezer Mudge. Originally it contained only two runs of stone; but during the improvements which were made a few years since, two more were added, making it one of the largest and best mills in the county. The greater portion of the wheat that is ground at this mill is purchased in the northern and southern portions of the State, as also from the southern part of Canada. During the past year there were ground at this mill about twenty-eight thousand bushels of wheat.

There were shipped from the Cortland Railroad station, from April 1, 1855, to March 24, 1856, to the different stations on the Syracuse, Binghamton and N. Y. Railroad, five millions eight hundred and eighty-three thousand one hundred pounds of freight.

We have elsewhere remarked with reference to the productive results of the dairy business—a prominent branch of agriculture, which has already superseded the others in practical importance. The amount of butter purchased and shipped by gentlemen in Cortland, reaches an aggregate amount which is certainly excessively large. The amount paid out in 1855 by James Van Valen, J. D. Schermerhorn, James S. Squires, and J. A. Graham, exceeded $249,000.

Cortland is a pleasant and prosperous village, with a population (as per census of 1855) of 1,576 persons. There are few villages in central New York, more favorably located, or in which may be found a more active and energetic class of enlightened citizens. In

1813 Port Watson numbered twenty-five inhabitants, and Cortland, twelve.

MARATHON is remarkable for its health and beauty, is pleasantly situated on the Tioughnioga river, and is surrounded by a densely peopled, rich, and highly cultivated country. It has a ready and cheap communication, not only with middle and western New York; but with Pennsylvania, Ohio, the Canadas, and indeed with the ever prosperous and growing West, by railroad, canal, and the great chain of northern lakes. The mass of its inhabitants are characterized for morality and intelligence, sobriety, industry, and enterprise.

The positive proof of her prosperity may be seen in the result of the numerous transforming influences which for the last few years have attended her healthful growth and permanent strength—in the newly erected public and private residences, as well as the commodious and truly valuable mercantile and mechanical establishments. That Marathon is exceedingly "favorably located, both in regard to the value of the country by which it is surrounded, and the area likely to be tributary to its business interests," is no longer a question admitting of a doubt.

Of the village of M'Grawville, we have remarked in another place. Cincinnatus, Truxton, East Homer, Preble Centre, and Scott Corners, are pleasant and prosperous villages.

CHAPTER XIII.

GENERAL REMARKS ON EARLY HISTORY—PAST AND PRESENT COMPARED.

Times change—one age succeeds another,
  And pining want and grim despair
Are left behind, and fairer, brighter
  Scenes the pioneers do view.

The history of Cortland county from the day when Amos Todd first planted the standard of civilization in this then "western wilderness," is but a record of such incidents as the faithful annalist is usually called to record of the rural or gradually improving agricultural districts of a naturally rich and fertile country. The early pioneers were mostly from the New England States, and were imbued with the Puritan habits of their fathers. In 1800, this inland, obscure, and almost inaccessible region had become dotted with log cabins and small clearings. The burning of huge log-heaps served as land-marks to guide the weary wanderer or returning hunter, as he neared the rustic home of the pilgrim pioneers. Clouds of smoke ascended from hill and valley as the old forest monarchs bowed before the invincible axmen. The wilderness vanished before the hand of civilization. It was scathed with fire, and ruthlessly torn with iron harrows. While the lowlands were being brought into suitable culture for corn, wheat, and potatoes, the crusaders ascended the hillsides and even made war with the hemlock highlands. This was the heroic age—an age of iron fortitude and persevering industry. The pioneers went forth armed with the conquering axe, impressed with a determined will, and inspired with a devotional feeling for home and country. Years of toil and privation succeeded, and occasionally penury and want communed together. Instances of this character, however, were not often allowed to be repeated, without an effort at prevention ; for the liberal hand of the more fortunate brother did not withhold the alleviating charities, especially if the means were in his power. Unlike their modern rivals in wealth—the golden barons of the present day, who are hoarding up means to procure Grecian, Gothic, and Italian finery—they were most happy in relieving the wants of their industrious neighbor. Unlike the present day, the means of subsistence were scant, and not easily obtained from a distance, and consequently want was not a stranger, even in the Tioughnioga valley. As settlements increased, and improvements spread, hope and joy began to realize the anticipated benefits which they saw in their day dreams and nightly visions. The products of a generous soil were garnered in their various depositories, and peace and gladness reigned in the pioneer's home.

What a change has been wrought in fifty years? Then the majority of the inhabitants were found located in our valleys. How changed the scene! Now the majority are found upon the more elevated lands. The huge log-heaps, sending forth their red-hot flames, like fiery serpents coiling around some proud old monarch, eating out its very vitals, the charred stumps, and rough brush fences, are no more seen as in days past. The change is hardly to be realized. Then a thousand unsightly scenes met the laborer's eye—the timber was felled in every conceivable form, or as best suited the purpose for the more ready application of the crusader's torch. Here and there were seen half-haggled outlines, and blackened trunks of stately trees, while the sun, half hid from sight, only occasionally glimmered through the thick hemlock boughs, as the rosy-cheeked maiden wandered in pursuit of the favorite cow, listening to catch the well-known sound of the tinkling bell, so frequently heard by the brave old pioneer. Now beautiful and well-cultivated farms, bedecked with the tranquil abode of the husbandman, mark the rapidly-improving aspect of the once hated and shunned highlands. Valuable horses and fine fleshy cattle graze upon the productive meadows. A thousand lights are seen at night from the windows of tasteful and elegant mansions. Carriage wheels rapidly roll upon the roads where once were seen only the Indian trails. The cheering light of science has ascended the hillside, and education erected her standard on the higher summit. A hundred school-houses, within whose walls literature and learning love to linger, as in some royal academic edifice, send forth an intellectual influence of far more service than the entrenched embattlements of a thousand warriors.

An intelligent and enterprising population of twenty-four thousand souls are now living within the boundaries of Cortland county. Mills and machinery are adding wealth and elegance, while the agriculturists are turning up the golden sands of an almost unrivaled soil, and the dairymen are shipping to eastern markets heavy consignments of butter and cheese. The heavy goods of our merchants are not now, as once, "dragged in logy wagons" from Albany and Utica, but the huge monster, clothed in iron mail and steel clad armor, belching fire and smoke, rushes with wild discordant shriek over the iron rails which are laid down through our valley, forcing, as with superhuman speed, heavy trains laden with every variety of merchandize for the retail trade—the sugars from the islands of the ocean, the teas of China, the silks of Calcutta, and the thousands of valuable products from oriental looms and spindles. The *Republican*, *Gazette* and *Banner* enter weekly almost every dwelling, even in the rural districts.

There has been a uniform indifference, and an almost entire absence of correct information, through the western divisions of our State in regard to a correct knowledge of this county, as well as with respect to the intelligence and rapidly increasing wealth of the inhabitants ; and we are very sure that no other portion has been so generally misunderstood and decidedly misrepresented. Indeed, Cortland county has been singularly unfortunate in this particular. And yet, through the active and enterprising exertions of her citizens, she is quietly and rapidly growing to be second to none in the State in all the elements of wealth and prosperity. Her agricultural resources and lumber trade are of considerable importance. The dairy business has increased to an almost unparalleled extent. Beside the home consumption, we have, for several years, sent to eastern markets large quantities of butter and cheese—of the former, upwards of $400,000 worth. There were shipped from the three stations—Homer, Cortland and Marathon—during the past year, 1,500,000 pounds of butter. There is still another item of increasing magnitude. We refer to the sale of cattle. There cannot be less than $220,000 worth of cattle driven out of the county annually. Our grain fields, though not in all respects equal to Tompkins, Yates, Ontario and Monroe, yet are generally very productive, while the grass lands are matters of astonishment to every one. We frequently cut from two to three tons of hay per acre. We refer now more particularly to the back and hill lands, which in times past have been regarded, by certain descriptive geographers of our State, as being only suited to the growth of "wild Yankees and tall hemlocks."

But "we were not aware until recently that the waters of the Tioughnioga had ever been the highway of so much commerce as to render it a part of the journalist's duty to publish a "marine report." We knew that great quantities of whiskey, grain, potatoes and other products of this wild region, were "sent down the river" to Harrisburgh and Baltimore ; but we did not suppose the commerce was of so much importance as the following would indicate. We copy literally :*

INLAND NAVIGATION.

PORT WATSON.

Highwater—Monday, 6th inst.

CLEARED.

Bark *Exporter*, G. Rice, master, for Harrisburgh, laden with cheese and gypsum.

* See "*Cortland Democrat*," of August 2, 1855.

Bark *Crazy Jane*, L. Rice, gypsum, for Harrisburgh.
" *Dutch Trader*, Shapley, gypsum, "
" *Navigator*, Parsons, gypsum, Columbia.
" *Brother Jonathan*, Taylor, gypsum, Columbia.
" *Gold Hunter*, Sherwood, " "
" *Indian Chief*, Billings, " "
" *Resolution*, May, gypsum, Marietta.
" *Perseverance*, Wakefield, gypsum, Marietta.
" *Phœnix*, " "
" *Enterprise*, " "
" *Lazy Tom*, " "
" *Sour Krout*, " "
" *Yankee Rogue*, " "

We doubt not the memory of our venerable friend, Major SHAPLEY, whose recollection is not altogether dimmed by age, of "hair-breadth 'scapes" from shipwreck, of the dangers of "taking in" too much freight—of passages over dams, and other adventures incident to the life of the Susquehanna raftsmen—will be greatly refreshed by the foregoing list. But the glory of the Tioughnioga has departed—the "ship yard" of Port Watson has gone to decay—the earth whereon those jolly barks were built, is now made to yield to the labors of the gardener and husbandman—the contest between nature and art has resulted adversely to the former, and the raftsman's song has given place to the shrill scream of the steam whistle, and the products of our county are whirled to other markets, at a speed somewhat greater than two or three miles per hour. Many an "old craft" has smoked his last pipe and uttered his last oath; and those who are left behind cling closer to the chimney corner as the frosts of age gather around them, while they recount to incredulous youth the deeds which wrought the hut into the mansion—the forest into the hamlet—and extended to their descendants the benefits of schools, religion, and the comforts and refinements which prosperity and wealth produce.

The few remaining relics of the "olden time" are now trembling on the verge of an hundred years, and treading, as it were, the confines of another world. As they look back upon the mighty changes which time and industry have wrought, they seem overwhelmed and bewildered. But, after resting a moment to collect their scattered thoughts, they enter into a warm and interesting disquisition on the moral and industrial habits of the present generation, as compared with the more active and laborious life of their fathers. They feel conscious that a very great change has taken place in the moral and social habits of the people, and that although the age in which we live is marked by the hand of progress, and an enlightened civilization, they do not perceive the same union of sentiment pervading the various associations, or cementing the more endearing ties of fraternal friendship. When they first landed from their canoes upon the banks of the Tioughnioga, they regarded themselves as being beyond the boundaries of civilization, and as having cast their destiny in the far distant West. They can hardly comprehend the means by which new territories are settled and admitted into the union of confederated States, with an energetic population of two years' growth, christened with the name of "State."

The inhabitants of this county are, in many respects, quite dissimilar to those of some of the sister counties of the State, being principally made up of Connecticut and Massachusetts people, or their descendants, though there is an occasional sprinkling of the Dutch ; yet the peculiar characteristics of the universal Yankee are predominant. The agriculturists are proverbial for their frugality and propensity to hoard money, yet with extremely few exceptions, are affable, courteous, and dignified in their deportment.

Our merchants, too, as a class, are a very worthy portion of community—intelligent, high-minded and honorable, and such as would be creditable to any country. Many of them are in the enjoyment of considerable wealth, honorably acquired.

And last though not least, the clergy deserve a passing notice :—distinguished alike for liberality of sentiment, generosity of purpose, and commanding powers of mind. The religious sentiments, greatly liberalized by the descendants of the pilgrims, and cultivated by the early pioneers of Cortland, are properly appreciated by the enlightened clergymen who conduct public religious worship in our various temples of christianity.

Of the legal fraternity we have remarked in another place.

The first military organization, embracing portions of the territory of this county, dates back to 1796. In March, 1794, after the erection of Onondaga county from Herkimer, various appointments were made for the new county ; and especially for the battalions, of Majors John L. Hardenburgh, Moses De Witt and Asa Danforth. The latter battalion, in 1796, was made a regiment, and comprised the townships of Hannibal, Lysander, Cicero, Manlius, Pompey, Fabius, Solon, Cincinnatus, Tully, Virgil, Camillus, Sempronius, Locke, Dryden, and the "Onondaga Reservation." Asa Danforth was made Lieutenant Colonel Commandant.

The act of April 8, 1808, authorizing the erection of Cortland county, provided for the holding of three courts of Common Pleas and General Sessions of the Peace, which were to be held on the second Tuesday of April, and the first Tuesdays of September and December, in every year after the due organization of the county. These Courts were to have the same jurisdiction, powers, and authorities as the Courts of Common Pleas and General Sessions of the Peace in the other counties of the State have in their respective counties. Suits previously commenced, however, were not to be affected so as to work a wrong or prejudice to any of the parties ; nor were any criminal or other proceedings on the part of the State to be in the least affected ; but on the contrary, all such civil and criminal proceedings were to be prosecuted to trial, judgment, and execution. The act also provided that the Courts "should be held at the school-house on lot No. 45, in the town of Homer." John Keep received the appointment of first Judge, April 3d, 1810.

Cortland county was made to form a part of the Western Senatorial District, and part of the Thirteenth Congressional District, and was entitled to one member of Assembly, and so continued to be up to 1823, when Daniel Sherwood and John Gillett were elected. By a change of Representation, in 1846, Cortland was reduced to one member, and in 1847 Timothy Green was elected to a seat in the Assembly. Ephraim Fish, the first member, was elected in 1810, and took his seat at the opening of the 33d Session.

The first court-house was erected on a commanding eminence west of Cortland Village. Various sites were examined by the locating commissioners, there being numerous interests operating upon the minds of the people in the different localities. Homer, Cortland, Port Watson and M'Grawville, were equally interested in securing the location of the public buildings, and the good citizens were, apparently, equally certain of success. The commissioners, however, after examining the different locations, and listening to the fervent and eloquent appeals of interested individuals, finally stuck the stake at the south-west corner of where the venerable old relic of a passing age now stands, "solitary and alone," a monument of other days and of the yet remembered differences of an excited people. The decision, as was naturally expected, did not meet with the general approbation of the community. A ludicrous representation of the commanding structure, and of some of the opposing interests, was prepared by a wag, which was rendered, from existing circumstances, somewhat amusing. The "was to be" elegant and dignified edifice appeared quite accurately drawn on old-fashioned foolscap, rearing aloft its bold outlines of pine and hemlock, and looking down with defiant scorn on the outraged citizens of Homer and Port Watson. Two lines of heavy cordage were attached to it; one leading to Homer, the other to Port Watson; and to each of these ropes were clinched the firm hands, as with a tiger's grasp, of several of the prominent and most influential leaders of the aggrieved parties. There they stood, pulling as if for life, resolved upon at least bringing the stupendous fabric to their notions of right, inasmuch as they had failed in securing the good will and approbating judgment of the self-willed commissioners. If they could not bring them to correct judgment, they could, at least, pull the magnificent structure down. But look again. On the other side of the *legal pile*, stands William Mallory, grasping a still heavier piece of cordage, determined on contesting the skill and strength of the opposing forces. There he stands, a proud representative of the immortal Wallace, of enormous form and determined will. His heels are imbedded in the earth, as he braces himself to the work of preservation.

But the scene was suddenly changed on turning the paper over, though the ludicrous picture was measurably the same. There it stood, an unyielding mass of timber,—of tenons and mortises. There stood the venerable Mallory, holding on to his undissevered rope, while a smile, peculiar to him alone, played over his flushed countenance. But where were his hitherto unyielding opponents? Their cords had parted, and forced them into the unpleasant attitude of turning double semi-circles down the declivated pathway.

The venerable pile that in former days

> "O'erlooked the town and drew the sight,"

long since failed to attract attention or gratify the pride of an enlightened and prosperous people. And in order to properly secure the ends of justice, the old structure was condemned and pronounced "unsafe," and measures were taken, which in due time resulted in the erection of the present court-house, which was completed in 1836.

The clerk's office was erected in 1819. The first county clerk was John Ballard, who was appointed April 8, 1808.

The county house, with one hundred and eighty-eight acres of land, was purchased in 1836, for $5,000. The house was originally erected by John Keep, at a very early day. It has been enlarged and variously improved at different periods.

At the time of our visit to the county-house, there were in all fifty-one paupers. The average number for several years past, as shown by the keeper's book, is a fraction over fifty-eight.

The ages of those bending under the weight of years, were variously classed as follows : two, fifty-five—one, sixty-six—two, sixty-nine—two, seventy-nine—three, eighty-five—four, eighty-nine—and one, ninety-two years.

Randall Bank, organized December 3, 1853. Capital $50,000. William R. Randall, *Banker.* Jonathan Hubbard, *Cashier.*

The Cortland County Medical Society was organized in 1808. The officers and members were as follows :

Lewis S. Owen, Homer, President.
John Miller, Truxton, V. President.
Jesse Searl, Homer, Secretary.
Robert D. Taggart, Preble, Treasurer.
Luther Rice, Homer.
Allen Barney, Homer.
Ezra Pannell, Truxton.
Elijah G. Wheeler.

Dr. John Miller, of Truxton, is the only living member of its original organization. The Association, with occasional amendments of by-laws, has been continued to the present day.

The Cortland County Agricultural Society was organized October 1, 1838. William Berry, President ; Jesse Ives and C. Comstock, Vice Presidents ; C. P. Jacobs, Recording Secretary ; H. S. Randall, Corresponding Secretary ; Rufus Boies, Treasurer ; Paris Barber, C. McKnight, Israel Boies, Morris Miller, and C. H. Harris, Executive Committee.

The Union Agricultural Society of Truxton, Willet, Marathon, and Lapeer, was organized in the winter of 1856.

The post-offices organized at various periods, are as follows :

Blodget Mills,	Willet,
Cincinnatus,	Cortland Village,
Cuyler,	East Freetown,
East Homer,	East Scott,
East Virgil,	Freetown Corners,
Galatia Valley,	Harford,
Homer,	Kinney's Settlement,
Lapeer,	Little York,
M'Grawville,	Marathon,
Messengerville,	Preble,
Scott,	Solon,
South Cortland,	Taylor,
Texas Valley,	Truxton,
Union Valley,	Virgil.

County Judges.

John Keep, appointed	April	3,	1810.	Fed.
William Mallory, "	Jan.	31,	1823.	Buch.
Joseph Reynolds, "	March	9,	1833.	Jack.
Henry Stephens, "	May	17,	1838.	Dem.
Daniel Hawkes, elected	June,		1847.	Whig.
Lewis Kingsley, "	Nov.	7,	1851.	Whig.
R. Holland Duell, "	Nov.	6,	1855.	Rep.

County Clerks.

John Ballard, appointed	April	8,	1808.	Dem.
Reuben Washburn, "	"	3,	1810.	Fed.
John Ballard, "	March	4,	1811.	Dem.
Mead Merrill, "	April	2,	1813.	Fed.
William Mallery, "	March	2,	1815.	Dem.
Joshua Ballard, "	July	7,	1819.	Clin.
Matthias Cook, "	Feb.	14,	1821.	Clin.
Sam'l Hotchkiss, jr., elected			1822.	B.
Orin Stimson, "			1834.	Whig
Gideon C. Babcock, "			1840.	Whig.
Sam'l Hotchkiss, jr., "			1843.	Dem.
Rufus A. Reed, "			1849.	Whig.
Rufus A. Reed, "			1852.	Whig.
Rufus A. Reed, "			1855.	Rep.
Allis W. Ogden, "			1858.	Rep.

District Attorneys.

Augustus A. Donnelly,	1819.	Clin.
Edward C. Reed,	1827.	Dem.
William H. Shankland,	1836.	Jack.
Horatio Ballard,	1844.	Dem.
Augustus S. Ballard,	1847.	Whig.

R. Holland Duell,	1850.	Whig.
Edward C. Reed, appointed	1856.	Dem.
Abram P. Smith, elected	1856.	Rep.

COUNTY TREASURERS.

Justin M. Pierce,	Nov.	1848.	Whig.
Edwin F. Gould,	"	1851.	Whig.
Isaac M. Seaman,	"	1854.	Whig.
Horace L. Green,	"	1857.	Rep.

SCHOOL COMMISSIONERS.

Noah C. Dady, appointed	June	10, 1856.	Amer.
Dan C. Squires, "	June	10, 1856.	Dem.
Noah C. Dady, elected		1857.	Amer.
Daniel E. Whitmore,		1857.	Rep.

SHERIFFS.

Asahel Minor,		April	8, 1808.	Dem.
Wm. Mallery,	appointed	June	9, 1808.	Dem.
Joshua Ballard,	"	April	3, 1810.	Dem.
Billy Trowbridge,	"	Mar.	25, 1814.	Dem.
William Stewart,	"	"	2, 1815.	Dem.
Noah R. Smith,	"	Feb.	13, 1819.	Clin.
Moses Hopkins,	"	"	12, 1821.	Buck.
Moses Hopkins,	elected		1822.	Buck.
David Coye,	"		1825.	Buck.
Adin Webb,	"		1828.	Antima.
William Andrews,	"		1831.	Union.
Gilmore Kinney,	"		1834.	Whig.
E. W. Edgcomb,	"		1837.	Whig.
Alanson Carley,	"		1840.	Whig.
Christian Etz,	"		1843.	Dem.
George Ross,	"		1846.	Dem.

J. C. Pomeroy,	elected	1849.	Whig.
Frederick Ives,	"	1852.	Whig.
John S. Samson,	"	1855.	Rep.
Silas Baldwin,	"	1858.	Rep.

SURROGATES.*

John McWhorter,	app'd	April	8, 1808.	Dem.
Mead Merrill,	"	"	3, 1810.	Fed.
Luther F. Stevens,	"	March	4, 1811.	Dem.
Adin Webb,	"	"	9, 1816.	Fed.
Jabez B. Phelps,	"	"	27, 1823.	B.
Charles W. Lynde,	"	April	15, 1828.	Dem.
Townsend Ross,	"	March	9, 1832.	Jack.
Anthony Freer,	"	May	4, 1836.	J.
Adin Webb,	"	"	4, 1840.	Whig.
Anthony Freer,	"	"	4, 1844.	Dem.

MEMBERS OF ASSEMBLY.

Ephraim Fish,	elected	1810.	Dem.
Billy Trowbridge,	"	1811.	Dem.
" "	"	1812.	Dem.
" "	"	1813.	Dem.
William Mallery,	"	1814.	Dem.
S. G. Hatheway,	"	1815.	Dem.
Joseph Reynolds,	"	1816.	Dem.
John Miller,	"	1817.	Dem.
S. G. Hatheway,	"	1818.	Dem.
Joseph Reynolds,	"	1819.	Dem.
John Miller,	"	1820.	C.
John Osborn,	"	1821.	B.

* Since the adoption of the Constitution of 1846, this office has been merged in that of the County Judge.

Daniel Sherwood, elected	1822.	B.
" " "	1823.	B.
John Gillett, "	1823.	B.
Matthias Cook, "	1824.	C.
William Barto, jr., "	1824.	C.
Josiah Hart, "	1825.	B.
J. Chatterton, "	1825.	C.
John Lynde, "	1826.	B.
Augustus A. Donnelly, "	1826.	C.
Nathan Dayton, "	1827.	B.
Cephas Comstock, "	1827.	C.
Nathan Dayton, "	1828.	D.
John L. Boyd, "	1828.	D.
Gideon Curtis, "	1829.	Antima.
Alanson Carley, "		A.
Henry Stephens, "	1830.	W.
Chauncey Keep, "		W.
Fredus Howard, "	1831.	Jack.
Charles Richardson, "		J.
Andrew Dickson, "	1832.	J.
J. L. Woods, "		J.
David Mathews, "	1833.	W.
Enos S. Halbert, "		W.
Oliver Kingman, "	1834.	J.
S. Bogardus, "		J.
Barak Niles, "	1835.	W.
Aaron Brown, "		W.
Chauncey Keep, "	1836.	W.
Cephas Comstock, "		W.
Josiah Hine, "	1837.	W.
John Thomas, "		W.
John Osgood, "	1838.	W.

David Mathews, elected		1838.	W.
G. S. Green,	"	1839.	W.
George Issacs,	"		W.
Jabez B. Phelps,	"	1840.	W.
William Barnes,	"		W.
Nathan Heaton,	"	1841.	W.
Lovel G. Mickels,	"		W.
Oren Stimson,	"	1842.	W.
Jesse Ives,	"		W.
H. M'Graw,	"	1843.	W.
George N. Niles,	"		D.
J. Kingman, jr.,	"	1844.	D.
Platt F. Grow,	"		D.
John Pierce 2nd,	"	1845.	D.
Geo. J. J. Barber,	"		W.
Amos Graves,	"	1846.	D.
John Miller,	"		W.
Timothy Green,	"	1847.	W.
James Comstock,	"	1848.	W.
Ira Skeel,	"	1849.	W.
Lewis Kingsley,	"	1850.	W.
Alvan Kellog,	"	1851.	W.
Geo. W. Bradford,	"	1852.	W.
Ashbel Patterson,	"	1853.	D.
John H. Knapp,	"	1854.	W.
Geo. J. Kingman,	"	1855.	R.
Joseph Atwater,	"	1856.	R.
Nathan Bouton,	"	1857.	R.
Arthur Holmes,	"	1858.	R.

The interest manifested by numerous prominent political actors, with reference to our full and complete table of county officers, from its organization in 1808 to the present time, with the names of the various parties to which they were attached, has induced us to add a comprehensive list of State, Congressional, and Senatorial members which have been chosen from this county.

SECRETARY OF STATE.

Henry S. Randall, Cortland, elected 1851. Dem.

REPRESENTATIVES IN CONGRESS.

	Elected.	Session.	
John Miller, Truxton,	1824	19.	C.
Edward C. Reed, Homer,	1830	22.	D.
Sam'l G. Hatheway, Solon,	1832	23.	J.
Joseph Reynolds, Virgil,	1834	24.	J.
Lewis Riggs, Homer,	1840	27.	D.
Harmon S. Conger, Cortland,	1846	30.	W.
Harmon S. Conger, "	1848	31.	W.
R. Holland Duell,	1858	36.	R.

MEMBERS OF THE NEW YORK SENATE.

	Elected.	Session.	
William Mallery, Cortland,	1818	40.	D.
Samuel G. Hatheway, Solon,	1822	46.	B.
Chas. W. Lynde, Homer,	1830	54.	W.
Wm. Bartlit, Cortland,	1841	65.	D.
Geo. W. Bradford, Homer,	1853	77.	W.
Geo. W. Bradford, "	1855	78.	W.

In 1855 there were in the county 3,388 farmers and agriculturists, 95 merchants, 56 clergymen, 20 lawyers, 49 doctors, 32 inns, 184 school-houses, 6,426 names of pupils on teachers' lists—average attendance, 4,157.

No. of churches, 51—valued at $99,900. Real estate on which they are located, valued $18,100. Salaries of clergymen, $17,164. Argricultural products, 1,212,074 bushels. Value of orchard products, $24,613. Value of market gardens, $508. Gallons wine, 81. Dairy products, 3,087,936 lbs. Tons of hay, 56,769. Clover seed, 866 bushels. Other grass seeds, 1,585 bushels. Hops, 10,327 lbs. Flax seed, 1,978 bushels. Wool, 120,793 lbs. Maple sugar, 521,052 lbs. Maple molasses, 2,769 gallons. Beeswax and honey, 24,360 lbs. Cloth, 21,800 yds. Common school libraries, 184. Number of volumes in Dist. School libraries, 19,669. Aggregate population, 24,957. There were 245 persons who could neither read nor write ; there were 95 who could read, but not write. Number of colored persons, 30. Owners of land, 4,212. The oldest person residing in the county (1855) was Margaret Berry, of Taylor, age 106 years.

In 1840 there were seventy-nine persons entitled to pensions for Revolutionary or military services. Of these, twelve resided in Truxton, fifteen in Cortland, eleven in Homer, eight in Preble, two in Scott, fifteen in Virgil, two in Solon, six in Cincinnatus, two in Marathon, three in Freetown, and four in Willet. In 1855 there were none reported.

Assessed Valuation of Real Estate for 1855,	$5,352,153 00
Assessed valuation of personal property,	530,691 00
Aggregate taxation, 1855,	29,909 49
Military tax, do.	543 00

INCORPORATED COMPANIES LIABLE TO TAXATION.

Syracuse, Binghamton and New York Railroad, and Randall Bank.

Assessed valuation of Syracuse, Binghamton and New York Railroad, in the towns through which it passes, is as follows :

Cortlandville,	$30,000
Homer,	30,000
Lapeer,	1,000
Marathon,	18,000
Preble,	30,000
Virgil,	5,000
Assessed valuation of Randall Bank,	50,000

It is a matter of no little astonishment to the enterprising and progressive tourist, as he visits our county, —with 194,736 acres of improved land, her beautiful farms, green pastures, watered by lovely streams, and her quiet picturesque villages located in her rich valleys, like gems in a golden casket,—that so little attention should be given to the growing of fruit. In 1855, the Marshals reported the number of bushels of apples grown in Tompkins county at 417,757 ; in Cayuga, 522,751 ; in Chenango, 553,554 ; in Onondaga, 624,545 ; and in Cortland, 351,975. The reader will readily perceive that Cortland county falls far behind either of the sister counties above quoted. Our soil and climate is not as well adapted to the growth of the peach and quince ; but we believe that all the prominent fruits may be equally well grown here.

The wealth of our county does not lie in jewelled

skulls and golden shrines, but in a commerce which enriches our agricultural producers.

The neglect in the culture of the apple is attributable to several causes, but mainly to the want of good, healthy nurseries. Until within a few years, no permanent nursery had been provided from which to secure the various trees for transplanting into orchards. A second, and most excellent reason is, that the people have been sadly imposed upon by men of little or no experience in the science of grafting. The permanent nursery of Messrs. D. C. Hobart and E. H. Knapp, in the town of Homer, comprising about thirty thousand grafted trees, of the most choice varieties, must eventually add greatly to the wealth of the county, as well as to the convenience and comfort of those who purchase and propagate the more desirable qualities of fruit.

The first and only death-penalty inflicted in Cortland county, occurred September 2d, 1853, upon the person of Patrick O'Donohue, for the murder of Mrs. Jane Ann Kinney, of Truxton, September 3d, 1852. The particulars attending the bloody tragedy are briefly as follows: His daughter Elizabeth, a girl of ten years, had been forbidden to visit the house of Mrs. Kinney. But contrary to the expressed wish of the father, the little girl had disobeyed; and to escape the vengeance of his fiend-like temper, her two elder sisters secreted her in a ledge of ragged rocks, and then informed their father that she had been stolen away. O'Donohue hastened from his work in the woods, accompanied by his wife and two or three other children, all in a high state of excitement. He was falsely made to believe that the abductor was no other than the husband of Mrs. Kinney, whom he presumed to be his enemy.

Little did the daughters think of the sad and mournful tragedy that was soon to follow their improper deception. Little did they presume that their indiscretion was so soon to lead the father to imbue his hands in the heart's blood of an unwarned and unprotected mother and child ; that murder—black-hearted and fiend-like murder—was to be the result of their inconsiderate conduct, and in a few short hours to send the life current curdling to the heart of a whole community. What a reflection to be forced upon the mind of the erring girls—sad, mournful, and truly tragical !—a lesson to the young written in the warm blood of the innocent.

A search for the little girl was instituted, between the father and son, the former carrying a loaded gun. The search was not a prolonged one, as it was given up about the middle of the forenoon. At about this time Mrs. Kinney, and her daughter, Amanda Jane, were on their way to the residence of a neighboring family, and of necessity had to pass the house of O'Donohue. Just as they drew near the gate leading to the barn, they were met by the murderer, who angrily asked Mrs. Kinney if she had seen Elizabeth. Receiving a negative answer, he flew into a terrible passion, leveled his gun and fired at Mrs. Kinney; the contents of the deadly weapon, however, merely glazed her side, causing her to reel or stagger. His uncontrolled temper now raged with greater fury in his unrelenting and fiendish breast. Hastily reversing the position of his gun, he struck her several blows with the butt end, the second of which dislocated her neck, causing immediate death. Not yet satisfied, but like a demon hot from the infernal pit, he flew at the daughter, who in the mean time had fallen from fright, and plunged a bayonet into her body, from which spirted the vital current of life. And although the fatal instrument was seized by the wounded and dying girl, it was quickly wrested from her grasp, and with a desperation scarcely equaled in the bloody records of crime, was again and again plunged into her body. And while the younger victim of O'Donohue's cruelty was yet weltering in her warm heart's blood, Charles McKnight, who had left his house at or about 10 o'clock A. M., for the purpose of superintending some work, was attracted by certain suspicious actions of the murderer's son to the place where the horrid deed was committed. A most revolting and heart-sickening scene at once met his sight. There lay the wife, the mother,—bleeding, ghastly, dead! A few feet distant lay the mangled form of the daughter, struggling in the terrible agonies of expiring nature. He heard her death groans, and saw her raise her hand, wet with her own blood, to wipe the death damps from her marble brow.

When Mr. McKnight first approached the spot where the fatal tragedy was enacted, his life was threatened by O'Donohue; yet he managed to get a fair view of the murdered victims. The heartless wretch still thirsted for more blood, and called to his wife to bring him some caps that he might assassinate another of his presupposed enemies, and add still another blot to his soul already crimsoned with the darkest hues of crime.

Before leaving him, Mr. McKnight advised him to go to the village and give himself up to the proper authorities, presuming him to be crazy; and as men laboring under the horrible malady of a diseased mind were not always responsible for their acts, perhaps he might not be hung. The advice, it would seem, was finally accepted, for O'Donohue, with his wife and son, did pass over the hills to the village, where he was finally arrested. But before leaving, under a fresh impulse of Satan, and as if to make his work of assassination more doubly certain, he returned to the bleeding, ghastly, and death-struggling victim, and again plunged the crimsoned steel into her breast.

Grim scowls pass'd o'er his dusky face
Like shadows in the midnight sky;
Each fiend-like passion mark'd its trace
By muttered oath or deep-drawn sigh;
With rolling eye,
And stifled breath,
He thought of blood, revenge, and death.

He was indicted at the October term of the County Court, 1852, and tried at the following July Court of Oyer and Terminer,—Hon. Schuyler Crippin, one of the justices of the Supreme Court, presiding, with associates John S. Dyer and Noah H. Osborne. R. H. Duell, District Attorney, and Gen. Nye, appeared on behalf of the people. Horatio Ballard and Daniel Gott, counsel.

The charge of the Judge was able, forcible and pointed. The Jury, after an absence of forty minutes, returned into Court with a verdict of "Guilty of Murder."

The records of the Court contain entry of his sentence, [Aug. 3d, 1853.]

The sentence was duly executed, and the spirit of O'Donohue was ushered uncalled for into the presence of his Maker, wreaking with the blood of the innocent.

After the last and final struggle between the American Republic and the Kingdom of Great Britain, the pioneers of the Tioughnioga valley, and indeed of the yet infant county of Cortland, began to look forward to the successful achievement of such measures as the wisdom of our State legislature might devise for the better development of science and the progress of art.

It was most evident that the Tioughnioga river, as a commercial highway, could never be available to any great extent, and that other channels of communication must be provided in order to encourage enterprise and reward adventure. State roads had been laid out and were measurably improved ; and the county had been cut up into gores or townships, while each of these was made to resemble an imperfect checker board, being variously marked out by "bridle paths," or to say the least, very undesirable roads. Yet poor as they were, the brave pioneers regarded them as acquisitions of great importance. Post horses and post coaches once, and finally twice a week, gladdened the sight of the toil-worn laborer. The Erie Canal, commenced in 1817 and completed in 1825, established a more direct line of communication with the eastern cities. Previous to this, the heavy goods of our merchants were brought up to Albany by way of the North river ; were then conveyed by land to Schenectady ; then through the canal at Little Falls ; then through Wood creek, Oneida lake, Onondaga river and the Tioughnioga, or were transported by land-carriage from Albany or Utica.

Cattle were usually driven to the Philadelphia market; potash was sent to New York or Montreal ; wheat was shipped on rafts and arks down the Tioughnioga and Susquehanna to Baltimore.

In 1826 there was a charter granted by the New York legislature for the construction of a railroad from Syracuse to Binghamton. This was the first charter ever granted by the legislature of this State. Internally shut out from the natural advantages or the more remote benefits of artificial communication with which other sections of country were blessed, the citizens located on the rich flats of Cortland, Homer and Preble, were made thrice joyful in their exultations of success. The toils, the sacrifices, and the cost of building a railroad had not, however, been fully considered or counted, and hence the active projectors were doomed, like the inexperienced alchemist, to see their golden dreams fade away.

As the country increased in population and productive resources, renewed efforts were made to revive or obtain a new charter. But up to 1848–9 nothing of importance took place.

In the mean time the growing West had become populous, while her commercial products were of an almost unlimited magnitude. Trade east and west had materially increased, as the various avenues of communication fully evinced. The store-houses contiguous to the great northern lakes were filled to their utmost capacity with the valuable products of the fertile fields of a rich and vigorous soil. The Erie canal, then the most powerful artery of trade in the Union, and though practically of very great importance, was found to be insufficient for the demands. The New York and Erie Railroad was projected and was rapidly hurrying to completion, while connecting links were put under contract, or completed, with, in many instances, "only a remote possibility of appropriating" a very small portion of that constantly increasing trade. The coal fields of the Lackawanna valley were laid open, and the black diamonds, which were really of more importance than the bloated mines of the Pacific coast, were exhumed, and a railroad was projected and completed, which united them with the Erie road at Great Bend, fifteen miles from Binghamton. The city of Oswego sat like a golden gem upon the shore of the lake, bearing the proud appellation of "Ontario's maritime port." Syracuse, the central city, was admirably spread out like a great heart in the centre of the State, with her salt springs to "preserve and enrich the empire." And the village of Binghamton, with her ten thousand enterprising inhabitants, sat queenlike upon the classic shores of the beautiful Susquehanna and Chenango, "receiving tribute and homage from both." These important locations were regarded with very great favor, and especially, when glancing at the map of the United States, it appeared positively evident that they were located within the most eligible and certainly the best commercial route from the seaboard to the great lakes of the west. The result thus far most amply verifies the conclusion. A few of the original charter petitioners went to work with renewed energies. The legislature was again petitioned, and a second charter granted. Meetings were called in various sections, and the people were ably and eloquently addressed with reference to the propriety of immediate action in behalf of the laudable enterprise. Books were opened for subscription, and early in 1850 the footings seemed to warrant the necessary survey to be made. Thus encouraged, the enterprising actors, most of whom resided in the growing villages of Homer and Cortland, redoubled their exertions, and with their shoulders at the wheel, determined to push on the car of progress. W. B. Gilbert, Esq., an accomplished, and indeed one of the most competent and energetic engineers in the State, was employed to make the necessary survey.

It is not our province to refer to all the opposing influences that were brought to bear against the speedy organization of the Company, or the immediate construction of the road—of the difficulties and delays attending the former—the almost unexampled stringent monetary pressure threatening to arrest the latter. These are already matters of history. They have been set forth in the more than thrilling eloquence of a Baldwin, or the persuasive and touching language of a Lawrence. The shock, though it swept over our country like the destroying host of Attila over the plains of Italy, arresting the progressive labors "of most other companies that were struggling into being," happily had become too much weakened to produce a suspension, and the work went steadily on "from its commencement in 1852 to its completion in 1854." Great credit is awarded to the various efficient actors in Cortland county, for to them belongs the honor of having revived or called up from the tomb of the Capulets the old exploded sympathies which finally terminated in securing for the project enough of popular sentiment to place the completion of the road beyond a reasonable doubt. Nor were the active efforts of prominent citizens of Binghamton, Syracuse and Oswego unimportant or unappreciated. Their highly valued influence was productive of the most favorable results, and when their purse strings were unloosed, or their bank deposits called forth, the cheering word of "liberality" was echoed and re-echoed from one end of the Tioughnioga valley to the other.

The road having been completed, a formal opening to the public took place on the 18th and 19th of October, 1854. Returning from an eastern tour, with our family, we joined the excursion party at Binghamton. The train consisted of twenty-seven passenger cars, which were crowded to such an extent that it was impossible for only a portion to be seated. It was reported by the editor of the Railroad Journal as a "perfect jam, the people numbering twenty thousand." Our estimate fell somewhat short of this round number. The display at the various stations presented a somewhat truthful conception of the joy of the citizens. From every church that had a bell went forth a joyous welcome ; cannons were fired ; and bonfires and illuminations signalized the auspicious event.

The road passes through one of the most delightful and productive valleys in the State. The scenery on either side is picturesque and beautiful.

The stockholders number about two thousand.

The total cost of the road up to November 5th, 1855, is reported by Mr. Gilbert to be $2,274,394 33. Its length is eighty miles.

Aggregate miles run by all engines during the year, 272,777. Number of passengers carried in the cars, 234,560. Amount of earnings for the same number of months is reported at $159,489 91. Expense of operating the road, $136,981 62.

It will be readily seen that the earnings fall considerably short of the original estimates. This seeming failure is satisfactorily accounted for by the Superintendent. In our mind there is no depreciation of real value. We never supposed that the estimates would be reached under the existing circumstances.

The Lake trade has been realized only to a limited extent.

"When this work was projected, the invariable and strong argument used for its construction, in reference to profitable results, was a continuous line to Lake Ontario, by which alone it could derive the benefits of that trade.

"The Directors having been unable to attain this, through the existing road from Syracuse to the lake, another Company was organized under the General Act, for the purpose of constructing a broad guage road on the east side of Onondaga lake and the Oswego river. But the necessity of an arrangement with the holders of Mortgage Bonds of the Company, whereby they could agree to withold action under the existing mortgages during the construction of the new road, suspended operations.

"Up to 1855 no agreement had been effected, which the Directors regretted, as the delay increased the financial embarrassment under which the Company labored."

In 1856 the stockholders were unable to complete the road to Oswego, as contemplated, or even to the Erie Canal, for the delivery of coal and other freight, or to meet their bonded and other debts, and consequently the bondholders were obliged to foreclose and sell the road in October of the same year. The Company was subsequently reörganized, the road finished, and extended to the Erie Canal, and the track and machinery put in perfect repair. There was also an arrangement made at Binghamton with the New York and Erie Railroad Company, to accommodate the cars of the Delaware, Lackawanna and Western Railroad Company, for the transportation of their coal and other freight, making the Syracuse, Binghamton and New York Railroad the proper channel for the transportation of their coal to the Erie Canal at Syracuse, and to Lake Ontario at Oswego, the Canadas and the great west.

Since the road has been thus reörganized, it has already proven profitable as an investment to the holders thereof, having, as we understand, paid the interest on its cost, and will be, as it is designed, extended to Lake Ontario, at Oswego, forming a continuous line of broad guage road to New York and Philadelphia, and in the event prove one of the best routes for travel and freight, and will realize all that was predicted or expected by its early friends as a richly remunerating investment.

The Syracuse, Binghamton, and New York Railroad may, with propriety, be regarded as an invaluable link in the chain of communication between Lake Ontario and the Atlantic cities.

The lake trade is immense, and must continue to be for all future time. The inexhaustible resources of the great west, with her fertile fields, her agricultural and mineral productions, and the vast amount of eastern merchandise that is necessary to meet her unprecedented increase of population—the greater portion of which must pass east or west through the State of New York.

"The value of foreign imports from Canada at the port of Oswego was in 1845 $41,313, and in 1855 it was over $6,000,000. The whole value of import and export trade with Canada in 1845 was $2,350,409, and in 1855, over $12,000,000.

"Under the operation of the Reciprocity treaty, the trade both ways with Canada has more than doubled in 1855 over the preceding year, 1854. In 1845 the whole foreign and domestic trade of Oswego, imports and exports, did not exceed $8,000,000, and in 1855 it amounted to over $40,000,000. The tonnage of vessels enrolled and licensed at this port shows a corresponding increase."*

The free-trade principle of Canada gives to the port of Oswego a powerful increase of business.

"For six months ending September 30th last, the duties chargeable on imports arriving at Oswego, and going east in bond, were $186,009 87, in addition, the value of these bonded imports being $930,107 49."†

The flour of Oswego, the salt, gypsum, water and quick lime, and marble of Onondaga—the vast agricultural products of a wide and fertile surrounding country, with the iron and coal of the Lackawanna and Wyoming valleys, will give to the Syracuse, Binghamton and New York Railroad an amount of local tonnage which will surpass that of any other road of the same length in the Union.

* J. M. Schermerhorn's Report, 1855.

† W. B. Gilbert's Report, 1855.

The coal trade is to be one of great importance. If in the single city of Syracuse 2,000 cords of wood are used per day for the manufacture of salt, and otherwise, at five dollars per cord, what are we to presume will be the sum total of the coal that will be conveyed over the road when properly connected with Oswego ?

The road is regarded as being one of the best built and equipped in the State.

The agents have uniformly been enterprising and active business men ; the conductors attentive, obliging, and gentlemanly.

The retirement of the able and courteous president, Hon. Henry Stephens, was widely regretted, yet his post has been admirably filled in the person of Jacob M. Schermerhorn, Esq., to whose unremitting and laborious exertions the Company are mainly indebted for the final completion, and the present prosperity of the road. No man ever labored harder. No man ever succeeded under more, if under equally, discouraging circumstances. He should have his reward.

CHAPTER XIV.

HUNTING INCIDENTS.

Hound-like they scent the track.

In previous chapters we have incidentally referred to the various species of animals that inhabited the wilderness, and against whom the pioneers waged a crusade, even with musket ball and rapier knife. The repose of the settlers was frequently disturbed by the terrific howl of the wolf, the piercing scream of the great northern panther, and the unfriendly growl of the old shaggy black bear of the hemlock forest. The flocks and herds were often preyed upon to an alarming extent, and the bold pioneers were not unfrequently placed in imminent peril. They had left the happy hearth-stones of their native land, and had pitched their tents in the valleys and on the hill-sides of this then western boundary of civilization ; and, unpleasant as it was, were of necessity compelled to wage an exterminating war against these more than savage beasts of prey. The heart chills at the recital of the often narrow escapes from the jaws of the gaunt, hungry wolf, the more prowling, rapacious panther, or the unsociable hug of the unterrified, snarling old bear.

The tender-hearted might shrink back at the howl of a single wolf, even in the day time ; but it took a whole clan, headed by a huge grizzly chorister, whose discordant howls, snaps, and snarls made night—dark, tartarean night—tenfold more hideous, to make the veteran forest hunter quail, or feel for the particular location of his heart. The women, too,—the bold republican women,—were occasionally called upon to exercise all the energies of a bold and noble spirit. We are told of one who was pursued for a distance through a winding and unfrequented glen, by a panther, whose long, greedy proportions told too truly of his powerful strength. If she hastened her step, the animal did the same. If she stopped short, he instinctively squatted as if preparing to leap upon his unarmed victim. She saw her peril, and resolved to make one bold effort at deliverance. Seizing a bludgeon of wood, she flew at him in a menacing attitude, uttering several successive screams as she dealt him a severe blow on that point of the proboscis which brought forth a hasty snuff and a sneeze, and turning upon his well-practised and flippant heels, he made a number of enormous leaps, and then seated himself in the branches of a partially decayed hemlock. Remembering that she was near the cabin of a successful and fearless hunter, she screamed with all her might for the bow-legged marksman. The animal not particularly relishing his treatment from the hand of the fair patroness, began to exhibit the most unmistakable evidence of a preparation to leap upon the bold defender of her forest rights. A moment more, and he hoped to gorge his ferocious rapacity with her warm heart's blood. But the sharp crack of a rifle was heard some twenty rods distant, just as he drew himself back to leap, and the next moment the long proportions of the mountain veteran were stretched dead at her feet. In the trunk of the decaying ancient relic, a couple of nursling "*painters*" were found. But in the very instant of leaving with them, the father, an old crippled martyr, who had snuffed upon the breeze the fresh scent of blood, was rapidly approaching. Another leaden missile, hurled from the old blue barrel, brought him to the ground. But he was not yet prepared to yield, for the victory was not yet achieved. The hunter succeeded in only partially reloading his gun before the maddened animal had sprung to his feet, and was ready for a contest or measurement of strength. The youthful matron stood by the side of her deliverer, resolving to share in the glory of victory, or die with him in a noble effort at resistance. On he came, ten times more ferocious, but was defiantly met with such a succession of blows as to induce him to retreat and take a position in a small tree, where he might look contempt upon his assailants. The old blue barrel was again leveled with unerring aim, and in an instant the panther's brains were lying at the base of the tree.

At an early day, and at a period when Marathon was yet a wilderness, and when but a few families were located within her rugged confines, the bears, wolves and panthers made terrible havoc with the stock and poultry of the but partially protected and often unarmed pioneers. During the latter part of November, 1799, an old hunter, and native of Long Island, was passing through the country lying between the Tioughnioga river and what is now known as Freetown Centre.

Ascending the rugged elevation, he struck an Indian trail leading in a direct line for the "pine woods." He had, however, proceeded but a short distance before he heard a sharp, piercing scream, as if coming from a female in distress. In a moment it was repeated again and again. Hurrying forward he soon heard it much plainer, and at intervals could distinctly hear moaning, as if coming from some object in nature that was suffering from the infliction of some horrible treatment. His anxiety was soon relieved, for just as he reached the summit of a little elevation, perhaps three-fourths of a mile west of the "panther forest," he saw to his astonishment an enormous panther spring upon a deer that was floundering upon the ground, and almost covered with blood. The old and unarmed hunter paused for a moment, that he might observe the movements of the half-enraged animal, and the better concentrate his scattered thoughts ; and was pained to hear the moans of the wounded and dying deer, as the panther screamed and then suddenly sprang upon his prey, burying his claws in the sides of the deer, and his tusks in the neck, tearing the flesh from the body. He knew it would be very unsafe for him to attack the panther, as he was but partially gorged with blood, and he therefore chose the better part of valor and hurried on his way ; but he was suddenly startled by a noise behind him which appeared like the sudden springs of a panther. Remembering that he had a few pounds of fresh venison which he was carrying to a sick friend, and knowing the danger of an encounter with such an animal, he picked up a heavy bludgeon of wood and quickened his steps until he came to the "mammoth log ;" then hastily cutting his venison into three parts, he threw one piece just into the mouth of the log, and the balance at a short distance from each side of it. He had hardly taken a position to await his approach, before he saw the bloody panther within a few feet of him. It was now night, but luckily the moon rolled forth from behind a dark cloud as he saw the animal nearing the huge opening which he endeavored to enter, for he had scented the fresh meat. The old man suddenly sprang to his feet and dealt the animal a heavy blow on the back, which rendered him partially powerless. The panther drew back, uttering a horrible groan, which was followed by several screams ; these were, however, soon silenced by a few more well-directed blows.

His hide was hurriedly stripped from his body, and the dauntless pioneer retraced his steps, arriving home near midnight.

The next day a grand hunt was proposed and entered into, which resulted in the death of three panthers, five wolves, and six bears. Three of the wolves, however, were not taken until the morning of the second day, when they were holed near Chenango Forks, and hastily despatched.

Three persons started out in March of 1799 in pursuit of bears, which had committed unwarrantable depredations in the town of Scott. One of them soon gave out and returned, but the other two continued the pursuit, the trail leading in the direction of Skaneateles lake ; but the snow being very deep, they, too, finally gave up, and concluded to return home by a circuitous route, in the hope of meeting with an old bear which had wintered within a mile or so of their home. As they approached the place of concealment he was discovered. Both hunters immediately discharged their guns, but only wounded the bear. He hastily left for other quarters, followed by his pursuers, who after camping out near Skaneateles lake for the night, drove him into a clearing some eight miles from home, in Sempronius, where they took off his hide, out of which they made each of them a cap, as they had lost theirs the day before, and were therefore hatless.

There are numerous instances showing the firmness and forethought of many a matron lady. A single example will suffice to exhibit them in their proper light: David Scofield, of Virgil, informed us that when he was but a lad, and while playing upon a brush fence, he accidentally fell off into the brush. He was immediately seized by a bear about two-thirds grown, who hastened away with him. It being near the house of his father, his aged grandmother observed them, and hastily snatching up a hot loaf of bread hurried to his relief; and just as he was entering his den she threw him the bread, at which he dropped the child and secured the warm loaf, of which he made a hearty meal.

Wolves frequently followed the hunter's trail in droves, making the night hideous with frightful, fiendish howling. There is, perhaps, no other animal which exhibits so much of the real demon, as the half-starved, lean, lank wolf, as he pursues his intended prey, eager and anxious to surfeit on the warm, gurgling blood, of which he is particularly fond. We repeat, upon the authority of one who frequently engaged in the chase,—not merely for the sake of stilling their "eternal snapping and snarling," but because he liked the sport,—

a case in point, which, though it did not tend to immortalize his name, gave him great credit for the courage which prompted the encounter. He had been out on the border line of Cortland and Chenango; and while returning upon his almost indistinct trail through the snow, he was followed by a hungry gang of wolves. He was met by a huge panther, who appeared determined to contest the right of soil on which they had thus unexpectedly met. With the wolves snapping at his heels in the rear, while the unterrified panther had blockaded his advance progress, he paused but a moment's time for reflection. The moon, peering out from behind a dark cloud, enabled him to draw a close sight upon the barrel of his unerring rifle, when suddenly a leaden missile went whizzing through the panther's brain. A moment more, and the whole pack of wolves had seized upon the dead animal and were lapping up the blood and brains that were scattered around him. Taking advantage of this propitious moment, he hastily took refuge some thirty feet high in the branches of a bushy hemlock. Here he resolved to remain until morning, or conquer in the unequal contest. Hastily loading his gun, he again brought it to such a level as would enable him to see with exactness the forward sight, when the rifle cracked again, and the bloody ghosts of two of the ferocious wolves had departed; and thus he continued until he had impartially extended the same treatment to three more of the gang. The others becoming alarmed at the frequent reports of the death-dealing weapon, made a hasty retreat for the unexplored *lagoon*.

During the early part of the present century, the

antlered deer bounded through the forest, not doubting their right to the supremacy of the territory through which they thus proudly ranged. They were almost as numerous as the dairymen's cattle are at the present day. Authority of the most positive character might be referred to in support of the truthfulness of our assertion. Twenty, and even thirty, noble bucks have been counted in a drove, as they swept through the woods pursued by the hunter's well-trained dogs. One old hunter, a Frenchman, whose home was among the Wyoming hills, came to this county to spend the winter with a brother, and during his stay killed upwards of two hundred deer. We have been told by the grey-haired veterans of those stern days of toil and trial, of numerous instances of a hunter sallying out at daybreak, and before the hour of nine in the forenoon returning for lunch, having slain five, seven, and even as high as ten deer.

Notwithstanding the horrid crusade that has been waged for upwards of half a century against the graceful, sprightly, bounding deer, his progeny has not been fully exterminated, for even to this day, (1855,) an occasional buck, bearing aloft his noble antlers, may be seen bounding through the southern limits of this county. During the past autumn and early part of the winter, several were killed on and about Michigan Hill, in the town of Harford.

We remember how in our boyhood's days our young and ardent mind was inspired by the marvelous tales told by the hunters of our native county; and we have always had a strong desire to bring down a noble buck. But of the numerous droves that we have seen shaking their horns in the wild gorges of the North American forest, or as they tossed them aloft while they swept over the flowery glades of the sunny South, it has failed to be our luck to bring a rifle to bear directly upon them. The various interesting incidents told us by the stern veteran pioneers, would more than fill a volume of the size it is our province to write. And however interested they may have been in repeating them, we have seldom heard one told with more felicitous feeling than one which is related by Charles Hotchkiss, of Virgil.

A gentleman by the name of Turpening came up from Newburg, and felt very desirous to take a hunt. Mr. Hotchkiss told him that it would be very unsafe for him to proceed alone, for if he should happen to kill a deer it would bleat, and that would arouse every deer in hearing distance, and that they would assuredly kill him. His brothers, however, persuaded him to go. Having equipped himself in hunting order, he sallied forth for glorious war. Approaching the deer-lick south of Virgil Corners, he espied a young fawn just upon its outskirts. Keeping one eye on the gun and the other on the deer, he waited for the appearance of more, but not being gratified with their approach, he blazed away. As the gun cracked the fawn leaped several feet from the ground, gave a bleat, as is usual, and fell dead. Presuming the story of Mr. Hotchkiss to be true, and expecting a whole clan of mad, frightened deer to be upon him with their bloody antlers poised to gore him to the heart, he hurriedly made tracks for home, stripping off hat, coat, vest and boots, and hurling them to the ground; puffing and blowing for the want of breath, and with impeded powers of locomotion, he entered the pioneer's home declaring that every deer in the lick was at his heels, frothing and foaming; and that they had gored him almost to death.

John H. Hooker, son of Increase M. Hooker, an early pioneer of Truxton, now residing in New Brunswick, N. J., recently related to us some interesting incidents with reference to trapping the various animals of the wilderness. One plan was to dig a pit about six feet wide by twelve deep. Around this a pen, or kind of curb, would be raised from two to three feet high. Over the pit a pan would be placed, balanced properly, so that when an animal should spring upon it for the purpose of obtaining the bait, which was appropriately hung above it, the pan would turn and precipitate the monster into the pit. In this way Mr. Hooker and two other gentlemen caught in one night the very respectable number of five wolves. They were lassoed in the morning and led round and exhibited to the neighbors, after which they were dispatched.

In 1803, Mr. Hooker was watching at a deer-lick, and in consequence of the almost impenetrable darkness, was compelled to remain all night in the woods, a distance of five miles from his father's log cabin. During the night he heard the approach of an animal, and presently discovered, a few feet from him, two balls resembling liquid fire. The animal undoubtedly anticipated a warm meal. Mr. Hooker, not a little excited, raised his unerring rifle, looked quickly over the barrel, and fired. The monster gave a piercing scream and bounded away in the darkness. He was found at a little distance with his under jaw broken, and dead.

Mr. Hooker was much surprised on finding that he had killed a panther nine and a half feet in length. It was not an uncommon circumstance for him to be followed by panthers and wolves when in pursuit of his father's cattle. On one occasion he made a rather hasty flight from the sugar bush. A panther had made him a visit and desired to contest the right of soil; Mr. Hooker, however, preferred to defer the matter, and, as he informed us, if ever he made tracks he made them then, and he presumed them to be few and far between, for he could distinctly hear every jump of the huge monster behind him, and he was only relieved when within a few rods of the house by the watchful and ever trusty old dog.

CHAPTER XV.

LITERARY AND BENEVOLENT INSTITUTIONS.

"I'll note 'em in my book of memory."

THERE are but few, if any, counties in the State at present in the enjoyment of greater educational facilities than Cortland county. The Cortland and Cortlandville Academies—the former located at Homer and the latter at Cortland Village—are enjoying a good degree of prosperity. The New York Central College, located at M'Grawville, has had a somewhat chequered existence, and the Cincinnatus Academy, located in Cincinnatus, is in a flourishing condition.

The light of the sun was scarcely let in through the dense forests of Homer, upon its extended and fertile plains, ere the light of science sent its genial rays among her people.

The first settlers, being chiefly from Connecticut, brought with their books and their love of books, their school-master and their high regard for literary institutions.

Among the earlier school-teachers of Homer was Maj. Adin Webb. The active business men and the efficient housewives now living in Homer look upon that venerable priest of Minerva—still bearing high alike his whitened locks and his golden honors—with mingled feelings of gratitude and reverence.

From the common school, which he so long and so successfully taught on the spacious common in the centre of the village, grew the Cortland Academy, which has been, for forty years, nestled among the churches which adorn the same Common, and whose graceful spires so significantly point to the same great Source of Light and Love, as does the less pretending spire of the academic edifice.

Cortland Academy was incorporated by the Regents of the University of the State of New York on the 2d day of February, 1819. The first trustees were Dr. Lewis S. Owen, Hon. John Miller, John Osborn, David Coye, Chauncey Keep, Hon. Townsend Ross, Rufus Boies, N. R. Smith, Elnathan Walker, Andrew Dickson, Matthias Cook, Reuben Washburn, Jesse Searl, Martin Keep, Benasjah Tubbs, David Jones, and George Rice.

Of the original trustees, David Coye, Rufus Boies and Noah R. Smith have continued to serve as trustees—the places of the others having been made vacant by death or by resignation.

The present members of the Board of Trustees are Jedediah Barber, President; Hon. E. C. Reed, Secretary; Noah R. Smith, Treasurer; David Coye, Rufus Boies, Hon. Geo. W. Bradford, Hammond Short, John Sherman, Prof. S. B. Woolworth, Hon. Geo. J. J. Barber, Wm. Andrews, Ira Bowen, Caleb Cook, Geo. Cook, C. H. Wheadon, Rev. C. A. Clark, Noah Hitchcock, Thomas D. Chollar, J. M. Schermerhorn, Giles Chittenden, Esq., Wm. T. Hicok, Manly Hobart, and Rev. Albert Bigelow.

The late Rev. Alfred Bennett, Joshua Ballard, Charles W. Lynde, C. Chamberlain, A. Donnelly, Tilly Lynde, and Horace White, also served as Trustees.

The first Principal, under the charter, was Oren Catlin. He was, also, the sole teacher. To him succeeded successively Mr. Ranny, Noble D. Strong, Charles Avery, A. M., Franklin Sherrill, Oliver S. Taylor, M. D., Samuel B. Woolworth, A. M., (now LL. D.), and S. W. Clark, A. M.

Since 1821 there has been a Female Department connected with the Academy, under the supervision, successively, of Flavilla Ballard, Caroline R. Hale, Melona D. Moulton, Elizabeth Steele, Harriette A. Dellay, Catharine A. Coleman, Mary Bascom, Mary S. Patterson, Helen H. Palmer, Esther L. Brown, Anna J. Hawley, and Harriet S. Gunn.

Since 1830 the Musical Department has been continued under the supervision and instruction of Frances Rollo, Harriet Foot, Julia A. Gillingham, Abigail F. Moulton, Maria L. Reston, Mary Fessenden, Sarah E. Reed, J. M. Palmer, and Isabella Livingston Brunschweiler.

Of the Assistant Teachers there have served in the Department of Ancient Languages, Abel F. Kinney, A. M., Charles E. Washburn, A. M., (now, also, M. D.,) Henry A. Nelson, A. M., Ezra S. Gallup, A. M., J. M. Woolworth, A. M., and Heman H. Sanford, A. M.

In the Department of Mathematics, A. F. Ranney, A. M., Geo. R. Huntington, L. S. Pomeroy, A. M., Alvin Lathorp, A. M., W. H. Lacey, E. M. Rollo, A. M., A. J. Kneeland, Louis A. Miller, Charles S. Lawrence, and Joseph R. Dixon, A. M.

In the Department of Modern Languages, Augustus Maasberg, and Oscar M. Faulhaber.

In the English Department, there have been eighteen different teachers.

At the present term, (1859), the various departments are filled by the following :

TEACHERS.

Stephen W. Clark, A. M., Principal ; Miss Harriet S. Gunn, Preceptress ; Heman H. Sandford, A. M., Languages ; Frederick B. Downes, A. M., Mathematics ; Miss Harriet Taylor, Modern Languages ; James S. Foster, Natural Sciences ; Miss Lucy B. Gunn, English Department ; Mrs. Mary Lund and Miss Harriet D. Gaylord, Instrumental and Vocal Music ; Almon H. Benedict, Penmanship.

Of the sixty-six teachers who have been connected with the Academy, two only have died while at service. The first was Abel F. Kinney, " a man who will not cease to be loved and venerated so long as any live who felt the power of his soul, and observed the strong fellowship which existed between his principles and his life. It was his rare privilege to say, on his death-bed, that he *never received the slightest insult from any pupil* —a fact which those whom he taught may remember with gratitude, and which his biographer may record as eloquent praise on his character as an instructor. Mr. Kinney commenced teaching before he was twenty years of age, and died before he was thirty-five. Most of his life as a teacher was spent in Cortland Academy, and few persons have done more to make it what it is. Within our village burial ground his pupils have placed a marble monument to his memory. But still richer memorials of him are to be found in the personal recollections of those who knew him, and in the Wednesday evening meetings for prayer which he established.

The other was Louis A. Miller, a mathematician of rare promise, and a teacher of remarkable tact and energy. Beautiful and appropriate monuments, the offerings of grateful pupils, mark the resting-places of their dust in the village cemetery of Homer.

Since the organization of the Academy more than eight thousand different students have been instructed in it. Of these many are numbered among the most distinguished men in the State, in the Church, and in the various professions of science and art. "Many are now occupying places of usefulness and honor in their own country; others have gone to show the benighted millions of heathen lands the way of life, and others have gone to the land of rest and seraphic bliss, which knows no change, and where dwell the good, the pure, and the great."

Among the various Academies of the State, the Cortland Academy has been uniformly distinguished for its giving decided prominence to its Classical Department. During the last three years the average number of pupils in the department of Ancient Languages has been eighty, while the average number in attendance in all the departments has been 240.

The number of students annually reported to the Regents of the University, "as having pursued, for four months or upwards, classical studies or the higher branches of English education," has increased in each successive year to the present time—the report of 1858 showing 642 students thus reported :

The growth of the Academy has been gradual and healthful. The assets of the corporation are,

Value of land and building, . .	$5,100
" " library, . .	995
" " apparatus, . .	1,243
" " other property, .	6,375
Total, . . .	$13,713

Its annual income for 1858 from tuition bills, literature fund, and interest, was $4,449 58

Annual expenditure, ... 4,208 78

The Cortland Academy is pleasantly situated on the public square. It embraces various apartments for study and recitations, a well-selected library, philosophical apparatus, and every facility needed to impart a good, thorough, and practical education. Indeed, it is with much pleasure that we refer to Prof. S. W. Clark, the gentlemanly and accomplished Principal, and his able and competent assistants, under whose faithful discharge of duties the Academy is made an ornament to the place, as well as one of the best educational Academic Institutions in our State.

The Cortlandville Academy was incorporated by the Regents of the University in the year 1842, and commenced in August of that year.

The original officers were Joseph Reynolds, President ; Henry S. Randall, Secretary ; Joel B. Hibbard, Treasurer. The Trustees were J. Reynolds, Wm. Elder, H. S. Randall, Wm. Bartlit, James S. Leach, John J. Adams, Jno. Thomas, W. R. Randall, Asahel P. Lyman, Frederick Hyde, J. B. Hibbard, Horatio Ballard, Henry Stephens, Abram Mudge, James C. Pomeroy, Clark Pendleton, Anson Fairchild, Parker Crosby, L. S. Pomeroy, and Otis Stimson.

Among the first instructors were Joseph R. Dixon, A. M., Principal; Henry E. Ranney, Assistant ; Miss C. Ann Hamlin, Preceptress ; Miss Fanny M. Nelson, Assistant ; Miss Sarah M. Parker, Assistant during third term ; Miss Mary E. Mills, Teacher of Music.

The number of pupils reported August 1, 1848, was 216.

The Trustees made a very flattering report, and anticipated increasing prosperity. They congratulated themselves upon their good fortune in being able to retain their very able and popular Principal, Joseph R. Dixon. Mr. D. continued Principal for four successive years.

The present members of the Board of Trustees are Frederick Hyde, President; J. A. Schermerhorn, Secretary ; Morgan L. Webb, Treasurer ; Joseph Reynolds, Henry S. Randall, John J. Adams, Horatio Ballard, Henry Stephens, James C. Pomeroy, D. R. Hubbard, Henry Brewer, Ebenezer Mudge, Horace Dibble, Hamilton Putnam, Henry Bowen, W. O. Barnard, Madison Woodruff, Martin Sanders, Rufus A. Reed, James S. Squires, W. P. Randall, Thomas Keator, R. H. Duell, and George Bridge.

TEACHERS.

Henry Carver, A. M., Principal ; Miss Maria S. Welch, Preceptress ; Ridgway Rowley, Languages ; Miss Mary M. Bartlit, Primary Department ; Frederick Hyde, M. D., Lecturer ; Mrs. F. R. Mudge, Instrumental and Vocal Music ; Mrs. A. R. Bowen, Drawing and Painting.

The Academy is large and conveniently arranged, and is located in a healthy and pleasant part of Cortland Village, and the students in attendance number about 150.

The Institution is furnished with a new Philosophical and Chemical Apparatus, an extensive Library, and all the necessary means to impart a healthful and practical education. The prospects were, perhaps, at no time more flattering than at the present.

Prof. Carver, the accomplished Principal and instructor in Natural and Moral Science and the Higher Mathematics, is deservedly worthy of his well-earned reputation. His zealous and active efforts to promote and advance the interests of the Academy are justly and fully appreciated.

The well-arranged lectures of Prof. Hyde on Anatomy and Physiology, are like the sands which descend with La Plata's rushing torrent, rich with golden ore. They are, indeed, of marked importance to the Institution.

And it is but just to add that the Assistant Corps of Instructors are admirably fitted for their various positions ; hence the Academy will flourish, and continue to rank among the best educational institutions in the State.

New York Central College.—In 1846 the attention of

gentlemen of enlarged views and liberal sentiments, residing in this and other States, was turned to the necessity of establishing a Collegiate Institution which should be entirely free from sectarianism, while the tendency of its teachings should be favorable toward a true hearty christianity. They felt that the opportunity to gain a liberal education should be extended to all as impartially as are the light and air, and that the minds of students should rather be made free and independent, than moulded according to creeds or the dicta of fashion. They reflected long and earnestly upon the subject, and finally resolved to found an Institution of Learning, in which character, not circumstances, color, or sex, should be the basis of respect; in which the course of study should be full and useful to those who looked forward to a life in one of the learned professions, as well as to those who expected to devote their lives to honorable toil; in which labor should be regarded as eminently honorable, and facilities for engaging in it should be furnished as fully as practicable; in which the minds of students should be untrammeled by the restriction of the freedom of speech, and undarkened by the shadow of some great name; in which the most noble life of usefulness, and practical, impartial Christianity, and every incitement to such a life should be placed before the student. Calling upon those who sympathised with them in their effort for assistance, they raised an amount of money sufficient to found an Institution, and on the 12th day of April, 1848, a charter was granted by the Legislature to New York Central College, located at M'Grawville, and on the 5th of September following it was opened to students. The buildings were large and commodious, and to which was connected a farm of 167 acres, upon which students could labor for a fixed compensation, or, if preferred, might rent pieces of land to cultivate for themselves.

The number of students at first was small, and has not at any time been large. Everything that an able faculty could do to advance the interests of the Institution has been done, and yet the College has not prospered. Its friends are discouraged, and the Board of Directors disheartened. Present appearances indicate that the College will either pass into the hands of its colored friends, or be purchased by the citizens of M'Grawville, and be renovated and reörganised into a seminary or academic institution, or finally cease to exist as a College.

Prof. Leonard G. Calkins, the hitherto active and efficient Principal, has resigned his position, and entered an eminent law school in Albany, with a design to fit himself for the bar. He is a finished scholar, an accomplished orator, and a true gentleman ; a deep thinker, of active temperament, and is in all respects admirably qualified to fill the position to which he now aspires, and we doubt not he will prove an ornament to the legal profession.

Cincinnatus Academy owes its origin to the spirited efforts of a few of the citizens of Cincinnatus, through whose exertions a meeting was held in December, 1855, when a committee was appointed to solicit subscription for the purpose of erecting a suitable building for an academic school. A sufficient sum having been obtained, and plans and stipulations adopted, a building was erected by George L. Cole. It is delightfully situated in a retired part of the village of Cincinnatus, in the Otselic valley, and commands a beautiful view of the surrounding country. It is by far the most tasty educational edifice in the county. The rooms are spacious and airy, and are arranged with a due regard to comfort and convenience. In short, the building is in all respects an ornament to the town, and especially to the village in which it is located. And while it is honorable to the taste and enterprise of its founders, it reflects great credit on the architect.

On the 19th day of December, 1856, the Academy was first occupied as a school-room. Prof. Hatch, Principal, was a graduate of Madison University. Miss Mary T. Gleason, Preceptress, and Miss Mary Winters, Assistant. The school opened with the most flattering auspices, but for a variety of reasons, at the close of the first term Mr. Hatch resigned his position, and was succeeded by A. P. Kelsey, A. B.

In April, 1857, the Academy was incorporated by the Regents of the University of the State of New York.

Miss Gleason continued in her position as Preceptress until the 17th of March, 1858, when in consequence of the illness of her friends she resigned, and was succeeded by Miss A. A. Field, a graduate of Oneida Conference Seminary.

The institution is indebted to the liberality of the citizens of the village for a select library, consisting of 160 volumes, valued at $180 ; as also for a philosophical and chemical apparatus. The entire property owned by the corporation is $3,654 08. The entire income for the past academic year, ending September 7th, 1858, was $1,232 26. The number of different pupils in attendance during the year was 151 ; tuition bills made out for the same time, 247.

The present members of the Board of Trustees are—Jeremiah Bean, President ; Benjamin F. Tillinghast, Secretary; John Kingman, Jr., Treasurer ; Peleg Holmes, Matthew G. Lee, Waite Wells, Israel Gee, R. R. Moore, Oliver Kingman, John Potter, Adna Warner, Dayton Kingman, Jacob A. Ressegieu ; A. P. Kelsey, Register.

TEACHERS.

Ambrose P. Kelsey, A. B., Principal ; Miss A. A. Field, Preceptress ; Miss Cornelia J. Dutton, Assistant ; Frank Place, Mathematics ; Miss Cornelia Kingman, Music ; Almon H. Benedict, Penmanship.

The first apportionment of the Regents was $115 35 ; that of the present year is $184 34. There has been also apportioned the sum of $60 for the purchase of apparatus.

In November last this institution was selected by the Regents of the University to instruct a class in common school teaching, and the class is now in process of instruction.

At the time of our visit to the Academy, there were eighty students in attendance, and the various exercises were conducted with marked success. At the date of writing the number in attendance is much larger. The career of the institution thus far has been of unexampled prosperity. Not an instance of discipline has yet occurred. And from the character of the Board of Trustees, we cannot doubt but that it will continue to increase in popularity. They will use every laudable effort to promote its prosperity, and furnish every facility which the ability and talents of competent teachers can impart.

Prof. Kelsey graduated with high honors in 1856. He is a self-made man, having been deprived by death of his father when but five years old; he early learned to depend upon his own energies for success in life, and bracing himself for a career of emulation, he has gradually carved his way to his present honored position. With the faithful and accomplished principal at its head, the Cincinnatus Academy will soon rank among the best educational institutions in the State. Indeed, we believe that with the experienced and highly competent teachers, and the valuable philosophical and chemical apparatus, the academy offers every facility needed to impart a good, thorough, and practical education.

The Academy is entirely free from that baneful species of aristocracy so common in older institutions, and hence should be vigilantly guarded, that the pernicious influence so seriously felt in other localities may not be permitted to enter its honored halls.

Odd Fellows.

This Order was founded in Cortlandville, February 16th, 1847, by the institution of a Lodge; and again at Homer, March 30th, 1847, and now numbers six lodges, as will be seen by the following statistics:

Lodges.	No.	P. G's.	Memb's.	Receipts.	N. G's.
Tioughnioga,	50	8	37	102 26	Frank Goodyear.
Homer,	280	20	67	136 50	O. Porter.
Preble,	409	8	19	65 00	H. M. Van Buskirk.
Marathon,	415	4	24	171 00	John H. Preston.
M'Grawville,	459	8	28	75 92	Leander B. Palmer.
Virgil,	465	7	15	81 88	Henry Luce.

ASTROESSA ENCAMPMENT, NO. 19.

The Encampment is a higher branch of the Order, having a separate organization, but receiving its character from the Grand Encampment, and is otherwise responsible to the Grand Lodge of the United States. Its charter was granted January, 1848, and was instituted February 12th, 1848.

D. Hawkes, R. O. Reynolds, Seth Haight, J. S. Leach, J. D. Clark, E. M. Leal, L. Reynolds, charter members.

J. S. Leach, D. Hawkes, E. M. Leal, L. Reynolds, R. O. Reynolds, A. G. Bennett, G. K. Stiles, J. Freeman, I. M. Seaman, J. B. Fairchild, Z. C. Allis, S. R. Hunter, H. P. Goodrich, J. Price, W. O. Barnard, W. S. Copeland, P. G. P's.

This branch of the Order is in a very flourishing condition. "The door of the Patriarch's tent is never closed to the needy or distressed."

Cherishing the principles of love, purity and fidelity, temperance, benevolence and mutual aid, a galaxy of unrivaled briliants, the members of the various lodges have extended to the needy and distressed the more substantial means of comfort and social union.

In September, 1854, a Masonic Lodge was instituted in Homer by dispensation from the Grand Lodge of the State of New York, and the Hon. Ashbel Patterson was appointed W. M., Cornelius B. Gould, S. W., and Lyman Reynolds, J. W.

This lodge, under the most favorable auspices, is increasing in numbers and in means of usefulness, and we have no reason to doubt that a long course of prosperity is open before it.

CHAPTER XVI.

BIOGRAPHICAL.

"Lives of great men all remind us,
We can make our lives sublime;
And, departing, leave behind us,
Footprints on the sands of time."

It is one of the pleasurable duties of the annalist to record the names and services of the most active and energetic characters who have taken part in forming new settlements, originating and reducing to systematized order such plans and measures as appeared best calculated to secure union and harmony among the various discordant elements of which society is composed, to extend civilization and dignify virtuous character. A due appreciation of the blessings of civil and religious liberty that surround us, urges us to laudable efforts to perpetuate those privileges; and contemplate the circumstances that tended most largely to make us thus happy and prosperous. The noble spirits of other days who devoted their best energies to the achievement of the means of happiness with which we are surrounded, are deserving of our warmest gratitude. We honor them for what they were while living, and now that they are dead, regret that we can only pay them just homage by recording their worthy efforts in the furtherance of the progressive improvements of the times in which they labored, and in emulating their cherished virtues. And to those who still survive the stern strife of the enterprising and brave pioneer, we extend our warmest and heartfelt congratulations. It is not our province to record their names or virtues in marble or in brass, in poetry or in eloquence ; but we will hope to make a plain yet faithful record of a few of the more prominent characteristics which marked their course through life. True history is but a simple and unvarnished record of men's actions. The few usually originate measures of public policy which are adopted by the many, and when the projectors of those measures devotedly cherish a sympathy of feeling for those whom they are calculated mostly to affect, do their acts reflect credit upon themselves, and inspire us with a regard for their worthy efforts. The few names we have selected are such as best presented us with positive data regarding their lives. True, it has been difficult for us to discriminate between the many who appeared equally worthy of a brief notice from us, and of whom we should have been pleased to have recorded their generous efforts in the popular enterprises of the day, did not circumstances and the limits of our work preclude the possibility of extending to any great length our biographical sketches. We shall, therefore, be pardoned for selecting a few names only from among those who have labored equally, ardently and devotedly for the advancement of our happiness and prosperity.

Tom Antone, was born at Oquaga, (now Windsor,) in July, 1770. This place has been made famous in history on account of its having been the ancient dwelling-place of a respectable tribe of Indians—the proud old Romans of the wilderness. Being located upon the Susquehanna river, and but a little distant from "the north-east angle of the Great Bend," it naturally became a half-way resting-place for the Six Nations, as they passed and repassed upon the war-path, or as they more frequently propelled their canoes between the Mohawk and Wyoming Valleys.

The father of young Antone was a chief of great and commanding influence; and he reared his son in accordance with the strictest precepts of right. He was undoubtedly of French extraction, as many of his natural eccentricities were peculiarly French. He bore upon his person the certificates of his valor, for he had distinguished himself in many a hard-fought battle. His flesh had been cleft with arrows, and his bones had been shattered with leaden missiles. In 1794, though his hair had become whitened by the frosts of time, and his form bent with age, he bade adieu to the valley of Ohnaquaga, and united with his brethren in arms in Ohio, who were preparing to make a bold defence against the invading force of General Wayne.

At about this time, Tom came into the Tioughnioga valley, and erected his rude wigwam a little to the east, yet within sight of the present village of Cortland. His disposition was antagonistic to that of his father, who, when around the camp fire, took pride in telling his shrewd and often comic yarns, or practical jokes. On the contrary, Tom was strictly taciturn—a stern, cold Roman hunter. His path had been crossed by a northern trapper, whose polished steel pierced the heart of his young and cherished princess, and she fell a bloody sacrifice to his heartless inhumanity. Revenge, hatred deep and undying, settled upon his hitherto generous mind, and he resolved to avenge the wrong by pouring out the blood of his fiendish foe. Numerous instances are related of his cruelties inflicted upon wild beasts, in imitation of the horrible tortures which were to be visited upon the person of the murderous trapper.

And yet, Antone possessed many fine traits of character, among which stood preëminent an idolatrous affection for her whom he called "wife." His love, like the generous sympathies of the heart, was warm and ardent. Indeed, we might describe it as being purely reverential. He hoped entirely to exclude himself from the association of "the pale face," unless he could destroy the foe who had wrecked his happiness. As the refining hand of civilization appeared in front of his cabin, he drew his blanket more closely about his person, and was seen retreating back into the wilderness. The New Englanders, with their rifles, strode manfully through the Tioughnioga valley, or ascended the hillside in pursuit of game, without receiving the slightest insult from their savage brethren. Antone would have regarded their conduct with the greatest displeasure, had they conducted otherwise than in accordance with his expressed wishes. He loved fame—he loved glory; but he would purchase neither on any other terms but such as justice dictated, or honor required. His hate, really, was directed or cherished against only one person, and that was the murderer of her who had strewed his youthful path with the fairest of flowers.

Leaving Tioughnioga valley, he struck forward in the wilderness in a direct line for the highest elevation bordering the majestic Mohawk. Here by mere accident he caught sight of his mortal enemy. The war-whoop was instantly echoed from hill to hill, and Antone leaped from the threshold of his cabin and darted forward in hot pursuit of the fast disappearing and hated destroyer of his happiness. The pursuit was continued to the shores of Ontario, beyond the thundering Niagara, around the southern coast of Lake Erie, to the banks of the Great Father of waters, where he left the coward's heart upon the sandy beach, a foul and fetid thing.

He fought under the brave Tah-wan-nyes* at the terrible massacre of Wyoming. He was at the Genesee Castle on the approach of General Sullivan, and fled just in time to escape the vengeance of the troops. Standing at a little distance, his eyes beheld its utter annihilation. But his proud and noble spirit did not break. His mind went back to the achievements and wide desolation which marked the course of his brethren when they swept along the majestic Mohawk, bearing the torch of conflagration ; and his dark eye saw the ghastly spirit of massacre, charred and blackened, while the voice of lamentation was heard throughout the settlement of Cherry Valley. He clenched his tomahawk with a firm grasp, and with his long knife sheathed at his side, went forth to battle for glory and conquest in the fairer fields of the "sunny South."

And still Antone lives ; and he who visits the West-

* Gov. Black Snake.

ern Reservation may look upon his stooping form, and behold his unblenching eyes as they glare upon the objects around him.

He was never cowardly—never unmerciful, unless driven to the adoption of measures which, under other circumstances than such as those tending to utter extermination, he would have despised and detested.

Joshua Ballard was born in the town of Holland, Massachusetts, July 21, 1774. His early literary advantages were respectable, and by a close application to study he became an excellent scholar. The various refining influences under which he was reared were well calculated to fix their impress upon his naturally generous and impulsive heart. At the age of twenty-one, (1797,) he left his native town and selected a location in the town of Homer. The next year he returned and moved in his young and interesting wife, who having enjoyed similar advantages in obtaining an English education, and in cultivating the moral and social virtues, was rendered an agreeable and cherished companion. They came in by way of Cazenovia. Their entry into the town of Homer, then a mere "dot in the wilderness," on horseback, and by a scarcely discernible "bridle-path," was hailed by the firm-anchored forester with sensations of heart-felt joy. He originally purchased about one hundred acres of land, but subsequently made several valuable additions. He was affable and courteous in his deportment. In intellect he afforded a rare combination of excellence. His judgment was sound and active. He read much—thought much, and as a natural consequence, usually arrived at correct conclusions. He became an active participant in the political strifes of the day, and few, if any, in our county, have acquired a greater or a more correct reputation as a practical thinking man. And few, perhaps, if any, for upwards of half a century have been more intimately connected with public affairs,—political or progressive,—than Mr. Ballard; and the numerous offices of trust and emolument to which he was at various periods elevated, furnish the most positive evidence of the confidence reposed in him as a just and worthy citizen.

He taught the first school in the old town of Homer, was one of the "projectors and directors of the Fifth Great Western Turnpike Company, whose road was built at an early day through this county. The Cortland Academy owes much of its present as well as past high reputation to the early exertions of Mr. Ballard, who was one of its founders and most permanent supporters. He was also a firm pillar in the Congregational church of Homer, of which he became a member in 1813. He was appointed Sheriff, April 30, 1810. He was an active member of the Legislature of 1816. He was appointed County Clerk, July 7, 1819, soon after which he located in Cortlandville. He also held most of the important town offices in Homer and Cortland. At one period of his life he took quite an interest in military affairs. He raised the first company of cavalry in the county, and was appointed its captain; and afterwards held the office of Brigadier Major and Inspector.

The greater portion of his life, however, was spent in agricultural and mercantile pursuits. The impulses of his heart were warm and ardent. His philanthropy gave ample evidence of a fellow feeling and sympathetic nature. Place and station never swayed nor influenced him from the path of duty. Kind and generous, his social and beneficent sympathies were always favorable to the unfortunate or oppressed. Frank and open, having no concealments, he was never charged with being time-serving. He never trimmed his sail to catch the popular breeze, but rather sought honest defeat than corrupt success.

He died January 10, 1855, having reached fourscore years. His illness was short but severe, yet his dying moments were like those of a child sinking into a calm and pleasant sleep, and his approach to the tomb was like that of one

> "Who wraps the drapery of his couch
> Around him, and lies down to pleasant dreams."

The hand that once aided in subduing the hoary growth of forest trees, and in planting and rearing the early germs of civilization, is cold and nerveless. The tongue that often spoke fervently and eloquently, is mute and dumb in the cold chamber of the grave. The reflection, pleasing and grateful, is forced upon the mind, and we justly exclaim—

> "He was the noblest Roman of them all;
> His life was gentle; and the elements
> So mixed in him, that Nature might stand up
> And say to all the world, this was a man."

John Albright, the pioneer of East Homer, was the son of a plain republican, who was originally from the land of the liberty-loving Tell. Of his ancestors we know but little—of his birth-place, nothing. Nor have we any definite information regarding his early advantages ; but, from his limited knowledge of letters, we are left to conclude that they were not of the most flattering character. His father died a little previous to the Revolution. He had, however, some time before been apprenticed to the tailoring business, to a gentleman whose only son was drafted at the commencement of hostilities into the American service. The young man not appreciating this favor, and his father not relishing the idea of his son being made a mark for British fusileers, consented, after due reflection, that young Albright, who had offered to volunteer, might go in his son's place. The matter being thus settled, John Albright, then only in his sixteenth year, with a heart full of patriotism which neither difficulty nor danger could chill, entered into the service of his country, and went forth to win laurels upon the ensanguined field of military glory. We have not the records at hand from which to glean the name of the commanding officer of the detachment to which he was at first connected. Numerous commissions were tendered him, but declined. In the office of Quarter Master he officiated for some time. He remained in active service until the fall of Montgomery, when he was taken prisoner by the British and carried to New York. He remained there eleven months, suffering all the hardships to which prisoners in the hands of the enemy were exposed ; but his uniform good behavior and honorable deportment won for him many friends. At the time he fell into the hands of the enemy he had an excellent dog, to which he was much attached. After repeated efforts the dog was separated from his master, and taken possession of by a British officer. He was occasionally permitted to visit his sister Elizabeth, who was living in the family of an English surgeon. Just before he was exchanged he was on his way thither, and was very much startled by something springing suddenly upon his back ; turning quickly around he was greatly surprised at beholding his own dog, the officer then being at head-quarters. At the time the animal was taken in custody the officer requested Mr. Albright to tell his name, which, for certain reasons, he refused. But finally, being assured that no harm should occur to him in consequence, he told him that his name was Liberty—a name that was dear to the oppressed, though hateful to tyrants.

After being exchanged he again entered into the service of his country, and continued an efficient actor until after the taking of Fort Stanwix. Soon after this event, he and a few other soldiers, being engaged at a short distance from the main army in picking berries, were surprised and taken prisoners by a company of tories and Indians, and were conducted to Canada. We regret that we are able to give but a few of the interesting incidents connected with his second captivity. During his toilsome march to Canada he was compelled to carry a heavy pack ; his shoes having become worthless, were left on the way ; and his feet, already blistered and torn, became so very sore that he could be tracked by his own blood. There were in the company an old Indian and an aged squaw, whom he had previously known,—the former he had befriended ; the latter called him "son," while he courteously called her "mother." They were consequently his friends. The young Indians appeared to take pride in vexing and torturing the prisoners. One of them sought every opportunity to follow close behind Mr. Albright, and tread upon his lacerated, bleeding heels. He feared to make any resistance, lest it should offend the chief and other influential Indians. But the repeated cruelties inflicted upon him at length exhausted his patience and forbearance ; he turned suddenly upon his persecutor, and with one powerful and well-directed blow of his fist laid him at full length upon the ground. As was natural, he expected to meet the indignant frowns of the Indians, but to his surprise they clapped their hands and laughed most heartily ; then, approaching him, they slapped him on the shoulder and exclaimed, "brave man ! brave man !"

At another time the march had been so rapid and protracted, and his pack so heavy, that he thought he must sink and die under it. He at length threw it down, declaring that he would carry it no farther. Again he expected to meet the angry displeasure of his enemies, and perhaps be tomahawked on the spot ; but, after they had uttered some angry words and exhibited many fearful gesticulations, an Indian was ordered to take up his burden, and he was permitted to proceed unmolested. When they encamped for the night he was tied to a tree, and during the absence of his protector, an Indian, whose hate seemed unrelenting, threw his tomahawk at him, which fortunately missed him and spent its force in a tree not more than three inches from his head. He was finally obliged to run the gauntlet. Then his face was painted jet black, indicating that his death had been determined on. But the squaw whom he called "mother" obtained access to him, and removed the filthy composition from his face ; and, through her influence, he escaped with only a few lacerating blows upon his back. Reaching the point of destination, he was thrown into the prison, the dampness of which soon brought on a fever. He was attended by a British physician, who gave him such large doses of calomel that the most fearful result was anticipated. His tongue became excessively swollen, and protruded from his mouth ; but by the kind interposition and skill of a French physician he was saved. After suffering every species of cruelty and hardship for nearly a year, he was again exchanged and returned to active service, in which he continued until the announcement of peace.

He was certainly a brave and heroic man, displaying the true characteristics of the reflecting and devoted soldier ; not the least of which were exhibited while accompanying General Sullivan during most of his skirmishes with the Indians and tories.

He married a young lady by the name of Catharine Smith. They spent several years in the city, but at length concluded to exchange the pleasures of city life for those of a more rural character ; and with his cherished wife, four daughters, and aged mother-in-law, he left with the determination to locate on the land which had been assigned by his country for services in her cause. He stopped and remained a year and a half at Charlestown, a little west of Schenectady. During this time, accompanied by his wife, on horseback, he came on and explored his "military" lot ; after determining to occupy it, they returned to Charlestown and remained until the spring of 1797. On the 12th of March, they reached Mr. Benedict's house in Truxton, where they remained until Mr. Albright could erect a small house on his lot. It was of the most primitive character, being composed of logs covered with bark.

His nearest neighbors were Mr. Benedict, on the east, near where Judah Pierce now lives ; and John Miller, on the west, where the willow trees have since grown. Toil and privation discouraged him not ; he had already passed through the trying scenes of life. Necessity compelled him to go to mill a distance of forty miles ; there being no road, he had to pick his way by marked trees. He was unaccustomed to agricultural pursuits, having no knowledge of farming, or the best mode to adopt in order to clear the heavy growth of forest trees preparatory to fitting the soil for the more common crops. Help was difficult to obtain,—his children all being girls, who from the nature of things could be of but little service to him,—and consequently he had to rely on his own strong arms and resolute will to sustain and accomplish what in the future crowned his persevering efforts. As his daughters grew up, they learned to do most kinds of out-door work ; and we are told, upon excellent authority, that his mother-in-law, then sixty-five years of age, and who had previously known nothing of country life, soon learned to chop, and would fell from six to eight old foresters in a day. Wolves and bears were plenty. But he paid little attention to hunting, save when rambling through the woods in pursuit of his cattle ; then his gun was his constant companion and trusty friend. At one time he discovered five bears in a tree gathering nuts, two of which he managed to bring down, and which served as a very good substitute for beef.

As a neighbor and friend he was universally esteemed. His benevolence was proverbial. Previous to his locating in East Homer, he was a member of the Reformed Dutch Church. In 1808 his house was opened for religious meetings. Subsequently himself and wife united with the Methodist order, and for several years meetings were held beneath the roof that sheltered the pioneer family from the storm-beaten blast. Favoring circumstances led others to locate near him, among the first of whom were James White, Samuel Greggs, David Lindley, and Samuel Crandall.

Mr. Albright lived on the most intimate terms with his neighbors, and to many he extended the hand of a father's friendship. If at any time they were in pecuniary difficulty, they hesitated not in appealing to him with an almost positive certainty of obtaining relief. He pursued an elevated course of action, entering into none of the speculations so common to new settlements ; and although he did not amass any great wealth, yet he secured a reasonable competence, from which he could draw.

Asa White was born in Monson, Mass., in the year 1774. His educational advantages were such as the common schools of his native State afforded. He early exhibited those traits of character which peculiarly distinguish the business man. Inheriting the energy and active habits of his father, he soon learned to rely upon his own efforts for self-advancement in the world, and thus by persevering industry, economy, and a just appreciation of an emulous reputation, he became the artificer of his own fortune and the moulder of his own character. In 1798, at the age of twenty-four, he emigrated to Homer and located on lot 45. He erected a house on the site now covered by the residence of Jedediah Barber. The farm is the same as now occupied by him, except that Barber has added to it on the north two small pieces of land which were known in an early day as Maj. Stimson's orchard, and Judge Ross' pasture. There has been sold from it the plot of ground lying between Main street and the creek, bounded on the north by the Stimson tavern property, and on the south by what was known as Dr. Owen's orchard.

He was married in 1800 to Miss Claricy Keep, daughter of Caleb Keep, who purchased and settled in 1798 on the farm now occupied by Noah Hitchcock.

At the date of Mr. White's advent into Homer, a gristmill frame had been raised and was partially enclosed. The proprietors were Solomon Hubbard and John Keep. The interest of the latter was purchased by Mr. White, and the enterprise speedily pushed to a final completion. The bur-stones, or rather rock-stones, were procured from the bank east of the residence of Lyman Hubbard, and were drawn by thirteen yoke of cattle to their place of productive labor. The bolts were purchased by Mr. White, of Utica. The mill, though finished as originally designed, produced only a very ordinary specimen of flour. But as there was no other mill in the county, the people, sensitive of their wants, were not disposed to find fault. The interest of Mr. Hubbard was subsequently purchased by Mr. White, and the mill was thoroughly renovated and improved. When it was fully completed, the people believed that they had reached a great attainment. In it they held their public meetings, their Sabbath worship, and social gatherings. Here the young folks held their balls. We have in our possession a record dating back to that period. Mr. White was a manager of one of these entertainments. The managers were placed in a rather unpleasant predicament. Neither rum nor molasses was to be had in town. And as a failure to procure such a *desideratum* would be an unpardonable lack of gallantry in gentlemen, a special messenger was sent post-haste thirty-three miles to Manlius Square for a gallon of rum and a half gallon of molasses, from which they made blackstrap for the company. The Maine Law had not then passed. The grist-mill, now owned by Messrs. Cogswell and Wilcox, covers the site of the original or first mill erected in the county. The various kinds of grain ground at this mill exceeds thirty-one thousand bushels per year. It is a fitting landmark or memorial to be situated on the original site of the first mill erected in the Tioughnioga valley, whereby the people may be the better enabled to point out the spot where the olden relic stood. If the primitive settlers "rejoiced over the final completion of White's mill," with its single run of stone, how much more should their descendants rejoice at having a first-class mill, with its four runs of stones in constant operation, producing the very best quality of flour?

Mr. White was the owner of three-fourths of the first cotton factory erected west of Utica. It stood on the ground opposite the present building. It was built in 1813–14, and destroyed by fire on the 25th of December, 1815.

Mr. White possessed many valuable traits of character, and was especially serviceable in giving the embryo village an auspicious commencement. He possessed a clear, vigorous intellect, strong physical energy, and eminent business talents. His manners were modest, his habits social, and his temper genial and forgiving. He died December 22d, 1843, aged 69 years.

> "As weary, worn-out winds expire,
> Or night-dews fall gently to the ground,
> So calm his exit."

Mrs. White deceased February 23d, 1849, aged 75 years.

> "A light has gone from out the sky,
> A star has left its sphere."

They lie entombed in the new cemetery at Cortland Village, where an appropriate monument, reared by the hand of fond affection, marks the place of their sepulchre.

Horace and Hamilton White, two of the most wealthy and enterprising citizens of the Central City, are his sons. They have passed through a career of active life, public employment and private enterprise, having but few parallels ; and they are everywhere regarded with marked consideration and respect. Their educational privileges ended before they had reached the age of sixteen years, and yet they are gentlemen of education, —self-made men,—eminent in all the varied business relations of life. Their generous sympathies for the poor and friendless, their liberal bestowments in behalf of literary, benevolent, and religious associations, and their kind proffers of pecuniary aid to the really worthy, who were just entering upon the active duties of life, stamp them as men of eminently appreciative character, and it would be well for the young and enterprising to study their history, and like them learn to depend upon their own reliant powers for success in life. Horace went from home at the age of twelve years, and engaged for a limited period in the capacity of a clerk, with Horace Hill, of Auburn. In 1816 he was engaged in a store in which his father had an interest, in the city of Albany. He was subsequently employed by Jedediah Barber, of Homer, in whose store he remained about ten years. Here he acquired a business reputation unusual for young men at his age. His health finally failed, in consequence of which he retired to a small farm, a portion of which is now occupied by Mr. Schermerhorn. Here he was employed for several years in cultivating the soil and in regaining his health. In 1838 he removed to Syracuse, where, in connection with others, he assisted in establishing the Bank of Syracuse, of which he was cashier until his health made it necessary for him to resign the active duties. He is now vice-president of the institution.

The first great feat in the career of Hamilton White occurred at the age of sixteen, in successfully teaching a District school, in what was then known as the new district, in the west part of the now town of Cortlandville, at the *enormous* price of nine dollars per month, with the *pleasure* of boarding round. In the spring he emerged from the log school-house without mar or blemish, and withal greatly encouraged with his achievement. His success encouraged him, and hence he continued in that employment, teaching two more winters and one summer. At the age of twenty he went from home and engaged as a clerk in the store of William Randall & Co., in Cortland Village, with whom he remained two years—the first year receiving six dollars per month. He subsequently spent four or five years in the employment of Messrs. Webb and Edgcomb. In the spring of 1836 he went to Lockport, where he remained until August, 1839, when he removed to Syracuse to assume the duties of cashier of the Onondaga County Bank. His success in the District school, behind the counter and in the counting-room, prepared him for a career of extraordinary usefulness and enterprise. Mr. White is now engaged in business as a private banker on his own account.

Nathaniel Bouton, one of the early settlers of Virgil, was born in Pound Ridge, Westchester county, New York, October 4th, 1778. The family were suffering from the war of the Revolution ; and at its close, found themselves in deep poverty. The schools for children and youth of that time were inferior, and furnished but scanty means of instruction ; and many grew up and entered the scenes of active life and assumed its responsibilities, with a very limited education. The subject of this narrative experienced the inconveniences incident to the times ; yet, by the assiduous improvement of his opportunities, he acquired what was then called a "good common school education." In the spring of 1799, in the twenty-first year of his age, he set out on foot for the western country, intending to remain during the season, engaging in some employment that should offer, and view the country. He came to Solon, and remained a short time with Mr. Samuel Benedict. He afterwards came to Homer, and labored with a Mr. Lee, and aided him in clearing a part of the ground now occupied by Cortland Village. His next stay was with

Mr. Ebenezer Brown, in Milton (now Lansing), where he was engaged in chopping by the job. At the close of the season he passed through Virgil, where a brother of his had settled the same year, and returned to the place of his nativity. On the 22nd of March, 1801, he was married to Miss Rachel Stevens, of New Canaan, Fairfield county, Connecticut. Soon after, he came to Virgil and purchased a farm of one hundred acres joining that of his brother Enos, to whom allusion has been made. He commenced immediately to fell the trees on a spot next the "Bridle road," so called, which passed through it. Near the close of summer he put up the body of a log cabin, and returned to Connecticut. Preparations were then made, and he and his wife, accompanied by his younger brother—who came to take back the team—commenced their journey through almost impassable roads, to their new home in the wilderness, at which they arrived late in October. Mr. Bouton and his family participated in the various hardships, privations, exposures and struggles incident to the settlement of this region and common to the early pioneers, which have been sufficiently set forth in the biographies already given. They began to enjoy the comforts of life and to entertain hopes of future prosperity, when, on the 25th of February, 1805, Mrs. Bouton was suddenly taken away by death, leaving to her surviving companion the cares, maintenance and instruction of four children. The dispensation was afflictive; but he was sustained under it, and was enabled to keep his interesting charge together, and provide for their care and support. He was subsequently married to Miss Lydia Stevens, sister of his deceased wife. Mr. Bouton was much engaged in agriculture, and especially in the department of fruit, being the first in town to put out a nursery of grafted fruit trees, which was as early as 1808 or '9. He was also ardently engaged in the subject of internal improvements, which led him to suggest plans that by many were deemed visionary. In 1827 the idea occurred to him that a railroad might be constructed from the city of New York to Lake Erie. Whenever he proposed this plan, he was met with objections that would have disheartened one less decided, or less assured of its feasibility. He made a journey through most of the length of the route, and was confirmed in his opinion. He procured a piece to be written setting forth the plan, sketching the proposed route, with arguments to establish its practicability, and the advantage it would be to the people of the State, and especially to the city of New York and the southern tier of counties. This communication was published in the *Cortland Observer*, in February, 1828. It was copied by a few other papers; and soon the project gained so much public attention that conventions were called to consider it. After many long and arduous struggles, its friends succeeded in completing the New York and Erie Rail Road, which has opened the way for the construction of numerous railroads that now checker the State and furnish facilities to nearly all parts, for the accommodation of passengers and the ready transmission of freight. Mr. Bouton was a firm friend of education and did what he could for its promotion, and secured to his family all the opportunities within his means of supply. He encouraged the establishment of meetings for religious worship, in 1802—when they were first instituted,—and was ever after a constant attendant and a firm and generous supporter of all the institutions of religion. He did not, however, see his way clear to make a public profession of religion till 1831; when, in a season of religious interest, he and his companion came forward and united with the Congregational church, of which they remained consistent members until their death. He was ready for every reform as it presented itself, and was especially an early and earnest advocate of the Temperance and Anti-slavery causes. His unwearied advocacy of these reforms sometimes provoked hostility, and caused it to be said by some that he had many enemies,—which might be comparatively true, as few who have been faithful and constant in support of these reforms have escaped censure. Early in December, 1846, he took a violent cold, which brought on a fever which terminated his life. When he saw that he should not probably recover, he set himself to adjust his temporal affairs, which he did to the satisfaction of his family, and waited with great composure the summons that should call him away. His peaceful death occurred on the fourth of January, 1847, in the sixty-ninth year of his age.

Mr. Bouton reared an intelligent family of children, among whom we take pleasure in referring to Deacon Nathan Bouton, an enterprising and highly valued citizen of Virgil.

John Miller descended from the English stock of Millers, some of whom figured largely in the political annals of England two centuries since ; and others, at a later period, were the ardent supporters of the American Revolution. With the latter class Mr. Miller was more immediately connected. He was born in Amenia, Dutchess county, N. Y., Nov. 10, 1774.

Of his early years we know but little. His attendance at the district school did not exceed one year ; he however continued to pursue his studies, relying upon his own exertions for success in the worthy effort. His classical advantages were also limited, he having been enabled to spend but a like period in a private classical school in Kent, Conn., under the charge of Barzilla Slosson, a most excellent classical scholar, and a thorough disciplinarian.

He commenced his medical studies in Dutchess county, in 1793, and completed them in Washington county, in 1795. He attended one course of lectures in the University of Pennsylvania, where he listened to the valuable instructions of the celebrated Dr. Benjamin Rush.

Dr. Miller was originally blest with a remarkable mind and memory ; and many of the most valuable impressions which he acquired while listening to this profound and unrivaled lecturer, have remained with him through his long and useful life.

Immediately after his return from the university he became a partner of his friend and preceptor, Jonathan Mosher, in Easton, Washington county, with whom he remained till 1801. It was his original intention to settle in Geneva, where he had made an arrangement to become a partner in the practice of medicine with a distinguished practitioner who had preceded him there, and who had already secured a very lucrative practice. Circumstances, however, over which he had no control, precluded the final consummation of the arrangement.

The connection was therefore dissolved, and Dr. Miller made an immediate and permanent location in Truxton.* He soon acquired a very extensive ride, extending into Homer, Solon, De Ruyter, Pompey, Tulley, and Onondaga Hollow, attending in the families of Joshua Forman, Thadeus Wood, Asa Danforth, and Jasper Hopper.

Previous to his engaging in the study of medicine his health had been exceedingly good, and so continued for two years after, when an accident occurred which deprived him of that important blessing. He became ghastly pale and emaciated ; his friends regarded him as a more complete subject for the anatomical knife, than for the performance of even the slightest labor. And yet, enfeebled, disorganized as he was, he had determined to accept a commission of Second Surgeon in the American Navy, and risk his hopes of life, fame and fortune in the Tripolian war. And he may well thank his friend and protector, Dr. Rush, for withholding his consent from the precarious enterprise, otherwise his bones might have been bleaching upon the shores of the Mediterranean, or whitening on the plains of Tripoli. The advice of Dr. Rush was given in candor and kindness, and had a most favorable impression on the mind of Mr. Miller. He was invited to the Doctor's home, where he was received by Mrs. Rush with appreciative attention. Here he had access to a very large medical library, in which he spent the greater portion of his time. He, however, occasionally accompanied Dr. Rush into the country on his professional visits—a distance, sometimes, exceeding fifty miles.

* Then Fabius.

His hitherto clouded mind gradually gave way to glee and gladness ; and, to use his own expressive language, in six weeks he was a new man.

Ardently attached to his profession, prompt and attentive to his patients, he soon acquired the most extensive practice ever secured by any practitioner in the county.

When the Cortland County Medical Association was organized in 1808, Dr. Miller was chosen Vice-president, and subsequently succeeded Dr. Lewis S. Owen to the office of President. He is the only living member of the original organization. In February of that year he was elected an honorary member of the State Medical Society.

He was married in 1805 to Miss Phebe Adriance, of Troy, a lady of rare accomplishments, and of great moral worth.

In 1805 he was appointed post-master, and retained the office for twenty consecutive years.

He was appointed Justice of the Peace in 1812, and continued in the administration of its duties until 1821.

He served with eminent ability in the New York Assembly during the years 1817–20 and '45.

In 1824 he was chosen a Representative in the United States Congress.

In 1846 he was elected a delegate to the State Constitutional Convention, and during the entire session exerted a commanding influence over that deliberative body.

Dr. Miller moulded his own character, and has been the architect of his own fortune. He has ever possessed a strong and vigorous mind, a clear and retentive memory; an unusual degree of energy and vivacity, blended with wit and generous sympathy.

He loved his friends, his profession, and his country; and ardently labored for the improvement of each. He was free and frank in manner ; generous and friendly in disposition, engaging in address, of active temperament, and indeed possessed all the social qualities of the gentleman, and the stirring energies of the man of business.

Dr. Miller located on lot 93 ; he did not, however, purchase until 1806, when he selected 450 acres at six dollars per acre. He still retains 150 acres of the original purchase. He also owns two hundred acres of a later purchase, on lot 64. He continued in the practice of his profession up to 1830 when he turned his attention to agriculture.

His great energy, determined will, and prompt action in every emergency of life, stamps him as a man of no ordinary character. His great power of endurance enabled him to undergo incredible fatigue in his laborious practice. When the roads were almost impassable, and the nights fearfully dark, he has been known to travel by torchlight through the wilderness, a distance of several miles, even though he had no hope of reward for his professional visit. At a later period, when his ride extended over a large portion of Cortland and Onondaga counties, he rode in one day upwards of fifty-five miles, making thirty-three calls upon the sick.

But the energetic perseverance of Dr. Miller was not alone confined to his professional duties ; it was exhibited in the more extended sphere of business, and in the social relations of life.

The venerable patriarch, now at the advanced age of eighty-four years, is enjoying in a remarkable degree his physical and mental powers; is still a man of unusual vigor.

Of the Doctor's surviving children, one daughter, the wife of Alfred Purdy, resides in Truxton; another is the wife of Rev. Henry Riley, residing at Montrose, Pa.; and Morris, his son, is located at Momentz, Illinois.

Deacon Thomas Chollar was born at Pomfret, Windham co., Conn., October 24, 1778. In his youth he received such advantges as his native town afforded. The Puritan habits of the people were well calculated to prove serviceable to a young man possessing the many benevolent and social traits of character that were assiduously cultivated by Mr. Chollar. It was his pride and pleasure to emulate the virtues of the great and good.

Mr. Chollar came to Cortland county in February, 1802, having but partially considered the privations of pioneer life—of the toils of the industrious settler while contending with the rugged wilderness of nature; the almost insurmountable difficulties to be overcome; the ills, the suffering and perils that often occur to those who venture beyond the boundary of civilization there to rear a domicil and a home. After viewing various portions of the unclaimed wilderness he selected a lot which is at present known as the Northrop farm, in the south-east part of the town. He was not, however, fully pleased with the location, and soon after disposed of it. At different intervals of time he extended his examinations, but did not make a positive and permanent selection until the latter part of 1804, when he made choice of seventy acres, being a part of lot No. 17. Soon after, he returned to his native home in Connecticut, where he remained for nearly five years. He was married March 5th, 1805, to Miss Sally B. Dresser, a young lady who in after life adorned and dignified the name of wife and mother.

He returned with his family to Homer in 1809, and lived one year near the County House, after which he moved on to his place and commenced its improvement. Abram Franklin drew the lot, for services rendered in the Revolutionary struggle. He sold it to Henry Franklin by whom it was subsequently transferred to a Mr. Cushman. The purchase price paid by Mr. Chollar was $3 25 per acre. His disposition was not of that unsettled kind which continually seeks for change, as is sufficiently evidenced in the fact of his having spent nearly a half century on the very spot where he first permanently located, living an honored life, and exhibiting the various virtues which fully adorn and dignify the Christian character. His conversion occurred while in Connecticut. He united with the Baptist Church, in May, 1810 ; was chosen deacon in 1812, and discharged its duties with eminent ability and usefulness until 1847, when a decline of health precluded the further performance of the required services.

In the truthful, eloquent and admirable funeral discourse of Deacon Chollar, pronounced by Elder Harvey, occurred the following tributary remark :

" He was a man of strict integrity in the business relations of life. The apostolic injunction, 'owe no man anything,' perhaps has seldom been more strictly observed. No man ever had occasion to complain of misrepresentation or overreaching. Though providences beyond his control sorely tried him in earlier life, he never had those perplexities and embarrassments that many Christians bring upon themselves by attempting a style of living beyond their actual means, or by careless, reckless speculations in order to increase their property. He rose early, worked hard, and trusted God to reward his diligent labor. The result was, his farm was always well cultivated ; and Providence gave him a competence to the day of his death. 'Diligent in business, fervent in spirit, serving the Lord' was a text fitly illustrated in his course of life."

Those who knew Deacon Chollar best will fully subscribe to the sentiments we have quoted. To have said less would have been excusable in Mr. Harvey, only on the ground of a misconception.

There is not a more sublime and interesting contemplation than the death of an aged, consistent believer. We behold the glorious setting of a sun which had grown brighter through its long-continued day, till, without a cloud to intercept its splendor it sinks into an ocean of light.

The radiant beams of Christian experience and character thus reflected by the venerable saint at the close of life's career, seem to throw back a hallowed lustre on all around. As we gaze on the prospect every faculty and affection of the mind is absorbed—we breathe the atmosphere of eternity—the concerns of the world are forgotten—its mightiest events are reduced to their absolute insignificance ; and the powers of the world to come fill the soul with the most impressive interest. We feel ourselves to be " quite on the verge of heaven."

We say to our companion, "Mark the perfect man, and behold the upright; for the end of that man is peace;" or pour forth the fervent prayer, "Let me die the death of the righteous, and let my last end be like his."

To the number of those whose departure has inspired such reflections, and who have lived for full half a century on the promises of the gospel, we add the name of Deacon Thomas Chollar, who, on the 6th of August, 1855, united his testimony to that of millions who have gone before him, "that the just receive their reward in a brighter and better world." His illness was long and severe; the disease having assumed the worst form of spasmodic asthma, terminated in death sooner than his friends had anticipated, and though not marked with ecstacies his end was peaceful and happy.

Fervent in his sympathies, gentle in his communion, consistent in his affections, the records of his Christian excellence live in the hearts of all to whom he was known, by whom he could but be beloved. Though declining years had much confined him to his dwelling, yet "Faith and Hope" were with him, and his "Charity never failed." Misery plead not in vain. He passed not by on "the other side" when want and sickness, cast forth on the highway of a pitiless world, turned toward him an imploring eye. The widow and fatherless did not breathe to a listless ear their tale of sorrow, when they appealed to his compassion. But he was especially distinguished, like the excellent Lydia, whose heart the Lord had opened to receive the faith and to show hospitality and kindness to those that preach the gospel. He spent not the "precious ointment" on himself; but broke it at his Saviour's feet, and the incense of his heart went up with it.

When bowed with age and sickness, still he "gloried in his infirmity," that the power of "Christ might rest upon him," and although he felt with the Apostle "that to depart and be with Christ is far better," yet he humbly resolved with patient Job, "All the days of my appointed time will I wait until my change come." In his house the weary herald of the cross has often found refreshment, and his heart has ever been opened to the destitute ; so that while we mourn his loss, which is severely felt by his relatives and friends and the church of Christ, we joy upon the reflection that our loss is infinitely his gain. "Blessed are the dead that die in the Lord—they rest from their labors."

The fond wish of this aged disciple has been realized—the pilgrim has safely passed through the waves of Jordan, and has reached the promised land of life and peace eternal.

And while we contemplate the bright example he has left behind him—his faithful profession of the Christian verity—his conscientious discharge of relative duties—his ardent desire for the salvation of souls, and the glory of God : in a word, his life of unspotted holiness, and his death of sainted serenity, and then turn to his glorious resting-place in the presence of his Saviour and his God—we pause, and seem to say :

He now holds converse with the Patriarchs
Of old—with Prophets, who foretold of all
That since has shaken empires, and made way
For the dominion of the Prince of Peace.
His voice unites with David's in the song

Of "Praise the Lord"—with David's harp, his harp
In concert joins the chorus of the skies.
He sits with the Apostles, and recounts
The eternal wonders of redeeming love.

Deacon Chollar was one of those who are justly termed "the Light of the World." And that same light which he had so steadily emitted during his Christian life for the illumination of others, shone not less brightly at the hour of death.

He reared a numerous family of children, among whom is Dea. Thomas D. Chollar, of Homer.

Mrs. Chollar, the aged sainted mother of Israel, still lives, her "lamp trimmed and burning," like a beacon light to the world of happiness, aged 80 years.

Deacon Asa Bennett was born in Mansfield, Ct., July 10, 1778. His education was strictly moral. He was early taught to fear God and to attend to the external forms of religion, and the parental instruction and prayer bestowed upon his youthful mind exerted a salutary influence upon his subsequent life.

At about the age of sixteen he embraced the Christian religion, and in 1800 evinced his catholicity of spirit by uniting with the Baptist church, in Hampton, Ct. He removed to Homer in 1803, and united in 1806 with the church of the same faith, of which he became an active and influential member. Early in 1807 he was chosen Deacon, though not ordained until 1815. His Christian character was well calculated to command respect and veneration, and most eminently fitted him for the high duties of Deacon, which relation he sustained to the church until the insatiate archer, Death, sped his shaft, and the venerable pillar was called to his eternal home.

His house was a home for the preachers, and a place for the people of God to meet. He gathered in and "built up souls," who will no doubt mingle their joys with his in Heaven.

He was affable and courteous, and in all the benevolent associations of the day he exhibited a zealous and enterprising spirit. His chief study seemed to be the eternal welfare of his brethren. And while his hand was engaged in dispensing blessings, his prayers were ascending to the Throne of Grace for the redemption of his fellow beings.

He was a subject of long and severe affliction. But up to the hour of dissolution he evinced all the powers of patience and resignation to the will of his Divine Preserver.

Eld. Alfred Bennett was born Sept. 26, 1780, in Mansfield, Windham co., Ct. He received an early religious education, and for which he always felt deeply indebted to his pious parents. The buds of a bright intelligence were early put forth, hopefully indicating a rich development of mind ; the spring of youthful piety had begun to flow along the opening channels of the tender heart with much assurance of high excellence of Christian character and deep devotion to his Maker. A mild and ardent temperament, warm social virtues, buoyant spirit, and winning address, tempered and refined through the chastening influence of his early education, made him a great favorite, and entwined him closely about the hearts of his devoted parents and friends, and prepared him for the higher duties of moral excellence just as he was entering the stage of rational life.

In 1800 he united with the Baptist church in Hampton, some fifteen miles distant from his home. Here he married, in 1802, Miss Rhoda Grow.

In 1803 he located in the town of Homer. His dwelling was a rude structure composed of logs ; the external and internal appearances were not of the most inviting character. Yet to the early pioneers these unhewed tenements were of valuable importance, and contained within their limited enclosures as much moral virtue and social benevolence as ever flourished within the gorgeous citadels of crowned monarchs. The valley was yet a comparative wilderness, the hills a dense forest, visited only by the fearless hunter and wandering savage. Here Mr. Bennett, with a strong arm and a resolute will, engaged in felling the forest. In April, 1805, he became deeply exercised upon the subject of the Christian ministry, and finally gave himself up to God and the church, and commenced his labors as an itinerant preacher. He was ordained Feb., 1807. His subsequent labors were arduous, but he appeared to be happily adapted for the promotion of the cause in which he embarked ; he labored with remarkable ability and eminent success. As a preacher his talents were respectable, but in the gift of exhortation few persons excelled him ; his appeals were made to the hearts of his hearers with remarkable effect.

He died May 10, 1851.

The demise of this good man was a loss never to be repaired ; and although it fell with peculiar weight upon his family and near friends, yet the Baptist church of Homer, over which he long presided, and the poor, shared very largely in the bereavement, for in him they always found a constant and untiring friend.

The closing period of his life was calm as a peaceful river. His inspiring hope of immortality found expression in the triumphant language of "Glory! Glory!"

MALACHI CHURCH, was born in Brattleborough, Vermont, May 15th, 1769. He enjoyed very limited advantages for literary pursuits; yet, by diligent application, he acquired a knowledge of the elementary branches which qualified him for the practical duties or business transactions of public life. A portion of his time, when a young man, was occupied in cultivating the soil, and in acquiring a knowledge of the blacksmith's trade. At the age of twenty-two years he married Lucy Blakeslee, and reared a large family of children—four sons and six daughters. In the winter of 1804–5, he emigrated to the present town of Bainbridge, Chenango county, N. Y., and in September of 1805 he removed to that part of the Tioughnioga valley now included in the town of Marathon, a distance of about forty miles. This journey was accomplished in three days with hard toil. Here he found but a few scattering residents, and no reasonable encouragement was presented to the patronage of a mechanic. Hence it became necessary, as the means of supporting his family, to engage in agricultural pursuits, in clearing and cultivating the soil. The lands lying in the valley being more feasible of tillage, were first cleared and improved; but gradually, as other settlers arrived, the contiguous hill lands were taken up; but the process of cutting and burning up the heavy timber and fitting the land for growing crops was a work of severe toil and of slow progress.

Mills for sawing lumber for building, and for grinding grain, were greatly needed, but for the want of adequate means none were erected till the year 1810. These structures called into requisition the aid of mechanics. The first framed edifices were erected on the land where Marathon village is now located. Mr. Church, some ten or twelve years after his arrival here, built a frame house and shop on the west side of the river, a few rods from the present railroad depot; where, assisted by his sons, he successfully carried on the blacksmithing business for several years. About the year 1815 Mr. Church was solicited to become a candidate for the office of Justice of the Peace; and although a large majority of the inhabitants were opposed to his political opinions, yet entertaining a high regard for impartiality, integrity, and capacity, his name was presented as the unanimous choice of the people. It will be recollected that all judicial officers at that time were appointed by the governor; and when a petition was presented for the appointment of an individual by constituents known to be favorable to the State administration, there could be no hesitancy in complying with the wishes of the petitioners. Mr. Church was accordingly duly appointed, and held the office for quite a number of years, discharging the duties thereof with ability equal to the confidence which the public had reposed in him. In the year 1823 Mr. Church made a public profession of religion and became a member of the Baptist church, and for his zeal in the cause, his talents and christian character, he was soon after appointed a deacon of the church,—an office which he filled with honor to the cause by an exemplary life to the time of his decease, which occurred November 20th, 1846, at the age of seventy-seven years. His widow survived him a few years. At his death, he left four sons and three daughters. His sons were all distinguished for military talent, and each of whom received a Colonel's commission; three of them also served as Justices of the Peace. His daughters were, by marriage, connected with respectable families.

MAJOR ADIN WEBB was a native of Scotland, Windham county, Conn. His father, Christopher Webb, was an industrious and enterprising agriculturist. At an early period of the American Revolution he embarked in the arduous struggle, and devoted his best energies to the acquisition of liberty and an equality of rights. He held the office of Sergeant, and discharged with marked ability its responsible duties. He was with his brethren in arms during the cold and stormy winter so memorable in history, when they were encamped on the hills back of Morristown, suffering the most severe privations; half fed, half clothed, and much less than half paid. His bravery and heroic devotion to his country was exhibited on various occasions, and especially in the bloody conflict at Bennington, and in the capture of Burgoyne, near Stillwater. He died a professor of religion, March 1, 1837.

Adin Webb, the subject of this notice, was born March 31, 1780. While still a mere child, his father concluded to change his place of residence, and located at Canterbury, where he remained until June 4, 1804.

His early literary advantages were respectable, having received a good academic education. He was reared to the business of agriculture, though he frequently engaged in teaching school. He taught eight winters in Connecticut—the first at the age of sixteen.

Modest and unpretending in his manners—strictly correct in gentlemanly deportment—diligent in the pursuit of his various duties, he secured the esteem of his pupils, and enjoyed a large share of the best affections of his near friends.

He was married October 15, 1800, to Miss Deborah Carter, in whose person were united in the extremest sense the various accomplishments of an intellectual lady. She too, was devoted to the profession of teaching.

He removed with his parents in 1804 to Cazenovia, N. Y. He came in with an ox team, by way of Hartford, Albany, Utica, Whitestown, Westmoreland, and Lenox. Approaching near Manlius, he turned to the left and bore to the head of Cazenovia lake, where his father purchased one hundred and fifty acres of land.

He spent one year and a half with his father, and then, through the urgent solicitations of a friend, was induced to come to Homer and take a school for a term of four months, as also a singing-school. Gratified with his success, and pleased with the attractive beauties of the county, he concluded to locate. And it is certainly complimentary of him to remark, that with one exception he taught seventeen successive years.

In 1808 he erected a dwelling-house on ground now occupied by Mr. Barber's new block. A few years after he disposed of it and purchased a lot of Captain Hezekiah Roberts, and erected a dwelling on ground at present covered by the Baptist church. Subsequently he sold this to Chauncey Keep, and spent two years in the vicinity of Mr. Kingsbury's. He next purchased a situation of Mr. Asa Kendall, where he lived until 1823, when he removed to Cortland.

In 1826 he purchased a lot on which now stands the jewelry store of Mr. Stiles.

At this time he entered into copartnership with Mr. Eleazar W. Edgcomb, in the mercantile business. The copartnership continued about ten years, when the latter disposed of his interest to Mr. Calvin Bishop. These gentlemen were sons-in-law of Mr. Webb. He continued for about fifteen years in the prosecution of the mercantile trade.

In 1809 he was elected Town Clerk of the old town of Homer, and continued in the discharge of its duties for twenty years.

He was appointed Surrogate in 1816, and held the office till 1823.

In 1827 he was elected Justice of the Peace ; and in 1828 elevated to the responsible office of Sheriff.

In 1840 he was elected Surrogate, and served the people for four years.

In 1845 he was elected Town Clerk of Cortlandville, and continued to discharge its duties till 1856.

His inclinations partook but little of a military cast ; yet in 1809 he was elected a Lieutenant. The next spring he was chosen Captain, in place of Benjamin Andrews. He served four years, and was then elected 2nd Major.

He joined the Congregational church in Homer in 1813, and led the choir for fifteen successive years.

In 1823 he united by letter with a church of the same order in Cortland.

In private life he has ever exhibited the true characteristics of a gentleman. In his public career he has adorned and dignified his position, alike creditable to himself and his country. A true pattern of integrity and worth, he is revered, not as a laurel-crowned hero, but as a noble specimen of the Great Architect. If

"'Tis infamy to die and not be missed,"

Major Webb will go down to the tomb an honored relic of an iron age, leaving behind him an unblemished reputation, which, like the cruse of oil, will gladden many a cherished heart.

The habits of Major Webb have been most remarkably correct. The numerous exhilirating beverages, alike destructive to the physical and the mental faculties, have had little or no influence over him. He has usually risen early, and always been active and energetic ; and to those influences he attributes much of his usually excellent health.

We doubt whether there is another individual in the county who has more warm personal friends, or whose sympathies and virtues have taken a more lasting hold upon the affections of the people.

And now, at the advanced age of seventy-eight, he exhibits the activity and sprightliness of the man of sixty.

Mrs. Webb died February 27, 1850.

Samuel Gilbert Hatheway was born in Freetown, Bristol county, Mass., July 18, 1780. He is descended from those Gilberts of whom Sir Humphrey was one, and from the Puritans, Bradford and Alden. He was the youngest son of Shadrach and Hannah (Chase) Hatheway. His only brother was lost at sea with the vessel he commanded. His sister married and died in New England. The father deceased while the son was yet in infancy, and soon after he was placed under the care of his paternal grandfather, with whom he remained for a period of nine years. His early education was derived principally from the primary schools of his native State. He possessed great energy of character, a clear, active mind, and was resolved to succeed in life, and hence he achieved a triumph over every difficulty. His early habits of industry were in after time exhibited in the unbending perseverance of the young New England farmer. His self-reliant powers were regarded with almost idolatrous respect. His energy was his capital, and he invested it with pleasure in approved pursuits. The limited amount of learning which he acquired in the common schools was subsequently greatly enlarged by private study and extensive reading. Thrown upon his own resources, he first presumed that the mariner's life would be congenial with his feelings, but, after making a voyage to the West Indies, he readily concluded that it would neither promote his interest nor be propitious to his feelings.

In 1803 Mr. Hatheway migrated to Chenango county, designing to make a permanent residence ; he was not, however, well pleased with the country, and after spending two years in the settlement, removed to Cincinnatus, (now Freetown), and located on lot No. 2. Soon after, his mother, a woman of great mental and physical energy, joined him, and remained with him until her death, which occurred Aug. 14, 1826. He purchased 300 acres of Robert Smith, a Revolutionary soldier. Mr. Smith drew the lot and had located on it some ten years previous. At this time Mr. Hatheway was eight miles distant from his nearest neighbor on the south, four to the north, and about a like number to the east and west.

In 1819 he removed to Solon, and settled on the eastern part of lot 71. Here he remained until 1842, when his buildings were devastated by fire, and he changed his residence to his present location on lot 73.

In 1810 he was appointed by the Council of Appointment, Justice of the Peace, which office he has held forty-eight successive years. He has also been honored with every office from Supervisor down to Commissioner of Highways.

In 1814, and again in 1818, he was elected to the New York Assembly. These were periods of marked importance in the political annals of our State, and Mr. Hatheway fully sustained the confidence reposed in him by his party and friends.

In 1822 he was elected to the State Senate, and in 1832 chosen a Representative from the 22d District to the United States Congress.

His early tastes led him into political life, and he soon acquired great influence in the Democratic party. A deep thinker and of active temperament, he was well calculated to plan and execute whatever business of a political and social nature he might undertake. Few citizens, if any, in the county, have acquired an equal influence in the control of party movements, or who could with so much exactness predict its majorities. It is believed that he has in no instance swayed from his political predilections, and has never compromised a right for the achievement of a temporary success.

In 1852 he was elected a Presidential elector. In 1804 he voted for Thomas Jefferson at his second election to the Presidency, and has voted for every Democratic candidate since.

He was a delegate to the National Democratic Convention at Cincinnati, in June, 1856, when James Buchanan was chosen as the national standard-bearer of the party he represented.

In 1808 he received a captain's commission in a battallion of infantry, under the command of Major John Kingman. He was appointed Major in 1814, and Lieut. Colonel by Gov. Tompkins in 1816; Colonel in 1819; Brigadier General in 1820, by Gov. Clinton; Major General in 1823, by Gov. Yates. The last appointment he still holds.

On the 13th of May, 1846, an Act was passed by the Legislature of New York, for the encouragement of the formation of uniform companies, and to provide for the enrollment of the militia. In accordance with this Act, Gov. Wright, on the 21st of October of that year, directed Major General Hatheway to divide the Sixth Military Division into two brigade districts, according to representative population as ascertained by the State census of 1845, and as required by section 3d of that law.

The duty was promptly attended to. He divided the division into two brigade districts, as follows: the first he composed of the counties of Oneida and Oswego, and the towns of Sterling, Victory, Ira, Cato, and Conquest, in the county of Cayuga, and the towns of Lysander, Van Buren, Clay, and Cicero, in the county of Onondaga; and the second, of the counties of Cortland, Tompkins, and the remaining towns of the counties of Cayuga and Onondaga.

The Report was fully approved by the Commander-in-Chief, and was regarded as an improvement on the original suggestion of the Adjutant-General, R. E. Temple.

Under the direction of Gov. Young, General Hatheway divided the Sixth Division into four Brigade Districts, according to representative population.

Previous to the passage of the Act referred to, the State was composed of thirty-two divisions—two brigades in each. The new law reduced them to eight.

The Sixth Division was composed of the counties of Oneida, Oswego, Onondaga, Cayuga, Cortland, and Tompkins.

General Hatheway, being the oldest Major General in the Sixth Division, was retained ; thus extending to him a compliment, not only for his venerated worth as a man, but for his zealous efforts as an officer.

During the entire period of a half century, General Hatheway has witnessed the gradual increase of the country from a wilderness to a populous and prosperous district ; and he has during the same period been intimately concerned with its business and its interests.

In the various civil and military capacities, he has been equally useful. His persevering energy rendered him valuable as a public officer, and prosperous in his private affairs. He has accumulated a very large property. His land consists of upwards of 3000 acres. The Home Farm between eleven and twelve hundred. His elegant residence was erected in 1844–5.

General Hatheway was married October, 1808, to Miss Sally Emerson, of Solon. She died April 28, 1832. Mrs. Hatheway was a lady of education and refinement, and possessed many eminent qualities. The inhabitants of the town where she passed her married life still speak of her many virtues, her genial kindness, and her untiring energy.

In November, 1848, Mr. Hatheway was again united in marriage to an educated and refined lady, in the person of Miss Catherine Saxton, of Groton.

General Hatheway is the father of eleven children—of the six sons, two only survive. Colonel S. G. Hatheway, Jr., is a prominent attorney and politician, residing at Elmira. Colonel C. L. Hatheway, his fourth son, is the active man of business at home. The accomplished and so much lamented Major John S. Hatheway, of the United States Army, was the second son. George R., the third son, was just admitted to the bar, when his career of promise ended. Charles R., the fifth son, was still a student. The sixth son died in childhood. Of his five daughters, three are living.

And now General Hatheway, at the venerated age of seventy-eight years, exhibits a remarkable degree of health, energy and vivacity ;

"His age like a lusty winter, frosty, but kindly."

Thurlow Weed was born in Cairo, Green co., N. Y., Nov. 15, 1797, and at the age of eleven years removed with his parents to Cincinnatus. In his youth he failed to enjoy the advantages of a good education. The limited means of his father required the most laborious exertions to support his family with even a moderate degree of respectability. His educational privileges were therefore as ample as the circumstances of his parents would permit. He attended school "one quarter" in Catskill, "part of a winter term" in Cincinnatus, and "three months" in Onondaga Hollow, paying for board and schooling, in the latter place, by working in the garden, chopping wood, and doing chores, morning and evening, for Jasper Hopper. He possessed a healthy, vigorous physical constitution, and an inflexible, abiding determination to excel. Though he was for the brief period of his minority doomed to constant physical toil; and though he might for a time be tossed about by the fickle breezes of external circumstances, he would at least make efforts to take that elevated rank to which it was his right and his duty to aspire. He felt the pressure of poverty; he knew the extent of his father's purse; he possessed talents, genius, and self-confidence, and he resolved to accomplish his purpose. He was never reckless, never an idler, and always conscious of his ability or self-reliant powers to advance. If he relinquished one enterprise, it was but to achieve another.

In the summer of 1806 he was employed in the capacity of cook and cabin boy on board the sloop *Ranger*, Captain Gager, of Catskill, and on board the sloop *Jefferson*, Captain Bogardus, in 1807. In the winter of 1808 his father removed to Cincinnatus, and our young aspirant found himself quartered in an ashery, where he learned the mystery of converting lye into black salts. During the winter of 1807 he first worked in the printing office of Macky Croswell, at Catskill, and was honored with the title of "*Printer's Devil.*" In 1811 he was employed in the "Lynx" office, at Onondaga Hollow. The next year he was engaged as a half-way journeyman in the office of Thomas Walker, of Utica, and worked on the "Columbian Gazette;" and in 1813, for Colonel William L. Stone, on the "Herkimer American." From this time until 1815, he was employed for short periods, at full pay, in offices at Auburn, Spring Mills, Sangersfield, Cazenovia, and Cooperstown; and for longer terms in Utica and Herkimer, when he went to Albany, and New York, working as a journeyman until 1819. He then went to Norwich, Chenango co., and established a weekly newspaper entitled "The Agriculturist." In 1821 he removed to Manlius, Onondaga co., and established the "Onondaga County Republican." In 1822 he removed to Rochester, and was employed in the office of Everard Peck, for whom he worked two years, when he purchased his paper, the "Rochester Telegraph." Mr. Weed took strong ground in favor of De Witt Clinton, who was elected Governor in the November election of 1824, and again in 1826. After the abduction of William Morgan, in 1827, he discontinued the "Telegraph," and commenced the publication of the "Anti-Masonic Enquirer," which soon became the leading anti-masonic paper of the State. The "Telegraph," under the supervision of Mr. Weed, had exerted a commanding and wide-spread influence. The controlling power of the "Enquirer" was far greater. Over the party of which it was the great head, its influence was almost unlimited. In 1830 he removed to Albany, and established the "Evening Journal," which for upwards of a quarter of a century he has conducted with signal ability and success.

During the last clash at arms between Great Britain and the United States, Mr. Weed exhibited an inclination for a more intimate association with the valorous spirits who warred for fame, glory and independence. In the winter of 1813 he volunteered, and served six weeks as a private in Capt. Ashbel Seward's company, then stationed at Adams, Jefferson county. Nothing of particular importance occurred, and he was discharged when the apprehensions of an attack from the British, a body of which were supposed to be preparing to cross on the ice, had subsided. He was a private three months in Lieut. Ellis' company of Artillery from Utica, and stationed at Brownville, in the same county. The regiment was commanded by Col. Metcalf, of Cooperstown. Mr. Weed also served at Sackett's Harbor as Quarter Master Sergeant in Col. Myer's regiment, of Herkimer, from August till October.

In 1824, and again in 1829, he was elected to the Assembly from the County of Monroe. He made an active and influential member.

He was married to Miss CATHARINE OSTRANDER, of Cooperstown, in April, 1818.

In 1843 Mr. Weed took a tour to Europe, visiting England, Scotland, Ireland, Wales, France and Belgium. In 1852 he took a second tour, and extended his visit to Switzerland, Germany, Saxony, Austria, Sardinia and Italy. During his travels he furnished for the columns of the *Evening Journal* a series of exceedingly interesting and valuable letters, which were extensively copied throughout the State, and indeed throughout the Union. They exhibited a complete daguerreotype of the habits, customs and national characteristics of the people of those countries.

Mr. Weed possesses a strong, clear and well-balanced mind. His career thus far has been an eventful one.

From the cook and cabin boy on board the sloops Ranger and Jefferson, he worked his way to a position the most worthy, dignified and appreciable. From the black salt manufacturer of Cincinnatus, or the young salt boiler of Salina, we see him gradually progressing in the scale of the ascending series, until he has reached the highest round in the ladder of political sagacity and editorial preferment. The chore-boy of Jasper Hopper becomes repeatedly a member of the Legislature, State printer, and unrivaled political editor of the Empire State. The youthful volunteer in the second struggle for freedom escapes the maelstrom of voluptuous dissipation, and becomes a self-made great man ; great in intellect, and great in the achievement of an enviable reputation. Had he vacillated and yielded to the numerous discouragements with which he was surrounded, he would never have taken his station in bright conspicuity in the annals of the world. His resolution and firmness of character saved him. He not only astonished his friends with the extent and variety of his attainments, but he astonished even himself. He did not look for superior mental manifestations without effort or active exertion, any more than he did for manifestations of physical power without constant exercise of the physical system. The skill of the mariner is unknown to the world, and even to himself, until he finds occasion to spread his canvas to the fury of the tempest—until his vessel plunges amidst the foaming, boisterous billows—until he comes in fearful contact with the angry elements of the mighty deep. The same is true of all the numerous conflicts of the human mind ; and resolution and decision are the only sure guaranty of success and ultimate triumph.

The illustrious intellects from Homer down—the giant minds who rise above their fellow-men, and stretch out their hands to each other across the interval of ages, transmitting to succeeding generations the torch of science, poetry and art, have achieved their greatness of character through the active propelling agency of these progressive elements. They have distributed the energies of the soul through every fibre, shred and muscle of the human brain ; have given god-like energy to the human character ; filled the fair temples of fame, leveled forests, and converted the nations of the earth from savagism and barbarity to a higher state of moral and intellectual greatness. Resolution and decision are traits of character which we admire, and which we love to contemplate. We pay them homage in Xerxes and Alexander—in Hannibal, Scipio and Napoleon—in Nero and Caligula. Indeed, we can scarcely contemplate them even in a demon without doing it involuntary reverence. It is inconsistent with the nature of mind that it should rise to greatness and distinction without unceasing effort. Hannibal's name is immortal, because the towering Alps, whose lofty peaks penetrated the clouds of heaven, could not successfully resist the energies of his mind. He fearlessly marched with his invincible host over those rugged and dangerous steeps, where mortal foot had never trod before. Thurlow Weed, through a like unceasing effort, has braved the ills of poverty, voluptuous excitement, a thousand threatening disasters, and slowly carved his way to wealth and greatness.

John L. Boyd was born in Charlton, Saratoga county, N. Y., October 16th, 1783. His educational advantages were limited to the common schools, where he acquired the rudiments of his education, and such scholarship as the transient opportunities of the country afforded. He had, however, early laid a good foundation for a practical education, which in due time was honorably completed.

At the age of thirteen he left the parental roof and the common pursuits of the youth of that time, and was for the succeeding four years in the employ of William S. Packer, an established hatter in Galway. Having closed his apprenticeship, he entered into the hatting business on his own account, but discontinued the enterprise at the end of one year and a half. Soon after, he was employed by James Hamilton, and continued in his service in the capacity of bar-keeper for about two years, when he removed with his father to Irondequoit, Monroe county. Here he had hoped to secure permanent employment, but failing in the effort, he engaged with a Mr. Seymour, and spent two months in surveying the large tract of land lying between Rochester and Lake Ontario. He was subsequently employed in the store of Messrs. Tryon and Adams, where he remained two years, and then returned to Saratoga county, and was for a like period engaged in agricultural pursuits. We next find Mr. Boyd in Albany, employed in the forwarding house of Hugh and Hamilton Boyd. At this period (1808,) the embargo made a serious change in commercial affairs, and darkened for a time our politcal horizon. The restraining influence extended beyond the shipping interest, and, indeed, paralized almost every branch of industry. The forwarding business was in the main closed, or very greatly limited, and in consequence Mr. Boyd again returned to his agricultural labors--an avocation in which he has since continued.

Mr. Boyd was married in 1809 to Miss Electa Bacon, of Williamstown, Mass., an early class-mate of Mrs. Col. Canfield in the Litchfield Academy. He removed to Solon in 1811; purchased 119 acres on lot 98. He subsequently added 251 acres to his farm, and at present retains 225.

In 1812 he was elected Lieutenant in a company of Infantry, commanded by Capt. Hedges, of Truxton. He afterwards rose to the rank of Colonel.

Previous to 1821 he received two commissions of appointment to the office of Justice of the Peace, but declined the honors. After the revision of the State Constitution, he was repeatedly elected to the same office, as also various other responsible positions in the gift of the people.

In 1827 Col. Boyd was elected to the New York Legislature, and made an active and efficient member. His first vote was cast for Thomas Jefferson at his second election in 1804.

In 1823 he united with the Union Congregational Society of Cincinnatus and Solon, and has since filled numerous prominent positions in the church, serving for many years in the capacity of deacon. He was a zealous pioneer in the early temperance reformation, and, indeed, an active participant in most of the social reforms of the day; and has successfully discharged the duties of Sabbath school superintendent for upwards of twenty-eight years.

He has reared an intelligent family of nine children. Louise M. is the wife of James Thompson, Esq., Cashier of the Camden, White Creek Valley Bank. John W. is an honored member of the Wisconsin State Senate—now serving a second term.

Colonel Boyd is emphatically a self-made man. Stout-hearted and sanguine, he felt that if blessed with health and the ordinary advantages common to the pioneer period in which he was reared, he could succeed in life and ultimately carve out for himself a respectable competency. His early reverses and embarrassments, instead of impairing his youthful energy, served but to stimulate him to greater activity. And when he had accumulated by honest industry and untiring energy a small fund, with his young and interesting wife he sought this wild region of country, and became an occupant of a log cabin. Here they spent many years of primitive happiness—though, strictly speaking, they were years of unremitting toil and privation. Surrounded by the deep, dark forests ; undismayed by the howl of the wolf, or the panther's scream, he grasped

> " The axe, that wondrous instrument
> That, like the talisman, transforms
> Deserts to fields and cities,"

and with a strong arm and a resolute will he went forth to war with the stern old monarchs of the forest. His Utopian dream has been realized ; his enterprise fully rewarded ; and now, at the age of seventy-five, we find him surrounded with broad and productive fields, in the full enjoyment of all the conveniences and comforts of life, an honored pioneer of an iron age ; still living upon the ground where his primitive cabin was reared, and still cultivating the soil over which, previous to his early adventure the footprints of civilization had scarce traversed the trail of the red man ;

> " Where nothing dwelt but beasts of prey,
> Or men as wild and fierce as they."

Joseph Reynolds was born in Easton, Washington co., N. Y., September 14, 1785. Some years after, his father removed to Galway, Saratoga co., from which place Mr. Reynolds migrated to Virgil, in 1809. He was eight days on the road. With his wallet of bread and cheese on his shoulder, he left his home for the promised land of the Tioughnioga valley. He drove in two cows; and, as yet having no land, or provision made for their keeping, he gave the milk of one for the keeping of both. Having made the necessary arrangements for his young family, he engaged himself in clearing land for his neighbors, at the rate of seventy-five cents per day.

In the spring of 1810 Mr. Reynolds purchased a small farm, mostly on credit ; and, with a determination to prosper through the means of honest labor, commenced felling the forest trees, that the virgin soil might yield to the hand of productive toil. Success followed his industrious and economical pursuits.

In 1814 he was elected to the office of constable. Soon after, a company of riflemen was organized, and he was made Captain. The company proposed entering into the service of the country in opposition to the encroachments of Great Britain. Having been reported to the proper quarter as being fully equipped and ready to march, they were in turn directed to remain as "minute men," lest a sally might be made on Salt Point by way of Oswego. Peace was however declared before the fierce war-spirits were crowned with laurels. The organization was discontinued. In 1817 he was appointed Major; in 1818, Colonel; and in 1823 he was chosen Brigadier General. This post he held with much credit for seven years.

In 1815 he was appointed Justice of the Peace in the town of Virgil, by the Old Council of Appointment, and held the office for about twenty-three years. After the Council of Appointment was abolished, he was elected by the Democratic party, to which he has ever been attached.

In 1818 he was elected to the Assembly without opposition: such an election has not happened in the county since. He was present when the division of parties took place; a portion of the Democrats or Republicans went over to the Clintonian party. The parties stood divided—fifty-one Clintonians, headed by Obadiah Germain; forty-four Bucktails, headed by Wm. Thompson; and twenty-eight Federalists, headed by Wm. A. Duer. After two days balloting the Clintonians and Federals fused, and elected Mr. Germain, Speaker.

In 1821 he was appointed Judge of Cortland county, which office he filled for nearly eighteen years—five of which he occupied the honorable position of first Judge.

In 1825 he was elected Supervisor, and continued to discharge its duties until 1835.

In 1832 he was elected a Presidential Elector, and cast his vote for the Democratic candidate.

In 1834 he was elected to the 24th Congress of the

United States, from the counties of Tioga, Tompkins and Cortland.

In 1839 he came to Cortland Village, and erected the splendid residence which he now occupies.

Judge Reynolds is emphatically a self-made man—a man of character and influence. There are but few who have made greater exertions in early life—who have labored harder, or who, through self-exertion, have carved their way to fortune, honor, and just respectability.

William Randall was born in the year 1782. His brother, General Roswell Randall, was born in 1786. Their father, Robert Randall, was a native of Stonington, Connecticut. William was reared to farming pursuits. Roswell obtained a superior education, and studied law with Stephen O. Ranegan, of Oxford. He was admitted to the bar, but never practised. The brothers engaged in merchandise together in Madison county, but removed to Cortland Village about the year 1812, where they continued the business. Their store was on the site now occupied by that of James S. Squires. They were highly successful in trade, which continued for a number of years. They at length dissolved their partnership, and William erected a store, which is now the Randall Bank. Roswell built the Eagle Store, now un occupied. When they finally discontinued the mercantile trade, the former engaged in banking and farming, and the latter in cultivating his farm. William Randall was emphatically a man of mark in his day. He possessed a clear, strong, and vigorous intellect, a firm and resolute mind, a warm and generous heart, and was, in short, a valued citizen. He died December 23, 1850.

Roswell Randall was an early Post-master of Cortland Village, and has honorably filled various other positions. His military rank of Brigadier-General was attained through the several gradations, commencing with fourth Corporal. He was much admired as a military officer. And now, at the age of seventy-two, with his physical and mental constitution unimpaired, has but partially retired from the active duties of life.

William and Roswell Randall were energetic business men. The monuments of their memory may be seen in the elegant residences, erected at their expense, which adorn and beautify the village.

George W. Bradford was born in Cooperstown, Otsego county, N. Y., May 9, 1796. He is of English descent, and of the sixth generation from Governor William Bradford, one of the Pilgrim Fathers who, in 1620, on board of the May Flower, braved the waves of the stormy ocean, preferring to seek an asylum in the rude wilds of America rather than endure the persecution of religious fanatics and political tyrants in the land of his birth, and who for twenty years was the great head or ruling spirit of the Plymouth Colony. The ancestors of Dr. Bradford were of families of distinction in the early annals of Massachusetts.

His father was an agriculturist and manufacturer, and gave his son the advantages of a common school education. He early impressed upon his mind the actual necessity of self-reliance ; and this has ever been an element in his character.

In 1812, at the age of sixteen years, he was sent to the academy of Woodstock, Ct., and placed under the charge of the principal, the venerable Rinaldo Burleigh, father of Wm. H. and C. C. Burleigh, whose literary achievements have made them ornaments to the age in which they live.

In 1814 he entered a classical school at Clinton, N. Y., and became a classmate of the Hon. Gerrit Smith. He pursued his classical studies until failing health required a relaxation from his studies. He abandoned for a time the study of Cæsar, Virgil, Livy, Sallust and Cicero, and made a general tour through the States and the Canadas, occupying about one year of time. Having regained his health, in 1816 he commenced the study of medicine with Dr. Thomas Fuller, of Cooperstown, and completed his professional studies in 1820. In the same year he was licensed to practice medicine by the Medical Association of Otsego county, and soon after located in Homer, where he united with the Cortland Medical Association, and commenced the practice of his profession. He soon acquired a varied and extensive practice, and devoted all his energies exclusively to it.

In 1846 he was elected a permanent member of the State Medical Society, and received the degree of M. D. in the same year. In 1847 he was made a member of the American Medical Association. In 1856 he was elected an honorary member of the Wisconsin State Historical Society, and of the American Association for the Advancement of Science in 1856.

In 1858 the Faculty of Genesee College conferred on him the honorary degree of A. M.

Dr. Bradford held a commission in the Medical Staff of the Militia of this State, under Major General Hatheway, from 1821 to 1832, occupying the different grades from Surgeon's Mate of the Regiment to Hospital Surgeon of the Division. In the fall of 1851 he was elected to the Assembly of this State, and in 1853 he was elevated to a seat in the State Senate, and in 1855 he was reëlected by a very large and increased majority. He served the three terms with great credit to himself and his constituents. He was Chairman of one of the important Committees of the House, and of two Standing and one Select Committee of the Senate.

"The interests of education, and the benevolent institutions of the State, found in Senator Bradford a warm supporter."*

He made an active and industrious member, having been absent only on one occasion—an evening session—during the whole five years of his legislative labors; and his absence at that time was caused by a detention of the cars. He framed and introduced several very important bills, among which we may mention the one for the appointment of Commissioners of Common Schools. Few Senators were more generally respected or possessed more influence among the members.

In the Congregational church (of which he became a member in 1832), in the Temperance Reform, and as a member of the County Bible Society, he was especially active. For the last thirty-four years he has served in the capacity of Secretary of the Medical Association.

The Cortland Academy owes its prosperity in no small degree to the efforts of Dr. Bradford, whose ambition has been to make it what it really is, a "model institution." For the last thirty years he has discharged

* Senator Kelley's letter.

the duties of Trustee. In the sick room he has ever exhibited a kind and generous sympathy ; to the poor and friendless he has been liberal and just.

His reading is varied and extensive. In the science of Botany, Geology, Mineralogy, and Zoölogy, he became a proficient.

He was married in 1818 to Miss Mary Ann Walker, of Middlefield. Of their three children—daughters—only one is now living,—the wife of William W. Northrop, of New York. Mrs. Northrop is a lady of extensive reading and of liberal education. She reads fluently in seven different languages.

Dr. Bradford is at present engaged in the practice of his profession, in which capacity he has been abundantly successful.

Samuel Nelson was born in Hebron, Washington co., New York, Nov. 10, 1792. His parents were John Rogers Nelson and Jane M'Carter ; both of Irish descent. Their ancestors emigrated from the north of Ireland to Salem, New York, about the year 1760. They came over in company with their clergyman, the Rev. Dr. Clark, a protestant of the strictest Presbyterian faith.

John Rogers Nelson married Miss Jane M'Carter at the close of the Revolution, and settled in Hebron. They were among the early pioneers in the settlement of that town,—its organization having occurred in March, 1788. Their eldest son, John Jay Nelson, only brother of the subject of this sketch, resides on the original premises.

Samuel Nelson was at an early age sent to the district school, where he made the usual progress in the primary branches. He fitted for college at a classical school in Salem, taught by the Rev. Mr. Gross; and at the Granville Academy, having for its principal the distinguished Salem Town. He entered Middleberry College, the Rev. Dr. Davis, principal, in the spring of 1811, and graduated in August, 1813, at the age of twenty-one. Adopting the legal profession, he studied law in Salem, under two eminent lawyers,—Messrs. Savage and Woods,—with whom he remained upwards of two years;—the senior partner being the late distinguished Chief Justice of New York.

In 1816, Judge Woods, the junior partner, removed to Madison county, where he settled in his profession. He was accompanied by Mr. Nelson, who, at the January term of the Supreme Court, 1817, was admitted to the bar. Soon after, he came to this county and located in Cortland Village, where he entered into the practice of law.

Cortland, though a small village, had become the county seat. The leading members of the bar were Oliver Wisewell, Henry Stephens, Samuel S. Baldwin, Townsend Ross, Edward C. Reed, and Augustus Donnelly. They commenced their profession unaided by fortune or legal reputation. They, however, belonged to a class of progressionists which seldom fail of ultimate success. Their intercourse was of the most friendly character. The principle of exclusiveness was not in those days cultivated, for selfishness was detested and discarded. In the southern portion of the county Messrs. Nelson and Stephens held the exclusive sway in the practice under what was then termed the Ten Pound Act, which was limited to the jurisdiction of Justices Courts. And here was laid the foundation of their professional ability and legal fame. Mr. Stephens had already acquired some notoriety as an able and successful lawyer. He defended the first suit brought by Mr. Nelson in the Common Pleas. It was on a stock note. The declaration contained a special count, and the common counts for goods sold and delivered. Stephens demurred to the special count, and put in the general issue to the common counts. Hon. John Keep occupied the bench. The demurrer was first argued, and a decision rendered against Mr. Nelson, followed by an execution for costs,—which very much astonished and chagrined him. At least, he felt that it was a most unfavorable beginning. However, in his despair he sought relief in his library, and soon discovered that it was erroneous practice to enter up judgment and issue execution for costs on the demurrer until the trial of the issue of fact, and the whole case is disposed of. Hence Mr. Nelson obtained an order to stay proceedings on the execution, and at the next term of court moved to set aside the execution for irregularity, which, with costs, was granted. He also tried the issue of fact, and recovered his suit; collected the note and costs, without having to pay any. This Judge Nelson remembers as having been regarded at the time as quite an achievement; and he has not since forgotten the practice.

The above incident fully illustrates how law may be learned even before courts not initiated into its mysteries.

The triumph of Mr. Nelson was of marked significance. It measurably established his reputation; gave him a higher position among his legal compeers, and opened for him a future bright and promising. If he was not actually "born a lawyer"—if he did not become a Hercules at a single stride, he at least rose rapidly in his profession, gathered fresh laurels, luxuriant in their growth, and which have neither been dimmed by the frosts of time, nor soiled by the touch of an enemy. His open-hearted frankness, liberal views and impassioned eloquence; his well-balanced mind and generous impulses,—eminently fitted him for the position he so creditably occupied, and combined to make him an ornament to the profession and a blessing to his country. Indeed, few young men of that day ranked higher, or received a more liberal share of business. The talents, ability, and stern integrity which he displayed on all occasions, made him a favorite with the people, from whom he afterwards received numerous political and social honors.

In the winter of 1820–1, he was appointed by the Legislature a presidential elector, and he voted at the Electoral College at Albany, for James Monroe, when chosen for the second term.

During the latter year he received the appointment of Post-master at Cortland Village. The peculiar circumstances attending the appointment are worthy of at least a passing notice. At that time Major Roswell Randall was the incumbent. Young Nelson was, through the kindness of the Major, boarding in his family,—and the appointment, being entirely unexpected by either, greatly perplexed Mr. Nelson, inasmuch as it left the implication that he had been undermining his friend while enjoying his hospitality. He, however, knew nothing about the appointment until he received the commission through the post-office. Hon. Elisha Litchfield, of Onondaga county, was then a member of Congress, and had, without consulting Mr. Nelson, procured the appointment.

He was a delegate in the Convention of 1821 for the revision of the State Constitution, and took an active part in the deliberations of that intelligent body. He advocated the abolition of the property qualification, which was upheld and defended by Chancellor Kent and Chief Justice Spencer. Unlike them, he could not see why men, because they might not possess a dollar's worth of real estate, were the less competent to exercise or enjoy the inalienable rights of citizens.

In April, 1823, he was appointed by Governor Yates one of the Circuit Judges under the new Constitution, which had the previous year been ratified by a majority of 33,330 votes. The court was composed of the counties of Otsego, Delaware, Chenango, Broome, Cortland, Tompkins, Tioga, and Steuben.

Having sustained himself throughout his eight years' service upon the bench, with ability and honor, he was on the first day of February, 1831, appointed by Governor Throop the successor of Hon. William L. Marcy on the bench of the Supreme Court of the State of New York,—Judge Marcy having been elected to the United States Senate.

On the 31st day of August, 1837, he was appointed by Governor Marcy and the Senate, Chief Justice of the State of New York,—Judge Savage having resigned that honorable position. Judge Nelson remained in that office until 1845, when he was appointed by President Tyler and the Senate, the successor of Judge Thompson, Associate Justice of the Supreme Court of the United States. Judge Thompson had adorned and dignified the office for a period exceeding thirty-eight years—"one of the longest and most honorable judicial careers on record."* And yet, Judge Nelson has thus far filled the seat made vacant by the death of Judge Thompson, in a degree so clearly eminent as to place him in the front rank of legal ability and judicial fame.

During his absence from Otsego county, in 1846, he was appointed a delegate to the State Convention, which convened at Albany on the first day of June of that year, for the purpose of revising the Constitution; but the duties of his office as Associate Justice of the Supreme Court of the United States, and impaired health, precluded his attending the Convention only for a brief portion of the time it was in session.

Judge Nelson received the degree of LL. D. from Columbia College, New York city; from Middlebury College, Vermont, his *alma mater*, as well as from Geneva College.

Mr. Nelson has been twice married. In the fall of 1819, he married Miss Pamela Woods, eldest daughter of Judge Woods, of Madison co. The union proved a very happy and agreeable one. The tie that bound them was not, however, permitted to remain unbroken. Death, the dread foe, envious of mortal bliss, "marked her for his own." She died in the summer of 1822. Her disease was consumption; and she bore her protracted suffering with resignation, and looked forward

* Van Santvord's Life of Judge Thompson.

to an exchange of worlds with Christian peace and hope.

In April, 1825, Mr. Nelson was again united in marriage to a lady of superior mind, genial temper and social worth, in the person of Miss Catharine A. Russell, only daughter of Judge Russell, of Cooperstown, where they now reside.

In the character of Judge Nelson we find much to admire; a combination of valuable characteristics which are seldom found united in one person. Originally endowed with genius and moral sensibility; with a grasp of intellect which seized as by intuition those stores of knowledge which others could acquire only by painful application, and with a full, rich flow of social feeling which early rendered him the fascinating centre of an extended circle of friendship, he braced himself for a career of emulation, and at once became an example and an ornament to the legal profession.

In all the positions in which he has been called to act, he has distinguished himself with marked ability.

His career upon the bench has been characterized by honesty, firmness, discretion, and liberal equity. His disposition of questions, even of the most embarrassing character, and involving the greatest responsibility, meets the general approbation of the bar and the bench. His opinions are clear, comprehensive and manly, and are pronounced with the scrupulous fidelity, the discretion and candor of a conscientious jurist. His great learning, eloquence and genius have secured him a pre-eminence in the profession and practice of law; and by his persevering attention to the duties of his office he has amassed a princely fortune.

Ira Harris was born in Charleston, Montgomery co., N. Y., May 31st, 1802. His parents removed to Cortland county, in 1808, and located upont he Preble flats. He remained with his father until he was seventeen years of age, alternately working upon the farm and attending the district school. He advanced rapidly in his studies, and devoured in the intervals of farm labor every work of interest that he could conveniently procure. In 1815 he entered the Academy in Homer, where he pursued his preparatory collegiate studies. In September, 1822, he entered the Junior class in Union College, and graduated with the first honors, in 1824.

Having determined to pursue the legal profession, he made the necessary arrangements, and at once entered the office of Augustus Donnelly, in Cortland Village, with whom he remained one year. His affable deportment, social habits, well-disciplined mind, and unremitting attention to his studies, secured him many friends, and most especially the good will of Donnelly. He left Cortland with a view of obtaining better advantages for the prosecution of his studies. His destination was Albany. Thither he went, an entire stranger, carrying with him a voluntary letter of introduction from his friend Donnelly to the late Chief Justice Spencer, whose office he entered ; and during the two succeeding years, completed his professional studies. Thus, in three years after graduating, he was admitted to the bar, and commenced the practice of his chosen profession in the city.

He had been a diligent and laborious student, and had fully qualified himself for his new position in life. He was ambitious and persevering, and soon laid the foundation for his future eminence.

> "On Fame's high hill he saw
> The laurel spread its everlasting green,
> And wished to climb."

The splendor of his genius, and the many noble and dignified traits of character for which he soon became distinguished, served in an eminent degree to enlarge his sphere of acquaintance, and urge him forward in his onward and upward career to fame and fortune. His careful preparation of authorities, his honesty of purpose, his chasteness of language, and his oratorical powers, were well calculated to make him successful. Business accumulated on his hands, and his reputation increased with each succeeding year, until at length he occupied a proud and even an enviable position among the most distinguished veterans of the Albany bar. He was

> "The forest-born Demosthenes
> Whose thunders shook the Philip of the seas."

He continued to practice in the city for twenty years, gathering fresh laurels and achieving new victories, until called by the voice of his friends to occupy a higher and a more responsible position.

On the first of July, 1847, he took his seat upon the bench of the Supreme Court, having, in the organization of the Judiciary of the Constitution of 1846, been elected and drawn for the term of four years. His arguments were clear, strong and logical, and tended greatly to enhance his reputation. In 1851 he was reëlected for the term of eight years.

At the general elections in the years 1844 and 1845 he was elected to the Assembly. He at once became a leading member of the house, and took an active part in its debates. His arguments were lucid and logical, and frequently exhibited the marks of the gifted orator, not surpassed " by the brilliant efforts of Ames, or the impassioned appeals of Hamilton."

In the spring of 1846 he was elected to the Constitutional Convention, which convened in Albany on the first day of June for the purpose of revising our State Constitution. He was the only member from the city, and took an active part in its deliberations. His mind appears to have been admirably adapted to the details of the business which of necessity came before the convention.

In the autumn of the same year he was elected to the State Senate, but resigned his seat in 1847, when elevated to the Supreme Bench.

Judge Harris has ever taken a deep interest in all matters connected with education. He has been a trustee in most of the literary institutions in the city,—in Union College, as also in the University at Rochester, in the founding of which he was actively engaged. His philanthropy is far-reaching. All the impulses of his heart are drawn out in sympathy for the oppressed and the friendless. He possesses a large share of legal experience, and hence the general correctness of his conclusions. Upon legal points, involving questions of right and wrong, his opinions have seldom been at fault ; and his suggestions have invariably been just and valuable. Indeed, he has discharged the duties of Justice of the Supreme Court with signal satisfaction both to the bar and to the public. His decisions command great respect, and are regarded as the end of the law.

In intellect, Judge Harris affords a rare combination of excellence. Traversing, as by enchantment, the path of public confidence and renown, he has gained those honored halls, where his graceful manner, impressive diction, and logical acumen have given him a position among the most attractive and eloquent men of the age. Nor is his history yet fully written ; the future annalist will erect to his memory a more enduring memorial.

William H. Shankland, late Judge of the Court of Appeals, was born in Montgomery county, N. Y., in the year 1804, and is of Scottish descent. His parents removed to Pompey, Onondaga county, in 1808. He received his English education in the primary or common schools of Onondaga, and his classical in the Academy at Pompey Hill. The late Joshua Spencer, of Utica, was his teacher for three successive years. He was admitted to the bar of the Supreme Court, in May, 1827, and during the same year commenced the practice of law in Cortland Village. Mr. Shankland was married, in February, 1828, to Miss Lucia Emeline Clark, of Onondaga county, N. Y. Soon after, Mr. Shankland was elected a Justice of the Peace, in which capacity he served four years. In 1836 he was appointed District Attorney, and discharged the duties of the office for eight successive years with marked ability and success, when he resigned, and was succeeded by Horatio Ballard. In 1847 he was elected one of the Justices of the Supreme Court under the new Constitution ; and in 1849 he was reëlected to the same office for the term of eight years. His faithfulness in the discharge of his duties was proverbial ; and the urbanity of his manners added to his constant patience and good humor, all regulated by a well-trained mind, a quick perception and sound judgment, enabled him to dignify the bench. His clear, logical and nicely discriminating powers of mind are prominently exhibited in all of his important decisions. He is now residing in the city of Syracuse, where he is devoting himself to his profession with all the ardor, enthusiam and vigor of youth.

Judge Shankland has ever been regarded as an able lawyer in both branches of the profession,—as a counsellor and as an advocate. He is remarkably industrious and persevering; possesses a high order of business talents, a thorough education, a clear, vigorous intellect, and he is in brief fitted to adorn and dignify any position to which he may aspire. He is a man of highly courteous and pleasing manners—of fine personal appearance ; and no Judge ever presided on the bench with a greater union of amenity and dignity.

But what adds the greatest lustre to his fame may be recorded in a single line. *He is a self-made man.* His talents, integrity and personal merit have given him a position among his brethren of the bench and the bar, above which ambition itself cannot wish to rise.

Hiram Gray was born in Salem, Washington county, N. Y., April 20, 1802. He early exhibited great activity of mind and energy of character. His preparatory collegiate studies were pursued at the Washington Academy, in Salem. In 1818 he entered the Sophomore class in Union College, and graduated with the usual honors, in July, 1821. In the early part of his senior year he entered the law office of the late Chief Justice Savage, and studied during the vacations.

On the 12th of February, 1821, Judge Savage received the appointment of Comptroller, and at about the time he entered upon his duties Mr. Gray came to Cortland, and entered the office of Messrs. Nelson and Dayton. On the 21st of April, 1823, Mr. Nelson was appointed Circuit Judge of the Sixth District. Soon after the appointment of Nelson, Dayton and Woods formed a copartnership, and Mr. Gray continued his studies in their office until the October Term, 1823, when he was admitted to practice. In the following December he went to Dryden and opened an office, where he remained until April, 1824, when he returned to Cortland county, and became a partner of Judge Ross, in Homer. He subsequently went to Elmira and commenced the practice of his profession. He made an active and energetic lawyer, and rose rapidly in professional eminence. He possessed a heart full of tender sensibilities and generous impulses; was never repulsive, and hence was easily approached. His political affinities were always Democratic, and to that party he early became attached, and was soon regarded as an active and prominent politician. In 1836 he was elected to the United States Congress. He made a ready and able debater—a prominent and efficient member of that distinguished body.

On the 13th day of January, 1846, Mr. Gray was appointed by Governor Wright, Circuit Judge of the Sixth Judicial District, and served under the Constitution of 1846 until the election in June, 1847, when he was elected one of the Justices of the Supreme Court—and he drew for four years. He was reëlected November 4, 1851. His term will expire June 1, 1860; after which he will retire with an honorable and a well-earned fame, to private occupation.

In person, Judge Gray is prepossessing; in stature, noble and commanding, with a frame robust, vigorous and athletic. Social in his manners, chaste and happy in his colloquial and conversational powers, with a strong, vigorous and well-balanced mind, he exhibits a combination of characteristics seldom found united in one man.

His range of reading has been varied and extensive. As a lawyer, he has ever exhibited a devoted attachment to his profession. His intellect has adorned it; and his scrupulous integrity given it honor and respect. As a Judge, he has proven himself eminently qualified to wear the ermine;—is distinguished for the correctness of his opinions, and the firmness with which his decisions are made. In brief, he is regarded by his brethren in the profession, and the public, as an eloquent advocate and a profound Jurist.

Lewis Kingsley was born at the upper village in Cincinnatus, December 15, 1823. In 1827 his father removed to the lower village, where he remained until his death, in January, 1857, having been a resident of the county about thirty-six years—twenty-five of which he was actively engaged in the mercantile business. The first rudiments of the education of his son Lewis, the subject of this sketch, were acquired at the common school. He afterwards attended select schools, taught by A. H. Benedict and R. K. Bourne, and subsequently he attended one term in the Sherburne Academy, where his schooling ended. He had, however, laid the foundation of a good classical education, which he afterwards continued to improve. In June, 1843, he commenced the study of law with Barak Niles, in

Cincinnatus, with whom he remained until October, 1844.

Hoping to obtain better advantages for study, he left Cincinnatus and entered the law office of Benjamin F. Rexford, of Norwich, Chenango county, N. Y., with whom he remained until July, 1846, when he was admitted to the bar by the old Supreme Court, then being held in Utica. In the autumn of that year Mr. Kingsley entered into partnership with Judge Niles, in Cincinnatus, with whom he remained until the spring of 1848, when the Judge went to Pennsylvania to reside. Mr. Kingsley continued the practice alone for upwards of a year, when he became a partner of Samuel C. Graves, and remained with him until 1851, when his official position made it necessary for him to change his residence for that of Cortland Village.

In the spring of 1848 he was elected Supervisor of Cincinnatus. In 1849 he declined a re-nomination ; but contrary to his wishes he was elected to the office of Town Clerk. At the November election of the same year, he was elected to the New York Assembly ; and in 1851 he was chosen County Judge and Surrogate. In January, 1856, he removed to Norwich, Chenango co., and formed a partnership with Benjamin F. Rexford, with whom he still remains.

Judge Kingsley possesses a sound judgment, discriminating mind, frank and manly urbanity, a warm heart, and a generous and self-sacrificing spirit. His habits of life have ever been active and enterprising. As a citizen, he has been held in high respect. As a politician, his opinions have always been the result of his own judgment and reflections; and when once formed, he has been open and free in their expression,—never swerving for expediency or party considerations.

As a lawyer, he has ever exhibited a high opinion of the dignity of the profession, possessing the true *esprit du corps*:—invariably accurate in his preparation of causes, and energetic and persevering in their prosecution.

As Judge and Surrogate, he discharged the duties with fidelity, ability, and to general acceptance.

And in all the varied relations of life, Judge Kingsley has adorned and dignified his position.

Rev. E. G. Holland, a gentleman of enlarged, liberal views, and of great intelligence, was born in the town of Solon, Cortland co., N. Y., April 14, 1817. His educational advantages, up to fourteen years of age, were such as the public schools of his native town afforded. His father, however, was a man of enlarged reading and of excellent education. He had also given much attention to the subject of teaching; and was therefore prepared to impart to his son the advantages of home tuition. He was early instructed in the various branches of good husbandry. His inclinations, however, induced him to turn his attention from that of the republican farmer to the more agreeable literary pursuit; hence he adopted the sentiment of the immortal bard, and resolved to

"Drink deep, or taste not the Pierian Spring."

Modest and unpretending in his manners, with the purest rectitude of principle, prompt and energetic, with warm social habits and gentlemanly demeanor, he was alike respected and cherished in the circle in which

Yours Truly
E. G. Holland.

he moved. He early exhibited a strong attachment to his books, and the scintillations emitted from his well-developed brain attracted to his side the intelligent and refined, by whom he was regarded with peculiar interest; for they saw in him the embodiment of a young immortal genius just bursting into the full fruition of glorious manhood.

His progress in study surprised even his most intimate friends. No question was so abstruse but he mastered it. No lesson too difficult for him to accomplish. His aspirations led from the dull, prosaic paths of life, and he sought for pleasure amid the flowery dales and classic fields through which the pure bright streams of knowledge flowed.

At the age of fourteen he entered the academy in Homer, where he studied the classics, Natural Philosophy, Chemistry, and Mathematics. The Grammar of the English language had been his favorite study, from the age of ten years; and when he commenced the classics, five different systems of the English grammar were familiar to him. At the age of twenty he was fully prepared for college; but was dissuaded from taking the college routine, partly from the conviction that it often sacrifices individuality, and partly from the opportunity offered to pursue his studies in private. Therefore the college course, which offers so many real honors to others, presents none to him. It has been a fundamental idea of his life, that man's education is never completed; that Nature, Experience, Consciousness, and the Great Masters, are the Four Faculties in the University which is world-wide, and wiser than all Professional Chairs. In this he has sought to study; entered years since, but has not as yet graduated.

The profession of the Rev. Mr. Holland is Literature and the Christian Ministry. Holding the religious sentiment to be universal in humanity, and believing that in Christianity it has found its highest and noblest expression, it has not been the sectarian form of faith to which he has been attached. It is Christianity radiating from its Divine Centre, the Christ,—as agreeing with the laws of the human spirit, its wants, weaknesses, and aspirations,—as harmonizing with all the truths of the external universe. It is in this form that he has represented the faith of Christianity. Sects he has regarded as being valuable, as fragments of Truth,—the catholicity so much desired being an attainment of the Future, not of the Present. We do not therefore regard him as being represented by any particular sect. He confides in the Church of the Future, in which all sectarian paths shall finally end.

Mr. Holland has contributed several exceedingly valuable volumes to American literature,—one, the leading subjects of which are the Life and Teachings of Confucius, the Chinese moral philosopher ; the Moral Genius and Literature of William Ellery Channing ; a Review of William Kinkade on Natural Theology, with essays on the Nature and Characteristics of Genius ; the Elements and Laws of Beauty ; the Infinite Harmony which pervades Nature and reveals in the Ages of History; the Immortal Life, as evinced by Analogies of Nature and the Facts of Consciousness ; and Human Rights as based in Human Nature. The essay on Channing was in 1856 translated into the German language, and was published by Bernard Shultze, a publisher at Leipsic. It was favorably received by the German press ; and, in connection with Channing's works, and separately, was sent over the States of Germany.

In 1855 Mr. Holland visited Europe ; he sailed from New York, June 10th, in the Germania, destined for Hamburg, one of the wealthy free towns of Germany, pleasantly situated on both sides of the Elbe. While here he visited the tomb of the German poet, Klopstock, at Ottensen ; his house and studio in Hamburg—reminiscences of the harbinger of the modern German poetic literature. His stay here was brief ; he did not, however, leave without seeing German civilization in its most attractive phases. He spent two months in Berlin studying German literature, and German manners and life as reflected in that metropolis ; studying the works of art there so numerously accumulated ; making the acquaintance of Alexander Von Humboldt ; Prof. Rauch, the famed sculptor ; Dr. Karl Ritter, and other German celebrities, by whom he was most generously treated.

In September he visited Dresden, its picture galleries, its varied objects of interest, as also its neighboring scenery.

From Dresden he went to Leipsic, the chief book mart of the nation ; Weimar, famed as the residence of Goethe, Schiller, Wieland and Herder. He was greatly interested with the reminiscences of the old "German Athens ;" went to Frankfort-on-the-Main ; Heidelberg, one of the old University towns of Baden, renowned for its sufferings in past wars, for its grand old ruins whose interest is never exhausted, for its University, and it may be added, for the exceeding beauty of the region about it. Here he remained one year, and during his studies in German literature he gave two courses of lectures on American literature to the citizens of Heidelberg—the first consisting of five, and the second of seven lectures, in which the romance writers, the poets, historians, orators and eminent thinkers of the country were represented. The most eminent men of the city were conspicuous in securing these valuable lectures. In Bonn he gave a course of nine lectures on American literature, landscape and institutions. The press, without distinction, referred to his lectures in the most favorable terms. The *Badishe Landeszeitung*, of April 3d, 1856, said : " We have been much pleased with the lectures of Mr. Holland, from America, which he gave here on American literature. These lectures prove how much the Americans have advanced in the poetic art, and in philosophy, and that the saying of an important author is true, viz.: that the American literature, though a youth in years, is a giant in form and vigor." The *Bonner Zeitung*, of September, 1856, said, "The writings of Mr. Holland are highly important and instructive. In style it is not too much to say that they may be compared favorably to those of Von Humboldt. His present course of lectures furnishes a rare opportunity to those who can appreciate a discourse in English."

He also visited Cologne, Belgium and France, remaining some months in Paris ; the Isle of Wight ; England, in her chief towns ; spent one year and a half in London, a part of the time being engaged in study at the British Museum, and in giving lectures on American themes. Passing to Scotland, he visited Glasgow, Ayrshire, the Highlands, and the scenery of the Clyde ; as also Edinboro' and its attractive scenes ; and finally completed his journey with making a tour through Erin-gobragh.

His lectures in London were highly lauded by the English press. The *London Chronicle*, the *Morning Advertiser*, *The Illustrated News*, *The Star*, and the *Journal of Arts and Sciences*, were prominent among the papers which thus favorably noticed him.

While in Great Britain he made the acquaintance of Thomas Carlyle, by whom he was kindly received ; of poet Mackay, Geo. Combe, as also various personages of the English nobility.

In July, 1858, Mr. Holland returned to New York in the steamer Indian Empire, after a three years' residence in Europe.

He remembers with reverential pride his native State, native county, and especially his native town. He possesses a richly-endowed mind, is a bold, vigorous and original writer, and always takes pleasure in dealing with practical themes. Indeed, he is regarded as one of the most remarkable men of the age,—"one of the few that were not born to die."

Mr. Holland is at present settled at Irvington, New Jersey, though his address is 151 Tenth street, New York.

Stephen W. Clark, A. M., the present Principal of Cortland Academy, third son of Joseph and Mary Clark, and younger brother of Myron H. Clark, ex-governor of New York, was born in Naples, N. Y., April 24th, 1810. After having spent his earlier years in agricultural pursuits in his native town, and in the capacity of a mercantile clerk in Canandaigua, he completed his preparatory studies in Franklin Academy, Prattsburgh, N. Y., and entered Amherst College in 1833. Here, under the care and instruction of the celebrated Dr. Hitchcock, he became specially devoted to the study of the Natural Sciences.

Having graduated with the usual honors in 1837, he immediately entered upon the duties of his chosen profession, which he has pursued without intermission to the present time, as Principal successively of Groton Academy, Monroe Collegiate Institute, East Bloomfield Academy, and Cortland Academy—a period of twenty-two years. He has been from his youth a member of the Congregational Church.

In addition to Prof. Clark's labors as instructor, he has written several popular and exceedingly valuable school books, among which are "Analysis of the English Language," "Etymological Chart" and "A Practical Grammar, in which words, phrases and sentences are classified according to their offices, and their various relations to one another; illustrated by a complete system of Diagrams."

These works, published by one of the most enterprising and successful houses in New York, have already reached a wide circulation, and have become deservedly popular throughout the Union.

His "English Grammar" has already reached a circulation of 30,000 per annum. In accordance with the recommendations of Superintendents of Public Instruction of various States, it has been adopted as the text book on Grammar, and it is rapidly finding its way into every State in the American Republic. "This original production will doubtless become an indispensable auxiliary to restore the English Language to its appropriate rank in our system of education. Indeed, we are tempted to assert that it foretells the dawn of a brighter age to our mother tongue."*

Successful as Professor Clark has been as an author, still he regards his chosen profession as a Teacher as his greatest business in life. To this he devotes his undivided attention and untiring energies ; and the success which attends his efforts gives evidence of his efficiency as a faithful Principal, and of his talents as an instructor. Cortland Academy stands second to no other sub-collegiate institution in the State of New York.

Professor Clark possesses a sound judgment, discriminating mind, frank and manly urbanity of deportment, high moral and social virtues, and a large-hearted generosity which endears him to the students, creating emotions which are always favorable to a healthful progress in study. His mode of government is calm and conciliatory, and may with propriety be embodied in a single word, that of *kindness*, which in influencing, controlling or directing the young aspiring mind is of more valuable importance than all the tyrant exactions of pseudo pedagogues, and may prove of a more lasting benefit to the country than all the golden sands of the Pacific coast. Happily would it be for our country were the various academic and collegiate institutes favored with as justly popular and courteous a principal as Professor Clark.

De Witt Clinton Glover, the eldest son of Daniel and Rhoda Gage Glover, was born in De Ruyter, Madison county, N. Y., in the year 1817.†

* Southern Literary Gazette. † Communicated by a lady.

His early advantages were such as the common schools of his native place afforded ; but while he loved the pursuits of literature, as tending to ennoble and purify the mind, he was not, strictly speaking, a student. Other aims possessed his soul; hopes, visions, and aspirations, such as haunt the pillow of Genius alone, were his daily visitants. A quiet, sensitive and shrinking boy, he shunned the boisterous sports and the noisy haunts of his comrades, and walked alone, and adored as one who has

> "Longings, yearnings, strivings
> For the good he comprehends not."

A love of the beautiful in all its forms was a marked element of his nature, and sometimes the bright visions that thronged his brain, took form and semblance upon paper. Well do I remember, when a child, he took me to his studio, and (himself but little else than a child) showed to me, in his boyish confidence, some of the sketches he had made. He had a room in his father's house where he sat hour by hour (when the green fields and sunshine tempted other boys abroad) at work upon some cherished task. Reared amid the seclusion and comparative isolation of a country village, (for it will be remembered that the march of improvements did not then keep pace with steam,) he was denied those outward helps which are now offered to the student in every career in our republic ; and by the force of his own genius alone he leaped over obstacles and accomplished results which many have vainly striven to attain, though surrounded by abundant aid and powerful patronage. He not only showed himself an artist in his

Your friend,
F. B. Carpenter

delineations upon paper, but even in boyhood, alone and unassisted, he commenced engraving upon wood and steel. Engraving for a pastime finally became a passion, and by the advice of some judges who pronounced upon his work, he adopted it as a profession. He executed orders for a time at home, but feeling himself in too contracted a sphere, he went to New York and entered the studio of J. W. Casilear, the eminent designer and engraver, where he made rapid progress.

That he excelled in the department of art he chose for himself, the works he left behind him, as well as the unqualified praise of his employers, abundantly testify.

In the midst of this career of hope and promise his health failed him, and he was forced to return to his native valley, in the hope that rest might restore his shattered frame to its early vigor ; but alas ! neither yearning love, fervent prayers, nor gentle ministrations could stay the footsteps of the Destroying Angel, and on the 3d of January, 1836, he sank beneath his fatal and insidious malady, trusting, as he said, "that he had made his peace with God." Let us hope that the noble talents which were here but expanding into flower, having been transplanted to the celestial gardens, may have ripened, and borne rich fruit to the glory of the Great Husbandman.

Francis B. Carpenter was born in Homer, Cortland county, New York, August 6th, 1830. His father, Asaph H. Carpenter, made his advent into Homer in 1800. His general characteristics are strictly Puritan, and they exhibit in a striking manner the self-reliant energy of the pilgrim spirit.

The educational advantages of Francis were limited

to the common school, and one term at the academy. He early manifested a desire to become an artist, and hence exhibited an aversion to farm labor,—not that he regarded it as a disreputable employment, but because he wished to become master of the limner's art. His father objected to his pursuing it as a profession, presuming that the success of his son in life would be better promoted by felling trees and in cultivating the soil. But the genius which shone in young Carpenter's face pictured a brighter future than this. He regarded agriculture as Tallyrand did the princess of Courlande, and would have made the same remark, 'You have but one fault, you are perfectly unendurable." He preferred to delineate character with the pencil and brush, or chalk ideal landscapes upon the fences and farm buildings. William Tell, in the act of shooting the apple from his son's head, and the capture of Major Andre, were among the first subjects which our young artist delineated in the vivid colors of chalk, brick dust, white lead and lampblack. The father little thought that in opposing the natural desire of his son he was for a time smothering that genius which has since made him famous, and crowned his aspirations with a victory of more value than the achievements of the laureled warrior. And the triumph is the more gratifying because achieved while unaided by fortune or family distinction. Indeed, it is doubtful whether there is another artist in America who, through his self-reliant energy, has so successfully conquered parental opposition, overleaped the barriers of poverty and prejudice, and in so brief a period carved his way to Fame's temple.

His mother, "ever sympathizing and appreciative,"

sat for his first bold effort at portrait painting. And it is worthy of remark, that the likeness, though wanting the artistic finish of the experienced limner, was yet so striking, that the father was reluctantly compelled to acknowledge its truthfulness ; he was never afterward heard to utter his oft-repeated expression concerning "the boy's nonsense," and was himself the next sitter for a picture.

Soon after the completion of the portrait of his father, he entered the studio of Sandford Thayer, of Syracuse, with whom he remained about five months, making rapid progress, and acquiring a still more exalted opinion of the profession.

During Mr. Carpenter's stay in Syracuse, Mr. Elliott, the distinguished artist, made a professional visit there. He perceived the genius of the beardless boy, and kindly imparted to him all the knowledge within his power; especially with reference to his mode of coloring.

In 1846, Mr. Carpenter, having returned to Homer, before he reached his sixteenth birthday opened a studio in the village. Relying upon his own exertions, independent of parental aid, he bravely launched his little bark upon the great sea of life. The citizens were suspicious of his ability, and hence gave him but slight employment; and it was long before he could see a clear sky in the ideal world he had fancifully created. The current of prejudice, however, soon turned in his favor. The first ten dollars which he received from any one source, was presented to him by Hon. Henry S. Randall, as a partial remuneration for preparing some drawings, with which he designed to "illustrate his valuable work on sheep husbandry." Mr. Randall subsequently sat for his portrait.

From this time forward, he rose rapidly in his profession, and previous to his locating in the city of New York, in the autumn of 1850, he painted, among other portraits, those of the nine surviving original trustees of the Cortland Academy. They were remarkably correct, and were consequently regarded with much favor. He subsequently executed and sent to the American Art Union several ideal pictures, all of which were purchased at appreciative prices. The first of these was one of twelve which were selected from four hundred pictures, and purchased by the managers of the Association.

Mr. Carpenter's success in the city has been commensurate with his talents and genius. He has been at various times commissioned to paint the portraits of some of our most distinguished men; among these we may mention those of Ex-Presidents Tyler, Fillmore, and Franklin Pierce; William L. Marcy, Lewis Cass, William H. Seward, Sam. Houston, Salmon P. Chase, and Caleb Cushing. The press of the country have given these pictures a wide notoriety. His crowning effort, however, is the recent admirable portrait of Henry Ward Beecher.

"The portraits by this artist are remarkable chiefly for their subtle *mentality;* for their faithful rendering of the inward life and disposition. His studio is hung around with statesmen and men of power, whose characters can be read as if the men themselves, in their most expressive moods, stood before you; and among them all this face of BEECHER shines like an opal among dull and hueless stones ; like a passion-flower among bloomless shrubs."*

Mr. Carpenter enjoys in an eminent degree the confidence and esteem of his early friends, and of all who know him. He is a man of delicate sensibility, of a lively and poetic fancy, and of unsullied purity of character. He possesses a noble, impulsive, and generous heart, which is ever alive to the good of those with whom he is associated. Lloyd Glover, of whom mention is made in this work, was one of his earliest and most sympathizing friends. Their acquaintance began about the time young Carpenter commenced painting, and very soon ripened into the warmest friendship. Mr. Glover's generous sympathy and proffers of pecuniary aid, though his own means were limited, were especially grateful at this period, to the young artist. He found also in Elliot Reed, another engraver, a kindred spirit ; and the intimacy between the trio was remarkable. They were felicitously termed the "Three Graces"—Poetry, Painting, and Sculpture.

Mr. Carpenter was married, in August, 1851, to Miss Augusta H. Prentiss, only daughter of Mrs. Frances Rollo Prentiss, formerly of Cortlandville.

Lloyd Glover.—Among those who have gone out from Homer, and who do honor to their native place, no one is more cheerfully mentioned than the subject of this notice. He was born in the village of Re Ruyter, in July, 1826. His father, Mr. Daniel Glover, appreciating the educational advantages of Homer, removed there the year following, and has since been numbered among its worthy and respected citizens. He pursued

* *N. Y. Evening Post.*

for several years the occupation of an amateur agriculturalist; his sons devoting their time to study. Lloyd, the youngest, was christened De Lloyd Gage Glover, but after he became an engraver, the similarity of the initials with that of an elder brother, who was also an engraver, induced him to obtain—while yet a minor—his father's consent to change his name to its present form. His academic course extended through several years, and he left the venerated halls of that valued institution, an able scholar, with the highest written encomiums of Prof. Woolworth, who, in public as well as private circles, has ever delighted to mention his pupil with honor As a youth, he was ingenuous and generous—the friend and defender of the weak—quick to resent and punish an affront, yet magnanimous and upright. He was full of hilarity and boyish exuberance of feeling, and evinced much shrewdness in planning roguery for his mates; which, however, was harmlessly humorous. Like his father, he possessed remarkable physical strength and courage; and his excessive vitality prompted him to give frequent demonstrations of the same; but the natural goodness of his disposition restrained him from anything like quarrelsomeness. His strength was frequently displayed in the novel method of *friendly battles*, at the odds of the best two against himself; and he often challenged the school *en masse*, to "throw" him by united effort; and in such contests his back was never known to touch the sod. His pranks with his most intimate friend and companion, Elliot, son of Judge Reed, who was ever ready to join him in any undertaking, however hazardous, will not be soon forgotten. On horseback they would roam fields, leap fences, scale aclivities, explore ravines, and swim streams; and it is on record, that on one of these expeditions both horses and riders came near being drowned. "The boy was father to the man." He exhibited at an early age much natural taste for engraving, and at eighteen went to Boston for the purpose of prosecuting his studies in that art. He made rapid progress; and has attained consummate skill in his vocation, second perhaps to no one in the profession. Successful in his business, which required but little capital, he embarked to some extent in commercial enterprise; and has secured the important position of commercial agent for the American Guano Company for the New England States. He has since served as a Director in the Board of Trustees of the same Association.

He was for several years engaged in the business of Bank Note engraving, as the head of the New England branch of the eminent house of Danforth, Wright & Co.

Aside from his skill as an artist, and his staid probity as a business man, he is esteemed for all those qualities which distinguish the true gentleman,—hospitable, courteous, liberal and generous to a fault, the life of the social circle, and fond of all manly sports and pastimes, particularly of yachting. At his residence at Lynn Beach, by the "ocean and its sounding shore,"—the beauties of which he has so well described,—his poetical taste greatly developed, and there his best pieces were composed. He loves the Poets, and revels with them, especially when genial friends are his guests.

He remembers Homer and its associations with the most affectionate regard. In one of his poems he pays, in the following stanzas, a beautiful tribute to the winding stream which is the pride of the valley.

"Tioughnioga! on thy buoyant breast,
In boyhood's time, how often have I lain;
Calm, as a mother with her babe at rest,
Thou bore me by thy banks sweet-scented train.
Tioughnioga! Mistress of the plain!
Thy cherished name is melody to me!
E'en though thy waters evermore complain,
Like spirit tones, of times no more to be,
Oft let me greet thee still with manhood's kindling 'ee.'"

Mr. Glover married Vaeilette Emogene, daughter of Benjamin Hitchcock, Esq., of Strong, Maine. He won, in her, a lady highly esteemed for the graces of her mind and person, and for her true womanly character.*

The various poems which he has delivered before literary associations, stamp him as a man of superior powers of mind. His "Jubilee Poem," a youthful effort, pronounced at the Academy, July 8, 1846, is intimately associated with the history of the Tioughnioga Valley. For elevation of style, nervous energy, strong imgination without the too common fault of excessive and far-fetched metaphor, together with an easy, natural and unlabored pathos, it may challenge comparison with any effort of a similar character. It will be read with pleasure by Mr. Glover's numerous friends, and, indeed, by all who can properly appreciate true poetic excellence.

The circumstances which led to its production are worthy of a brief narration. Prof. Otis, of Indiana, had been appointed Poet of the "Jubilee." He was prevented, however, from fulfilling the engagement, and Prof.

* Mrs. Glover died January 6th, 1859.

Woolworth was made aware of the fact only a day or two previous to the arrival of the auspicious occasion. Our young friend, then an apprentice in Boston, had returned to Homer to participate in the festivities, and learned the evening previous to the opening exercises that Mr. Otis would not be present, and he secretly resolved to supply his place. During the night he produced the poem. Determining to let its fate be decided by its merits, he sent it anonymously to Principal Woolworth, who was struck with its beauties and its appropriateness to the occasion, and requested the bearer to name its author, which was properly declined. Mr. Woolworth returned a befitting expression of his sentiments, informing him that the poem was accepted, and would be read at the Jubilee, and desired an interview with the author. The young poet acknowledged himself the author of the production, warmly thanking his honored teacher for former encouragement, attributing whatever merit he possessed to his influence and approbation. Mr. Woolworth, by this heartfelt tribute, was quite overcome, and evinced deep emotion. In his speech at the Pavilion he made honorable mention of the poet, and the circumstances which called forth the poem. Mr. Glover's modest appreciation of his effort induced him to withhold his assent to its publication in the Jubilee pamphlet; but, having at length overcome his objections, we now have the pleasure, for the first time, of presenting it to the public.

We have dwelt at some length upon the peculiarities of Mr. Glover, believing that our beautiful region will yet be hallowed by his muse, and cherished by kindred minds for his sake.

JUBILEE POEM.

Read at the Jubilee at Cortland Academy, July 6th, 1846.

Friends of our common country ! here ye stand
Once more among the scenes your childhood knew,
In the fair bosom of a happy land,
Beneath your native skies of gold and blue !
Like joyful pilgrims when the shrine is won,
When bosoms swell and tears impulsive start,
Ye come with love warm as this summer sun,
To this loved spot, this Mecca of the heart !

Ye may have roved your long and weary way
O'er the broad prairies of the distant west,
Where varied scenes cheer not the long, long day
Of death-like silence and oppressive rest,
Where evil spirits hold their hideous courts,
And range with furies on the midnight air,
Breathing fierce lightnings at their hellish sports,*
And leave their smouldering tracks of blackness there.

Ye may have roved afar 'neath other skies,—
Where the dark ocean beats a frowning shore ;
Where Nature's noblest works in grandeur rise ;
In Art's fair temples or in courts of lore :
But here, upon your own prolific soil,
How fair the landscapes to your sight unfold,
Teeming with increase for the sons of toil
In many a bounteous field of green and gold.

* An Indian superstition regarding the prairie fires.

Like loving halos ling'ring round the spot,
  Here dwell the memories of the cherished past,
Of scenes and joys which ne'er can be forgot,
  Too dear to die, too beautiful to last.
No dread simoon upon the breeze's breath
  Is blasting through Tioughnioga's vale,—
No fell disease, the herald stern of death,
  Doth seek its prey in this delicious dale.

Again ye view each well-remembered place,
  Dear in the morning of your youthful years,
Again behold each loved familiar face,
  And well-known voices greet your gladdened ears.
Yet all is changed unto our stranger view,—
  Time hath not spared, Dame Nature wends her way,
And many a form hath passed away, like dew
  Before the glory of the king of day.

Where is the good man Chamberlain? and where
  Our friend from thy cool shades, O willow tree!
Where are the bands that knew our mother's care,
  This faithful mother of the good and free.
In death's embrace lamented Lacy sleeps,
  And Kinney lives but in each bleeding breast,
Affection mourns, and pity, drooping, weeps
  Where Curtis* lies beside the "Dove at rest."

In their last mansion sleep the brothers Lynde,†
  Lulled by the murmurs of Lake Erie's wave;

* Over the remains of this lamented young man and his sister is reared a monument on which is inscribed, at the base,

"A LAW STUDENT WHO LIVED BY THE LAW OF LOVE."

And opposite,

"A DOVE AT REST."

Sweetly indicative of the character of the girl to whom reference is here made.

† The brothers Lynde, with all that talents, education and wealth could bestow, perished at the burning of the steamer Erie, on Lake Erie.

Quenched were the beamings of young Bennet's mind;
  De Witt,* the child of Genius, found a grave.
Peace to the sleepers! loved, regretted throng!
  Green be their memory to our latest years!
To them our freshest flowers, our saddest song,
  Like pilgrims at the shrine, our copious tears.

O, from the mind such memory never fades,
  Ne'er from the heart the love for such as these;
With us they live within these classic shades,
  Again their voices float on every breeze!
Where, where is Woolworth? Heaven's own bounteous hand
  Hath still upheld him in his works of good;
Crowned with rich honors, long may yet he stand
  Amid the places where he long hath stood.

He sowed the seed of wisdom in the mind,
  And richly doth the harvest yield, and well,
For every tare he scattered to the wind,
  And *marked* the ground wheron the seedlings fell.
And downward through the maze of future thought,
  Wide and still wider as it flows along,
Its genial influence with his genius fraught,
  Will live in wisdom, eloquence and song!

And here are aged men, whose locks of eld
  Float lightly in the valley's vernal breeze,
Who, on this spot, when pioneers, beheld
  The noon-day sun o'ertop the forest trees.
And here they felled the brave and sturdy oak
  Which ne'er before had known a white man's gaze,
And viewed the startled deer as forth he broke
  His covert wild in terror and amaze.

* De Witt Glover, whose undoubted genius gave promise of the most brilliant success. He was the friend and pupil of the eminent artist, Casilear, of New York city, and his early loss, at the age of nineteen, was deeply deplored.

With antlers high, and nostril widely spread,
  And quivering nerve, that form of beauty stood,
And snuffed the breeze from o'er the stranger's head,
  Then plunged, like lightning, through the pathless wood!
And where above is reared the gilded vane
  O'er the fair verdure of the velvet green
And the wide spreading populated plain,
  The wigwam of the Indian brave was seen.

Yet, when upon this new-born, sacred spot
  The men of wisdom and and of goodness trod,
Their own great cares and hardships they forgot,
  And built a house wherein to worship God!
Thanks, thanks, brave Sires! your children sing your praise
  Amid the shades of your own fragrant bowers,
And long they'll chant the soul-inspiring lays,
  And strew your pathway with life's sweetest flowers!

Here, too, the women who hath cheered them on
  Through dread and darkness, and through sorrow's night,
With pictured scenes of bliss, and laurels won,
  And dawning glories of a future light:
Still then for us, amid unnumbered woes,
  When hope seemed oft the shadow of despair,
They bravely wrought, until in beauty rose
  (To truth and learning reared) this temple fair!

O noble, noble Woman! thine the power
  To sculpture on the immortal, towering mind;
Man rules with wisdom the tumultuous hour;
  Thine is his wisdom and thy love combined.
Thanks, thanks, ye noble Mothers! grateful tears
  Still thank and bless ye o'er and o'er again;
Full be the measure of your blissful years,
  Unknown by sorrow, free from every pain!

There is a charm which binds the wandering one
  As by ten thousand bands of meikle might,

Tho' he doth wander 'neath the tropic sun,
  Or in the dismal gloom of polar night;
Tho' he doth bask amid ambrosial groves
  Where fields like magic and enchantment bloom,
Or drink his full of oriental loves,
  Or lave his breast in India's rich perfume.

Or when the Syren lures with winsome smiles,
  And artful glances and bewitching grace,
And with her honeyed tongue each sense beguiles,
  To prove each beauty of her borrowed face;
Or when Ambition twines the laurel wreath,
  And Wealth and Fortune deck his form with gold,
Or when a captive, bound with chains beneath
  The gloomy walls of dungeons stern and old,—

'Tis the charm of his childhood, the light of his home
That binds him and keeps him where'er he may roam,
This the voice of its spirit, so calm and so still,
That teaches him honor and shields him from ill:
Then we'll love our dear home, tho' Time's flowing wave
Is evermore bearing us on to the grave;
Its loves and its joys like green islands shall be,
Mid the surging of life's tempestuous sea,
And when from on high the dread summons shall come,
Our watchword from earth shall be "HEAVEN AND HOME!"

BRIEF NOTICES.

Among the first lawyers who located in the county, were Townsend Ross, Luther F. Stephens, Oliver Wisewell, and Samuel S. Baldwin. Ross and Stephens settled in Homer, and Wisewell and Baldwin in Cortland. Ross was an uneducated man ; but what he lacked in this point was amply made up in tact and genius. He had a clear head, was shrewd, witty and sarcastic, and in short, he was an able and successful lawyer. Stephens was cool and calculating. He died at Seneca Falls. Wisewell was educated for a clergyman, and followed for a time that honored profession. He had his faults to a liberal degree, and yet he possessed many good and liberal traits of character. Baldwin was prompt and energetic ; but his habits of inebriation rendered him less valuable to society and to himself than he otherwise would have been. The profligate habits of his wife, though a beautiful and otherwise an accomplished woman, tended to the perversion of the more noble faculties of the mind.

Henry Stephens, from Wareham, Mass., located in Cortland Village, in 1814, and immediately engaged in the practice of his profession. He possessed energy and integrity of purpose, a fearless self-reliance, a well-regulated ambition, and a just and definite end in view. He was appointed Judge in May, 1838, and honorably filled the position until June, 1847, when he was succeeded by Daniel Hawkes. Judge Stephens has filled various other public positions; and has devoted his best energies to the furtherance of the numerous public improvements of the county. He filled with eminent ability the first presidency of the Syracuse, Binghamton and New York Railroad.

Edward C. Reed came in from Fitzwilliam, N. H., in April, 1816. He entered into partnership with Ross, in Homer, where he still remains. He made an excellent office lawyer, and a valuable citizen. Mr. Reed has creditably filled various influential positions, among which are those of District Attorney, County Judge, and Member of Congress.

Samuel Nelson came in from Madison county, and settled in Cortland Village in 1817. He had been an industrious and energetic student, and hence he early acquired a successful and lucrative practice. His impassioned eloquence and finely rounded periods were regarded as a fair offset to the tact, genius, and scathing sarcasm of Stephens.

Not long after Nelson's arrival came Augustus Donnelly and Rufus H. Beach, who became joint partners in the profession. Donnelly was a large, portly man, of commanding presence and elegant manners. He died in Homer.

Next came Nathan Dayton, Jonathan L. Woods, Daniel J. Betts, John Thomas, and Hiram Gray. Dayton was born in Granville, Washington co., N. Y., in August, 1794. He had been well-educated and well-trained. He studied with Messrs. Sheperd and Barber, in his native village, until October, 1819, when he was admitted to the bar, and soon after settled in Truxton, but subsequently located in Cortland, where, after a year's residence and an ordinary practice, he became a partner of Samuel Nelson, and immediately found the area of his practice greatly enlarged. He was afterwards a Justice of the Peace, District Attorney, and Member of Assembly. In 1831 he removed to Lockport. Here he rose rapidly in the profession, and has at different periods held the office of first Judge of Niagara county, Circuit Judge of the Eighth Circuit District, and County Clerk; the latter office he still holds. Judge Dayton has ever been an active and enterprising man, universally respected in and out of the profession. Woods became his law partner in Cortland, where he gained an honorable reputation as a legal adviser. His personal appearance, genial temper and courteous demeanor weighed strongly in his favor, and certainly made him many warm friends. In 1831 he was elected to the Assembly, a position which he honored. He too went to Lockport, where he became deservedly popular. He also rose to the office of Judge.—Betts was well-educated, and possessed many attractive qualities, and was, in short, a general favorite. His brilliant career was, however, soon cut short. He died in the midst of his usefulness.—Thomas migrated from Connecticut. He soon established a just and appreciative reputation. He now resides in Syracuse.—Gray came from Washington county, and completed his studies with Nelson, Dayton and Woods. He is now one of the Judges of the Supreme Court of this State.

William H. Shankland, originally from Montgomery co., located in Cortland in 1827, where he soon acquired an excellent practice. He made an able legal adviser and an eloquent advocate.

Horatio Ballard commenced reading law in the office of Henry Stephens, in 1822, and completed his studies with Judge Jewett, at Skaneateles. He was admitted as an Attorney to the Supreme Court, in August, 1828; as Counsellor, in May, 1831; and soon afterwards admitted as Solicitor and Counsellor in Chancery. He became a partner of Stephens, and on the elevation of the latter to the bench, he succeeded him to the leadership at the bar. He is a gentleman of great purity of character, and is undoubtedly one of the most industrious, energetic, and thorough-read lawyers in the county.

Samuel N. Perkins, also, studied with Stephens, but at what particular period the author is not informed. He made a fair, average lawyer. He lies entombed in the Cortland Cemetery.

Next came Joseph D. P. Freer, Daniel Hawkes, and James S. Leach. Freer studied with Dayton and Woods. He was well read in the profession. He, too, died early. —Hawkes studied with Stephens and Ballard. He had been well-educated, and was a thorough student. He succeeded Stephens to the bench. Disease fixed its fatal grasp upon him, and he found an early grave.—Leach was born in Sangerfield, Oneida co., August, 1812. He was educated on a farm until sixteen years old. Spent two years at Union Academy, and a like number at a mathematical school at Clinton. He studied with Shankland, in Cortland, and was admitted to the bar in 1835. He entered into the practice of his profession in Cortland, where he remained until 1850, when he removed to Syracuse. He has tact, energy and genius, yet he takes the world easy, and neither mourns over his past or present achievements, but is looking steadily forward to what he terms the glorious future. He is now a prominent practising lawyer in the central city, and is highly respected in and out of the profession.

Henry S. Randall was born in Madison co., in 1811. Received his academic education in Cortland Academy, under Prof. Avery and Dr. Taylor. Graduated at Union College in 1830. Studied with Stephens and Betts, and was admitted as an Attorney in 1834; as Counsellor and Solicitor in 1844. Mr. Randall has not, however, practiced his profession. He served for several years as Corresponding Secretary of the State Agricultural Society, and first moved in the Executive Board to hold a State Fair. At one period he devoted considerable attention to farming, and at another, filled with credit and ability the editorial chair.

In 1839 he was appointed by the Secretary of State a visitor of Common Schools, and although he received no compensation for the arduous labor, he entered at once upon the duties of the office, and visited and reported to the Secretary the condition of all the schools in the county. He is the author of several valuable agricultural works; of one of these 37,000 copies had been sold several years since.

In 1843-4 he held the office of Superintendent of Common Schools, and his admirable reports were of great value.

In 1851 he was elected Secretary of State, and entered upon the duties of the office Jan. 1, 1852. He filled the office with acknowledged ability and success. He was subsequently employed for several years in gathering the materials and writing the life of Thomas Jefferson, which has been but recently issued, in three elegant octavo volumes. It is unquestionably the most perfect biography ever written of this truly great man ; is an honor to our national literature, and will, as it deservedly should, remain a standard work for all future time.

Isaac A. Gates is a native of the town of Scott. He was admitted to the Supreme Court, in 1841, and is now a prominent practicing lawyer in Homer.

Lewis Kingsley is a native of Cincinnatus. He studied with Barak Niles and Benjamin F. Rexford, and was admitted to practice, in 1846. He now resides in Norwich.

Hiram Crandall came from Plymouth, Chenango co. He was educated at Homer; studied law with William H. Shankland, and was admitted to the Supreme Court, and Court of Chancery, in January, 1846. He entered into practice with Shankland, with whom he remained until the latter was elevated to the Supreme Bench, when he became a partner of Robert O. Reynolds, and continued with him until his decease, in Sept., 1855. Mr. Crandall possesses good legal abilities, is prudent and cautious—two excellent qualities in an honorable attorney. In a military capacity he has risen from third Sergeant to Lieut. Colonel. He is now the popular and courteous Post-master in Cortland Village.

Samuel C. Graves commenced reading law in the office of Judge Reed, in 1844 ; was admitted to practice, in 1848, and soon after formed a law partnership with Lewis Kingsley, with whom he remained until 1851, when the firm was dissolved, preparatory to Mr.

Kingsley's removal to Cortland to assume the duties of County Judge. Mr. Graves is fitted to adorn either branch of the profession.

R. Holland Duell was born in the town of Warren, Herkimer co., N. Y., Dec. 20, 1823. His education was derived from the common school, with the exception of one or two years' attendance at the Syracuse Academy. He entered the law office of Charles B. Sedgwick, of Syracuse, in March, 1842, and remained with him until his admission to the bar in July, 1845. Commenced practice at Fabius, Onondaga co., during the same month, and remained there until July, 1847, when he came to Cortland Village, and formed a law partnership with Judge Stephens. In Nov., 1850, he was elected District Attorney of Cortland county, and in Nov., 1853, was reëlected to the same office. In Nov., 1855, was elected County Judge and Surrogate, and in 1858 was chosen a member of the 36th Congress, from the 21st district, to succeed Henry Bennett.

Judge Duell is possessed of finely developed talents, remarkable shrewdness, tact, and address, and in short, exhibits all the elements of an accomplished legislator.

James A. Schermerhorn is a native of Schenectady. He was educated in Cortland Academy and Geneva College. He read law with Daniel Hawkes, in Cortland Village, and was admitted an Attorney at Law and Solicitor in Chancery, at the quarterly term of the Supreme Court, 1847. Mr. Schermerhorn is a well-read lawyer; he however excels chiefly in the first branch of the profession,—as a legal adviser,—not caring to shine in the capacity of an advocate.

Edwin F. Gould was reared in Cherry Valley. He

received an academic education; studied law with Shankland & Leach; was admitted to the bar at the General Term of the Supreme Court, held at Ithaca, July 4, 1848, and commenced practice in Cortland Village. Mr. Gould is an accomplished writer and an eloquent speaker. As editor of the *Central New Yorker*, published at De Ruyter; *Madison County Journal*, at Hamilton; *Cortland County Whig*, at Homer, and the *Cortland American*, at Cortland Village, he exhibited a clear, vigorous intellect.

George A. White is a native of Cortland, where he was reared and educated. He studied law with J. D. P. Freer, and was admitted to practice, in January, 1848. He commenced practice in Homer, but subsequently returned to Cortland, where he has since remained. Mr. White has secured a very lucrative practice, and it is not saying too much, an enviable reputation as a lawyer. With care and application to his profession he may rank with the first class lawyers in the State.

Horace L. Green is a native of Virgil. He was educated at Cortland—studied law with Stephens & Duell—was admitted to the bar in 1852, and commenced practice in Marathon—was elected Justice of the Peace in 1854—removed to Cortland in 1856, where he has since continued to practice. In 1857 he was elected County Treasurer—an office which he has thus far filled to the general satisfaction of all parties. He is a gentleman of good habits, fair legal acquirements, and is deserving of great credit for his early political achievement.

A. P. Smith is also a native of Virgil. He was born

in the year 1831 ; received his academic education in Cortland ; graduated at the State Normal School, in 1853 ; commenced the study of law with H. L. Green, at Marathon, and completed his studies with Horatio Ballard ; was admitted to practice, at the January term of Supreme Court, 1856, and at the November election of the same year, was elected District Attorney of Cortland county. Mr. Smith was an industrious and energetic student. His career in the past has been eminently successful—the future is bright and promising.

Charles Foster is a native of Lansingburgh, Rensalaer co., N. Y. He fitted for college at the Pompey Academy, and graduated at Yale College in 1844. He read law in the office of Victory Birdseye, at Pompey, one year ; six months in the law school at New Haven ; one year in the office of B. D. and G. Noxon, Syracuse, and finally completed his studies in the office of Wood & Birdseye, at Albany. He was admitted to practice as Attorney, Solicitor and Counsellor at Catskill, in the fall of 1847. He commenced practicing in Pompey, in the office of Daniel Gott. In Jan., 1853, he located in Cortland Village, where he continues in practice. Mr. Foster possesses fine talents, tact and energy, with a fair prospect of professional success and eminence.

M. M. Waters is a native of Truxton. He was educated in the common school, with a brief attendance at the De Ruyter Academy. He studied his profession with Reynolds & Crandall ; was admitted to practice, in January, 1856. His business habits, unyielding energy and close application to study, are sure precursors of eminence in the future.—Alvah D. Waters was educated at Cazenovia ; read law in his brother's office, and was admitted to the bar, in November, 1858.

John S. Barber, from Broome county, was educated at Ithaca; read law in the office of M. M. Waters; was admitted to practice, in January, 1858, at Binghamton, and soon after opened an office in Cortland Village. The health of Mr. Barber incapacitates him for close application to his profession.

William Henry Warren studied with Ballard, and was admitted to practice, in November, 1858. He is industrious, possessed of a good mind, and has a laudable ambition to succeed in the practice.

Oliver Porter read law and was admitted to practice, in Delaware county. He opened an office in Homer, in 1855, and is now doing a successful and prosperous business.

Alanson Coats was the first permanent lawyer in Truxton; Palmer & Williams succeeded. Coats, though not decidedly brilliant, is nevertheless a good legal adviser. He went early to Syracuse, but subsequently returned to Truxton, where he still resides. Damon Coats, a practicing attorney in Syracuse, is his son.—Palmer & Williams were not very successful—went west, where the latter soon after died.

Amos L. Kinney received his academic education at Homer; collegiate, at Hamilton; graduated in 1843. He studied with Alanson Coats, and was admitted to practice, in 1848. He is pleasantly situated at Truxton Village.

Barak Niles located in Cincinnatus, previous to 1820. He possessed a good legal mind, and was a fair, average advocate. He was for several years an Associate Judge, and was much respected. He removed in 1848 to Pennsylvania.

Roswell K. Bourne is a native of Otselic, Chenango county. He was educated at Cazenovia; studied with Judge Niles; was admitted at the General Term of Supreme Court held at Utica, July, 1844. He commenced practice at Pitcher, but subsequently located at Cincinnatus, where he still continues in the practice of law. Mr. Bourne is a man of indomitable energy and force of character, and is every way fitted to dignify and adorn the profession.

Ira L. Little was born in Wallkill, Orange co., N. Y., July 26, 1830. He graduated at Harvard University; studied with Benjamin S. Bentley, of Montrose, Pennsylvania, and was admitted to practice in that State, in 1852. In 1854 he located in Binghamton, and was admitted to the bar of the Supreme Court of this State, at the general term of 1855, and soon after removed to Marathon, where he has since practiced with a good degree of success. Mr. Little is possessed of a superior education, fine literary attainments; is a well-read lawyer, and a worthy citizen. As a magazine writer he has won an appreciable reputation. Many of his poetical contributions have been regarded as gems of superior beauty.

George B. Jones is a native of Columbia county, N. Y. He was educated at Cazenovia and Homer; studied his profession with Horatio Ballard, of Cortland, and with Southerland & McLellan, in Hudson, and was admitted to the bar, May 9, 1848. In April, 1849, he opened an office in M'Grawville, but has recently located in Cortland Village. He possesses great energy of character, and hence applies himself with untiring perseverance to the duties of his vocation.

John S. Van Hoesen was born in Preble, May 11, 1833; was educated at Homer; studied with Judge Kingsley and Major Crandall; was admitted to practice on the 13th day of May, 1856, and commenced practice at Preble Corners. In October he removed to Minesota, landing at Hastings, a flourishing city on the Mississippi. Here he was favored with only a limited practice. Hence he turned his attention in the main to another branch of business,—speculating in land; and in the brief space of seven months he accumulated a "respectable little fortune." After visiting St. Paul, Mineapolis, and several other places of importance, he reëmbarked for his native land, on the 14th of May, 1857, and arrived at Preble on the 17th of the same month, where he is now doing a good business in his profession.

Luther W. Griswold, Darius Allen, Orson A. and Gavett Z. House, also studied with Reynolds & Crandall. Griswold is the able and popular Judge of Minneshick co., Iowa. Allen is engaged in a flourishing practice in Penn Yan, Yates co., N. Y. Orson A. House is now doing a prosperous business in New York, as a member of the firm of Bergen & House. Gavett Z. House, former editor of the *Dryden News*, is now practicing his profession in Buffalo.

Samuel G. Hatheway, Jr., studied with Dayton & Woods. He possessed a calm, discriminating, well-balanced, intellect, and rose rapidly in both branches of the profession. He became an early partner of Judge Gray, in Elmira, where he still remains, and is unquestionably one of the ablest lawyers in the State. Chief Justice Joseph S. Bosworth, of the city of New York, the able and distinguished lawyer—the profound jurist and enlightened citizen—the man who has risen meteor-like, resplendent in genius, reflecting honor upon his native *county of Cortland;* the late Robert O. Reynolds, the brilliant orator and gifted advocate ; Gardner Knapp, the polished student and acute observer—studied with Stephens & Ballard. H. S. Fuller, Charles G. King, Hon. H. S. Conger, Jerome Rowe, William Marsh, Augustus L. Ballard, and Ira D. Warren, studied with Horatio Ballard. Mr. Ballard retired a few years since from the profession he honored, and is now settled at Lakeland, Minesota. Mr. Warren is now in a lucrative practice in the city of New York, and is one of the firm of Cutler, Pennington & Warren. He is a gentleman of rare abilities, well read in his profession, which he pursues with great zeal, industry and success, and will undoubtedly become very eminent as an advocate Robert Stewart, now Governor of Missouri, Hon. H. L. Dunham of Indiana, Hon. A. P. Lanning of Buffalo, and W. H. Mallory, studied with Wm. H. Shankland. Hon. Levi F. Bowen, a native of Homer, studied with Joseph P. Morse, a distinguished lawyer of Lockport. Mr. Bowen has been elevated to various honored positions, having creditably filled the offices of Judge and Surrogate of Niagara county, and Justice of the Supreme Court of the Eighth Judicial District. Morse studied in Cortland with Dayton & Woods. He was a man of ability. Judge Ira Harris studied with Augustus Donnelly.

Perhaps no individual has done more for the welfare of the children and youth of this country, than Professor Chas. W. Saunders, the well-known author of the popular series of school-books that bear his name. He resided in the town of Cortlandville for almost thirty years, and spent much time in teaching. He is the author of twenty-five different works, all of which have been stereotyped from the manuscript. His text books have given him a just and an enviable reputation.

Among those who were born and educated in Cortland county, and who have not already been mentioned, and who by their talents and industry have risen to high positions, we may briefly notice John M. Keep, son of General Martin Keep, late of Homer, who is now a distinguished Judge of the Supreme Court of Wisconsin. William Keep, son of Hon. Chauncey Keep, is a prominent banker at Buffalo, residing at Lockport. Austin Fuller, of Freetown, is the popular State Auditor of Indiana. A. L. Pritchard, son of Garret Pritchard, of Solon, formerly a practicing lawyer in New Berlin, Chenango co., N. Y., is at present extensively engaged in the banking business in Wisconsin, residing at Watertown. He is a zealous and prominent citizen, highly respected for his active efforts in improving the place, having done more than any other person towards beautifying the town. Rev. William C. Boyce, son of Colonel Obadiah Boyce, is the efficient Principal of the Aurora Academy. Augustus A. Boyce (another son) is Clerk of the District Court of the Northern District of New York, residing in Utica. Charles H. Hunt, son of Dr. S. M. Hunt, of Marathon, is District Attorney of the United States for the Southern District of New York. John W. Hunt (another son) graduated as a physician, and moved to Wisconsin in 1849, and has for the greater portion of the time been Assistant Secretary of State, residing at Madison. Dr. Ray Hunt (also a son of Dr. Hunt) is residing at Madison, and is the Chief Clerk in the same office.

Charles H. Salisbury, son of Nathan Salisbury, of Scott, studied medicine, and graduated at the Albany Medical College. He was for several years employed as an assistant to Dr. Emmons, of Albany, in a chemical analysis of the soil and vegetable productions in different parts of the State, and the results are published in the agricultural parts of the Natural History of the State. He was regarded as one of the best analytical chemists of the State. He now resides in Ohio. His brother, Charles Salisbury, has acquired an enviable reputation as a portrait painter. He lived several years in the city of Albany, pursuing his profession with eminent success.

DeLay Glover, son of Daniel Glover, of Homer, has acquired a well-earned fame as a historical engraver. He resides in Syracuse.

Hon. Arthur Holmes and Alis W. Ogden: the former a resident of Cortlandville, is at present an active member of the New York Assembly; the latter was born and reared in Homer, and is the successor of the Hon. Rufus A. Reed, to the office of County Clerk.

There were seven delegates—emigrants from Cortland county—honored with seats in the Constitutional Convention of Wisconsin. One of them was Michael Frank, formerly of Virgil.

Of the physicians and surgeons who have at various times commenced the practice of their profession in the county, we can only notice a few, many of them having remained scarce long enough to acquire a residence,

John McWhorter, the pioneer physician, was a native of Washington county, in this State, and located in Cincinnatus in 1795. He was an excellent physician, but did not confine himself entirely to the practice. He entered into the political arena, and was honored with numerous official positions.

Lewis S. Owen was a native of New Lebanon, Columbia co., N. Y. He studied medicine with Drs. Stringer and McClellan of Albany; removed to Homer in 1799, and engaged in the practice of his profession. He was eminently qualified for the position he occupied. John Miller, from Amenia, Dutchess county, settled in Truxton, in 1801. His medical studies were pursued in Dutchess and Washington counties, under the direction of eminent practitioners. He attended lectures in the University of Pennsylvania, then under the direction of Drs. Rush and Shipper. Robert D. Taggart was a native of Colerain, and studied his profession with Dr. Ross, in his native town. He located in Preble in 1804. He remained engaged in the practice of medicine for about twenty-seven years, when he removed to Port Byron. He possessed a clear judgment; was regarded as a man of great moral worth, and eminent in his profession. Elijah J. Wheeler was a native of New Jersey, where he acquired his medical knowledge. He possessed a strong, vigorous intellect; was well educated, and eminently qualified to honor the medical profession. He located in Solon in 1805. His early habits of inebriation retarded his usefulness, and greatly afflicted his young and intelligent family of children, and withered and blasted the once brilliant prospects of his wife. Jesse Searl was from Southampton, Mass. His medical studies were pursued in the office of Dr. Woodbridge, of the same town. He settled in Homer in 1804, and went into practice, but subsequently turned his attention to politics, and engaged in conducting the *Cortland Repository*. His medical knowledge was good, his literary acquirements superior; and, in brief, he was an excellent citizen and an influential man. Miles Goodyear was born in Hampden, New Haven co., Conn.; graduated at Yale College; studied medicine with Professor Eli Ives, of New Haven; came to Cortland in the latter part of 1816, and was soon engaged in an extensive practice. His education was superior; his medicinal knowledge extensive; his habits social; his temper genial and forgiving; and hence he acquired warm friends in and out of the profession. Dr. Goodyear has been engaged in continuous practice for a period exceeding forty-two years—years of usefulness and of eminence—rendering service alike to the poor and the rich,—a noble and dignified trait in the character of the worthy practitioner. He is still devotedly attached to the profession, and ardently labors to alleviate the sufferings of the sick.

Lewis Riggs is a native of Norfolk, Conn. His medical instructor was Dr. Samuel B. Woodward, of Litchfield. He received his license from the State Medical Society, in 1812. He emigrated to Homer in 1818. As a practitioner, he has been prudent, skilful and successful. In addition to his local offices, he has been elected to and served in the United States Congress. He erected the Superior Mills in 1838. His history is closely identified with the history of the county; and he has in all respects maintained an upright and valuable reputation.

Robert C. Owen was born in Homer in 1802, educated at Cortland Academy, studied his profession with his father, Dr. Lewis S. Owen, and Platt Williams, of Albany, and graduated at the Harvard University, Boston, in 1820. He was for thirty-eight years a prominent practitioner in Homer, but for the last eight years has been, in the main, retired from the active duties of the profession.

George W. Bradford is a native of Otsego county. He received an academic education; studied medicine with Dr. Thomas Fuller, of Cooperstown; was licensed in 1820 by the Otsego County Medical Association, and soon after commenced practice in Homer, where he still remains in the active duties of his profession.

Horace Bronson was born in Catskill, Greene co., N. Y. His classical studies were pursued under the charge of Rev. C. Bushnell, and his medical in the office of Dr. Lewis Riggs. He attended medical lectures at the College of Physicians and Surgeons of the Western District, where he received the degree of M. D. He subsequently spent one season with Prof. Noyes, of Hamilton College, and another with Dr. Seth Hastings, of Clinton, Oneida co. He came to Virgil in 1821, where he has, with the exception of a brief period, remained in practice. Dr. Bronson has been eminently successful in the profession, discharging all its onerous duties, and devoting his best energies to the advancement of medical science, and to the perpetuity of a just appreciation of the high duties of the worthy physician. Hence he has gained the kind respect and affectionate regard of a long list of devoted friends.

Azariah Blanchard came in soon after Dr. Bronson

and settled in Truxton, where he remained many years, and "enjoyed to an eminent degree the confidence of a large part of the population of that town, and who, deservedly, was considered one of our most intelligent physicians."* Dr. Blanchard is now a respectable and influential citizen of Wisconsin.

Phineas H. Burdick received an academic education. Commenced the study of medicine in 1823, with Dr. Hubbard Smith, of De Ruyter, and completed them in the office of Dr. Jehial Sterns, of Pompey; attended lectures at Castleton, Vermont, in 1826, and was licensed by the Medical Society of Onondaga county in 1827. He commenced practice in Scott, May, 1827, and removed to Preble, January, 1823. He received the honorary degree of M. D. from the State Medical Society in 1851, and became a permanent member of the association in 1853. He has ever been regarded as an excellent physician, and maintained a prominent position among his medical brethren. He has an extensive practice, in which he appears eminently successful.

Samuel M. Hunt was born in Marathon, Oct. 30, 1798, being the first child born in that town. His first recollection of attending school was in a long barn, and subsequently at a log school-house, with windows of oiled paper as a substitute for glass. His classical studies were pursued at the Cortland Academy, commencing in 1819; studied medicine with Dr. P. B. Brooks, of Binghamton, was licensed by the Medical Society of Chenango county in 1823, of which Dr. Henry Mitchel was then President. He commenced the practice of medicine at Sharp's Corners, on the Otselic River, now Tri-

* Hon. George W. Bradford's Semi-Centennial Address.

angle, Broome county; has practiced mostly in Lisle, Union and Maine of that county. He served in the capacity of Justice of the Peace in Maine for about ten years, and for five years as Justice of Sessions for Broome county. Dr. Hunt has acquired considerable eminence in the profession; has been active in favoring the various benevolent reforms, as, also, in forwarding the educational interests of the county. His children have enjoyed the benefits derived from our academic institutes, some of whom have emigrated to other parts, and are now elevated to high public positions.

George W. Maxon studied his profession with Drs. Palmer and Haven of Oneida county, and E. S. Bailey of Madison, and completed his studies with Samuel R. Clark, with whom he practiced one year. He removed to Scott in May, 1832, where he remains in a lucrative practice.

Frederick Hyde was born in Lisle, Broome county; received a common school education; studied medicine in the office of Dr. Hiram Moe, Lansing, Tompkins co., and Dr. Horace Bronson, of Virgil. He attended three years in Fairfield Medical College, and graduated in 1836. The Faculty embraced an amount of learning and talent perhaps unequalled in the State, and we therefore record with pleasure the names of Drs. Westel Willoughby, James McNaughton, James Hadley, Theodoric Romeyn Beck, and John De Lamater. He commenced practice in Cortland, February, 1836. In 1854 he received a professorship in Geneva Medical College, which he still holds. Dr. Hyde possesses a clear, strong, vigorous mind, and is a ready, cool and skilful surgical operator. Hence it is with pleasure that we speak of him as having acquired considerable eminence in the several branches of medical and surgical science.

John H. Knapp was born in the town of New Fairfield, Conn. His academical education was received in the Sherburne Academy; studied his profession with Drs. Devillo White and Elijah S. Lyman; was licensed by the Chenango Medical Society on the 22d day of April, 1843, and located in Marathon. In 1845 he removed to Etna, Tompkins county, where he practiced until 1849, when he removed to Harford, where he now resides, and is engaged in the active duties of his profession. Dr. Knapp has held various local offices, and was in 1854 elected to a seat in the New York Assembly. He has by his own exertions carved his way to his present honored position, enjoying the respect and confidence of a very large circle of friends. If he has enjoyed much of the sunshine of this fleeting life, he has also passed through the fiery ordeal of affliction, having but recently buried his fourth and last child.

Homer O. Jewett was born in Madison county, in 1819; studied his profession with Dr. Shipman; graduated at the Medical University in New York, in 1843; commenced practice at Summerhill; came to Cortland in 1849, where he has since remained in the practice of his profession. He is eminently qualified for his position, and is regarded as an able and successful practitioner, enjoying a large medical practice.

Caleb Green was born at La Fayette, Onondago co., N. Y., in 1819; his medical pupilage was spent under the tutorship of Prof. Frank H. Hamilton, of Rochester,

N. Y. He graduated at Geneva Medical College, in January, 1844 ; commenced the practice of medicine in Homer, in March of the same year. He was elected Professor of Materia Medica and General Pathology in Geneva Medical College in 1855, and resigned his professorship in 1858. He is now engaged in a lucrative practice in Homer. Possessed of an active, well-balanced mind, a thorough knowledge of disease in all its various types and phases, of medicines, their virtue, power, and use, he is ever prepared to act wisely, cautiously, and successfully, having a fixed purpose in view—the restoration of the sick. His surgical skill has rendered him justly eminent.

Eleazer H. Barnes is a native of Broome county, N. Y.; studied medicine with Dr. E. Barnes, late of Geneva ; attended lectures at Geneva Medical College in 1837–8, and in the spring of the latter year commenced practicing as a partner with Dr. E. Lyman, at Great Bend, Pa. In 1839 he removed to Marathon, where he has since been an active practitioner.

Theo. C. Pomeroy was reared in Otisco, N. Y.; educated at Hamilton College ; studied with Drs. Goodyear and Hyde, and graduated at Geneva Medical College in 1844, and is now practicing his profession in Cortland with a good degree of success.

William W. Bradford is a native of Pitcher, N. Y.; acquired his education at the common school and the Fayetteville Academy ; attended lectures at Laporte, Indiana, with Dr. A. B. Shipman, formerly of this county, holding the Professorship of Surgery in the Indiana Medical College, from whom he derived much valuable knowledge ; also, attended two course of lectures at

Castleton, Vermont, and graduated 18th of June, 1851; practiced successfully six years in Lysander; came to Marathon in the fall of 1851, where he is now permanently located in the practice of medicine and surgery.

A. D. Reed was reared in Delaware county, educated at Roxbury; studied with Sherman Street; attended lectures, and was licensed at Castleton, Vermont, in 1848, and is now engaged in successful practice in Cincinnatus.

Scepter Smith is a native of Marathon; was educated at the Cortland Academy; studied medicine with Dr. Taylor in Alleghany, and was licensed in 1848 by the Alleghany Medical Society. In 1851 he partially retired from the practice of medicine and turned his attention to the profession of dentistry, in which he has become eminently skilful. He removed to Scott Centre in 1851, where he is now doing an excellent business.

J. C. Nelson was educated in Owego; attended three courses of lectures in Geneva Medical College, and graduated in 1848. He spent three years under the tutorship of that most eminent physician, Dr. Thomas Spencer; settled in Truxton in March, 1848. Dr. Nelson is an active, energetic man, engaged in an extensive and eminently successful practice.

Charles M. Kingman is a native of Cincinnatus. He received an academic education; studied with Dr. F. F. Maybury, formerly of Solon, now a prominent and skilful physician in Morrisville, Madison co., N. Y. Dr. Kingman graduated at Geneva Medical College in 1846, and commenced practice in M'Grawville, where he is much respected as a physician.

Charles S. Richardson is a native of Cayuga county;

studied with Dr. George W. Bradford, and graduated at the Medical Department of the Albany University in 1856; commenced practice in Homer in 1857. Dr. Richardson is a young man of excellent habits, is persevering, and, in brief, is well qualified to excel in the profession.

William R. Brown settled in Homer in 1845, having removed from Oneida county. He graduated at Fairfield College, and subsequently engaged in the homœopathic art of curing disease. He is a gentleman of good abilities, and is engaged in a good business practice.

Jay Ball attended lectures in Geneva Medical College, and graduated in the Medical University of New York City in 1848. He was at this time under twenty-one years of age. In 1853 he commenced in Homer the homœopathic practice of medicine, where he still remains.

H. C. Gazlay graduated at the Eclectic College in Syracuse, and commenced practice in Truxton in 1841. He subsequently removed to Fabius, where he practiced until 1847, when he returned to Truxton. In 1857 he came to Homer, and engaged in the practice of his profession. He is now a partner in practice with Dr. Ezra Loomis. He possesses an active intellect, is energetic and skilful, and has the necessary elements of success.

Henry A. Bolles is a native of Litchfield, Conn. He studied his profession with Drs. Loomis and Hobart; was licensed at the Eclectic Medical College in Syracuse, and commenced practice in McLean, Tompkins county, in 1852. He subsequently removed to Cortland, and is at present engaged in a lucrative practice.

There are a number of other prominent physicians

residing in the county: among these we may mention Dr. Lyman Eldrege, of Cincinnatus; Henry C. Hendrick, of M'Grawville; Squire Jones, of Homer; Franklin Goodyear, of Cortland; William Fitch, of Virgil; and Dr. Hubbard, of Scott.

CONCLUSION.

Our history now draws to a close, and is given to the reader in as perfect a form as the circumstances of the times will permit.

We have in no instance given publicity to statements of suspicious or doubtful character; and we have in all cases aimed to be impartial. Of the moral, social, political, educational, and religious associations, we have spoken frankly and feelingly. Of the local interests and natural advantages we have remarked as became our position, and in so doing we have hoped to do ample justice to the resources of the county. Traditions extending back for three centuries have been favorably regarded only when they were supported by the most warrantable chain of circumstances.

In the prosecution of our enterprise we have been materially favored by the voluntary assistance of gentlemen of acknowledged worth and ability; by the reading of written memoranda and valuable data, and by a free access to their extensive and well-selected libraries. To Hon. Henry S. Randall, for the liberal gift of voluminous publications, and other promoting circumstances; Dr. E. B. O'Callaghan, author of the "Documentary History of New York," Hon. Elias W. Leavenworth, for valuable publications, Hon. William

H. Seward, of the United States Senate, Hon. Charles P. Avery, late of Owego, now of Michigan, and Hon. Gideon J. Tucker, Secretary of State, for an exceedingly valuable work, we return our acknowledgments.

To enumerate the names of the numerous gentlemen who have given us verbal statements and interesting incidents, would be hardly possible. We are, however, none the less thankful for their favors and solicitous expressions, tending to enhance the value, correctness and truthfulness of our labors. To the Hon. George W. Bradford, for various State documents, Rufus A. Reed, Esq., for access to the county archives, Hon. Joseph Reynolds, Dr. H. S. Hunt, Hon. Walter Sweetland, Rev. John Keep, and Hon. Harvey Baldwin, are we especially indebted.

It is also our pleasurable duty to tender our reciprocal acknowledgments to Dr. Franklin B. Hough, author of the "History of St. Lawrence and Franklin Counties," Hon. Joshua V. H. Clark, author of an admirably well written history of Onondaga county, Deacon Nathan Boughton, the practical annalist of the town of Virgil, Hon. Dan C. Squires, of Lapeer, for valuable notes on that town, Messrs. Edwin F. and Cornelius B. Gould, late editors and proprietors of the *Cortland County Whig*, Mr. Joseph R. Dixon, of the *Cortland County Republican*, Myron S. Barnes and Anson Spencer, the former of the Mt. Morris *Independent Watchman*, and the latter of the *American Citizen*, Ithaca; Messrs. A. G. Chester and C. P. Cole,—the former of the *Syracuse Journal*, and the latter, of the *Cortland Gazette*. To Hon. Henry Stephens, late President, and Superintendent, William B. Gilbert, Esq., of the Syracuse, Binghamton, and New York Railroad, are we sensibly indebted, for the favorable facilities and kind courtesies which they have freely extended to us.

In brief, we return our grateful acknowledgments to all friends, and for the present, bid them an affectionate ADIEU.

www.ingramcontent.com/pod-product-compliance
Lightning Source LLC
LaVergne TN
LVHW020937110826
845150LV00004B/890

9781425551681